Make that Grade
Irish Tort Law

Make that Grade
Irish Tort Law

Kathleen Moore Walsh

Gill & Macmillan

Gill & Macmillan Ltd
Hume Avenue
Park West
Dublin 12
with associated companies throughout the world
www.gillmacmillan.ie

Print origination in Ireland by Carole Lynch

*The paper used in this book comes from the wood pulp
of managed forests. For every tree felled, at least one tree
is planted, thereby renewing natural resources.*

CONTENTS

Introduction   1
   I.   Historical background   1
   II.   Modern tort law   2
   III.   List of abbreviations   4
   IV.   Revision questions   5

SECTION 1: INTENTIONAL TORTS

Chapter 1 — Intentional torts to the person   8
   I.   Trespass to the person   8
   II.   Intentional infliction of emotional distress   17
   III.   Defences to intentional torts to the person   19
   IV.   Revision questions   26

Chapter 2 — Intentional torts to property   28
   I.   Trespass to land   28
   II.   Intentional torts to chattels   39
   III.   Revision questions   56

SECTION 2: FAULT-BASED LIABILITY

Chapter 3 — Common law negligence   60
   I.   General principles   60
   II.   Common law general duty of care   63
   III.   Special duty issues   74
   IV.   Duty may be limited by type of harm   92
   V.   Breach of the duty of care by defendant   103
   VI.   Causation   109
   VII.   Defences   126
   VIII.   Damages   130
   IX.   Revision questions   131

Chapter 4 — Statutory-based torts   135
    I.   Statutory standard of care   135
    II. Occupiers' Liability Act 1995   138
    III. Revision questions   144

SECTION 3: STRICT LIABILITY

Chapter 5 — Strict liability   148
    I.   Common law strict liability   148
    II. Statutory-based strict liability   164
    III. Revision questions   175

SECTION 4: MISCELLANEOUS

Chapter 6 — Nuisance   180
    I.   General principles   180
    II. Public nuisance   182
    III. Private nuisance   184
    IV. Causation   194
    V.   Defences   195
    VI. Remedies   198
    VII. Revision questions   200

Chapter 7 — Defamation   202
    I.   Historical background   202
    II. Present status of defamation   204
    III. Defences   214
    IV. Remedies   223
    V.   Proposals for change   223
    VI. Revision questions   224

Chapter 8 — Economic relations   227
    I.   Injurious falsehood   227
    II. Passing off   230
    III. Deceit   234
    IV. Interference with contractual relations   237
    V.   Revision questions   240

SECTION 5: THE EXAMINATION

Chapter 9 — Approaching the exam   244
    I. Where to concentrate revision   244
   II. Avoiding common mistakes   249

Appendix — Answers to revision questions   253
      I. Chapter 1 answers   253
    II. Chapter 2 answers   254
  III. Chapter 3 answers   256
  IV. Chapter 4 answers   259
    V. Chapter 5 answers   259
  VI. Chapter 6 answers   261
 VII. Chapter 7 answers   262
VIII. Chapter 8 answers   263

INTRODUCTION

I. Historical background

A. Tort comes from the Latin word tortus *meaning twisted.* **[1]**

1. Tort is found in the French language and means *wrong*.
2. Tort at one time was used in the English language as another word for *wrong*. (Similarly, the word *wrong* is said to be derived from *wrung*.) After the word *tort* left common English speech it continued to be used in the law.

B. Early torts **[2]**

Generally in the early English common law, remedies for wrongs depended on the issuance of writs to bring a defendant into court. The procedures were rigidly prescribed, and only two writs were available for tortious acts: namely *trespass* and *trespass on the case (Action on the case)*.

1. **Trespass** first emerged in the thirteenth century and was criminal in character.
   a. Directed at serious and forcible breaches of the peace.
   b. Courts were primarily concerned with punishment.
   c. If convicted a defendant was fined. If the fine was not paid the defendant was imprisoned. This is how damages first became awarded to an injured plaintiff.
   d. **Remedy** for all *forcible, direct* and *immediate injuries* whether to persons or property.
2. **Trespass on the case** is sometimes referred to as Action on the case and developed as a supplement to trespass. It was designed to afford a remedy for obviously wrongful conduct resulting in indirect injuries.
3. **Distinction between trespass and trespass on the case**
   a. *Trespass* dealt with immediate application of force to person or property.

1

b. *Trespass on the case* dealt with injury by some obvious and visible secondary cause.

Classic example: A log is thrown into the highway. If a person is struck when it is being thrown, that person could maintain trespass against the thrower. The injury is direct. If a person is injured because the log was tripped over as it lay in the highway, the injured person could only bring a trespass on the case action. The injury is indirect. Fortescue J. in *Reynolds v Clarke* (1725) 1 Stra 634.

c. **Damages**
   (1) Trespass required no proof of any actual damage.
   (2) Trespass on the case: No liability accrued unless actual damage was proved.

d. **Liability**
   (1) Trespass imposed liability without regard to fault.
   (2) Trespass on the case required proof of either a wrongful intent or negligence.

II. Modern tort law

A. *The historical classifications of injuries as direct or indirect is being abandoned.* [3]

1. **Focus** is now on the *intent* or *fault* (negligence) of the wrongdoer.
2. Old common law action of **trespass**:
   a. has given rise to some modern tort actions, and
   b. all may be maintained without proof of damages.
   c. **Examples:**
      (1) Battery
      (2) Assault
      (3) False imprisonment
      (4) Trespass to land
      (5) Trespass to chattels
      (6) Conversion
      (7) Detinue.
3. Likewise, **trespass on the case**:
   a. has given rise to some modern torts where damage is the basis of the action.
   b. **Examples:**
      (1) Intentional infliction of emotional distress
      (2) Negligence
      (3) Deceit.

B. *Definition of tort*   **[4]**

1. Generally, academics have difficulty in defining tort. However, all definitions of tort refer to the unreasonable interference with the interests of others.
2. Various definitions of tort:
    a. A tort is a civil wrong (other than a breach of contract or a breach of trust) for which the normal remedy is an action for unliquidated damages. (McMahon citing, *Secretary of State for War v Studdert* [1902] 1 IR 375 (HL), aff'g [1902] 1 IR 240 (CA). Unliquidated damages are damages not determined by the parties.
    b. A tort is a civil wrong, other than breach of contract, for which the court will provide a remedy in the form of an action for damages. (Prosser)
    c. Tortious liability arises from the breach of a duty primarily fixed by law; this duty is toward persons generally and its breach is redressable by an action for unliquidated damages. (Winfield)
    d. A civil wrong for which the remedy is a common law action for unliquidated damages and which is not exclusively the breach of contract, the breach of a trust or other merely equitable obligation. (Salmond)

C. *Function of modern tort law*   **[5]**

1. The protection of interests.
    a. **Examples:**
        (1) Defamation protects good name.
        (2) Nuisance protects use and enjoyment of land.
        (3) Battery protects bodily integrity.

D. *Goals of modern tort law*   **[6]**

1. Compensation for injuries to interests.
2. Loss Distribution for injuries.
3. Punishment of wrongdoers.
4. Deterrence against future injuries and retaliation.

E. *Modern tort liability*   **[7]**

1. This is generally divided into three main areas:
    a. Intentional torts
    b. Fault-based torts
    c. Strict Liability.

2. Not all torts fall exclusively within one of the three main areas.

F. Distinction between tort and criminal wrongs **[8]**

1. Tort
   a. Private dispute between individuals.
   b. Primary goal is to compensate for harm suffered.
2. Crime
   a. Public dispute between an individual and society.
   b. Primary goal is to punish the wrongdoer.

G. Distinction between tort and breach of contract **[9]**

1. Tort
   a. Breach of duty fixed by law.
   b. Duties owed to people in general.
   c. Primary goal to compensate for harm suffered.
2. Contract
   a. Breach of duty fixed by parties themselves.
   b. Duties only owed to parties in contract.
   c. Primary goal to enforce terms (promises) in contract.

III. List of abbreviations of commonly cited tort works [10]

A. Irish

1. McMahon	McMahon B.M.E. and Binchy W., *Irish Law of Torts*, 3rd edn., Butterworths, 2000.
2. Quill	Quill E., *Torts in Ireland*, Gill & Macmillan, 1999.

B. Other

1. Salmond	Salmond R.F.V. and Heuston B., *Salmond & Heuston on the Law of Torts*, 21st edn., Sweet & Maxwell, 1996. (English and Irish)
2. Street	Brazier B. (ed.), *Street, The Law of Torts*, 10th edn., Butterworths, 1999. (English)
3. Winfield	Rogers W.V.H., *Winfield and Jolowicz on Tort*, 15th edn., Sweet & Maxwell, 1998. (English)
4. Prosser	Prosser W. (ed.), Keeton W.P. (ed.) and Dobbs B.D., *Prosser and Keeton on Torts*, 5th edn., West, 1984. (American)
5. Restatement 2d	American Law Institute, *Restatement (Second) Tort*, (1966).

IV. Introduction revision questions

1. What is the primary function of modern tort law? *See* [5].
2. Distinguish between torts and criminal wrongs. *See* [8].
3. Distinguish between tort and contract law. *See* [9].
4. Distinguish between the ancient torts of trespass and trespass on the case. *See* [2].
5. What is the common thread running through all of the various definitions of tort? *See* [4].

SECTION 1:
INTENTIONAL TORTS

1

INTENTIONAL TORTS
TO THE PERSON

Chapter synopsis

I.   Trespass to the person
     Battery
     Assault
     False imprisonment
II. Intentional infliction of emotional distress
III. Defences to intentional torts to the person

I. Trespass to the person

A. Definition: Trespass to the person means direct and intentional acts of interference by the defendant with the person of the plaintiff.   **[11]**

B. There are three modern torts to the person that flow from the ancient principles of trespass: **[12]**

  1. Battery
  2. Assault
  3. False Imprisonment
    All three are crimes as well as torts.   **[13]**
    (1) Tort does *not* require the mental element of *mens rea*.
    (2) Criminal cases can often be used in tort as authority, *but* always note the different context of the decisions.

C. All three trespasses to the person have the following common *characteristics.*   **[14]**

  1. **Voluntary act by the defendant.**
    a. *Voluntary* meaning under defendant's *conscious control.* **[15]**
      (1) **Example:** A person who strikes another while suffering an epileptic seizure did not act voluntarily i.e. act with conscious control.

(2) **Classic case:** *Scott v Shepherd* (1573) 96 ER 525. Persons in a busy market who were throwing fireworks away from themselves were not acting voluntarily because they were acting in self-defence after a person had thrown the fireworks toward them.

b. The defendant's act must be *intentional* or *negligent*. [16]

   (1) It is not necessary for the plaintiff to prove that the defendant intended to injure the plaintiff.

   (2) However, it is necessary to prove that the defendant intended the act that lead to the plaintiff's injury.

   (3) **Example:** As a romantic gesture: if Tarzan swept Jane off of her feet but dropped her causing Jane to break her wrist, Tarzan did not intend the injury but he did intend the act.

c. **No transferred intent:** the intent to commit a tort against one victim cannot be transferred to another victim. [17]

   (1) Historically transferred intent applied to the five intentional torts of Battery, Assault, False Imprisonment, Trespass to Chattels and Trespass to Land.

   (2) Legal commentators appear to agree that transferred intent should *not* be applied in a civil case (although the concept is accepted in criminal law).

   (3) **Note:** negligence may apply. A person is always deemed to intend the natural and probable consequences of their actions. **Example:** Sally and Greg are in a crowded pub. Sally is annoyed with Greg and intends to throw her glass of red wine over him. If Sally misses and hits Danny with the wine she has committed a battery to Danny although she did not intend to hit him with the wine.

2. **Direct injury to plaintiff.** (*See* [2] for difference between direct and indirect.)

a. Injury can be a mere *contact* or *impact* to the plaintiff's person, property or rights (such as freedom). [18]

b. **Actionable *per se*:** No proof of damages is required to maintain an action.

3. **Causation:** The injury to the plaintiff must be caused by the defendant's voluntary act or some force set in motion by the defendant's act. [19]

Burden of proof [20]

   (1) The plaintiff must prove that the defendant's conduct caused the injury, contact or impact.

(2) The onus then shifts to the defendant to prove that the injury, contact or impact was not intentional or negligent.

Battery

Definition: Battery is the direct application of physical contact upon the person of another without consent. *Dullaghen v Hillen* [1957] IR Jur Rep 10 13   [21]
Required elements of battery   [22]
Voluntary act by the defendant
Physical contact (or impact) to the plaintiff
Intention or negligence
Causation
No consent

A. Voluntary act by the defendant

1. *Voluntary* meaning under the defendant's conscious control. [23]
    (a) **Example:** A person who strikes another while suffering an epileptic seizure did not act voluntarily i.e. act with conscious control.
    (b) **Classic case**: *Scott v Shepherd* (1573) 96 ER 525. Persons in a busy market who were throwing fireworks away from themselves were not acting voluntarily because they were acting in self-defence after a person had thrown the fireworks toward them.
2. Force is *not* required.   [24]
    (a) A hostile intent is *not* necessary for a battery, e.g. caressing or kissing.
    (b) However the least touching of another in anger is a battery. *Cole v Turner* (1704) 90 ER 958, e.g. hitting, striking, pinching or spitting on the plaintiff
3. Mere passive obstruction is not a battery, e.g. John is standing in the doorway of the shop, and Mary wishes to enter the shop. John has not committed a battery even if Mary brushes against him. [25]

B. Physical contact (or impact) to the plaintiff   [26]

1. **No harm or injury required**
    (a) The plaintiff is not required to suffer any harm or injury such as bruising, cuts or broken bones from the contact.
    (b) The contact (or impact) is enough. **Rationale**: Battery protects bodily integrity.

2. Physical contact [27]
   (a) Extends to *any* part of the plaintiff's body that is touched.
   (b) Extends to anything which is *attached* to the plaintiff's body and practically identified with it.

   Examples:
     (1) Removing an orange lily from a ladies coat by a policeman was held to be battery. *Humphries v Connor* [1864] 17 IR CLR 1 (QB 1964).
     (2) Striking the horse that the plaintiff was riding. *Dodwell v Burford* 1669 86 ER 703.
     (3) Pulling out a chair upon which a person was going to sit.
     (4) Grabbing a plate out of a person's hand, or knocking a hat off the plaintiff's head.

3. Impact: No actual contact between the defendant and the plaintiff is required. [28]
Example: If Fred hits Barney with a brick, Fred has committed a battery even though he did not actually touch Barney himself.

C. Intention or negligence

1. Intent [29]
   (a) It is *not* necessary for the plaintiff to prove that the defendant intended to injure or harm.
   (b) The plaintiff *must* show that the defendant intended the act(s) that constitute the battery.

2. Negligence [30]
Natural and probable consequences: Everyone is deemed to intend the natural and probable consequences of their actions.
Example: If Kitty hits a customer while practising her golf swing in a crowded sports shop, the contact with the customer would be a natural and probable consequence of Kitty's actions. Kitty owes a duty of care to the customer to act as a reasonable person (*see* [276] *et seq.*). It is not reasonable to swing a golf club in a crowded sports store. Kitty has acted negligently.

D. Causation [31]

1. Direct application
The contact (or impact) to the plaintiff must have directly resulted from the defendant's act(s). *Leame v Bray* (1803) 3 East 593.
2. Intention disposes of any question of remoteness of damages. *Quinn v Leathan* [1901] AC 495

Example: John intends or wishes to hit Ray with a stone. If John throws a stone at Ray, even if there is little chance of John actually hitting Ray because of the direction, John cannot argue that he should not be liable because the harm to Ray was remote or not foreseeable.

E. No consent (See Defences [75].)   [32]

1. **Express consent:** A verbal or written agreement to the physical contact.
   Example: A written consent form for surgery to be performed.
2. **Implied consent:** A presumed agreement to the physical contact based upon the plaintiff's acts.
   Example: Rolling up sleeve and offering arm to doctor for blood to be drawn.
3. **Exceeding consent**   [33]
   If consent, either express or implied, is exceeded a battery occurs.
   Example: *Nash v Sheen* [1953] CLY 3726. The defendant hairdresser caused a skin complaint when she gave the plaintiff an unwanted hair dye when the plaintiff had requested a perm. The plaintiff's consent to physical contact had been exceeded; therefore the defendant was liable for battery.

Legal dilemma   [34]

1. Practical jokes and other contacts of modern life have caused difficulties.
   Example: It is technically a battery to slap someone's shoulder in congratulations or to bump into another on a crowded sidewalk.
2. English approach: Such contact would only be a battery if the contact was *hostile*.   [35]
   a. **Leading case:** *Wilson v Pringle* [1987] QB 237; [1986] 2 All ER 440. A schoolboy was injured when another boy pulled his shoulder bag roughly.
   b. Hostile approach rejected by Lord Goff in *F v West Berkshire Health Authority* [1989] 2 All ER 545, 564.
3. American approach: Battery in the US has been restricted to harmful or offensive contact.   [36]
   a. Incidents of modern life such as patting someone on the back is not harmful or offensive and thus not a battery in the US.
   b. However, an unwanted kiss would be offensive.
   c. Intentionally blowing cigar smoke into the plaintiff's face for the purpose of causing physical discomfort, humiliation and

distress was found to be a battery. *Leichtman Communications v W.L.W. Jacor* 634 NE 2d 697 (OH 1994).

Assault

Definition: An assault is an act by the defendant that places the plaintiff in reasonable apprehension of an immediate battery.   [37]
Required Elements of Assault   [38]
1. Voluntary act by the defendant
2. Apprehension by the plaintiff
3. Intent or negligence
4. Causation

A. Voluntary act by the defendant   [39]

1. **Voluntary — under the defendant's conscious control**.
   a. See [23]
   b. **Assault example:** Mr Magoo is tired of pedestrians walking in the roadway instead of on the footpath. In an effort to teach Paul the pedestrian a lesson Mr Magoo drives straight for Paul only turning away at the last minute. Paul is frightened and thinks that he is going to be hit by the automobile. Mr Magoo performed a voluntary act i.e. driving toward Paul. However, if Mr Magoo had passed out and his automobile veered toward Paul, causing Paul to think that the automobile was going to hit him, Mr Magoo has not performed a voluntary act.
2. **Words as the Voluntary Act**   [40]
   a. **General rule**: No matter how harsh, lying, insulting and provocative words alone can never amount to an assault.
      Exception: In a particular context words alone may be an assault if the words induce a reasonable apprehension of an immediate battery. *Dullaghan v Hillen* [1957] IR Jur Rep 10
      Example: In a dark alley a man whispers to a young girl, 'Don't move or I'll get you!'
   b. **Circumstances:** Under certain circumstances, words alone *may* render some conduct harmless that would otherwise constitute an assault.   [41]
      Classic case: *Tuberville v Savage* [1669] 86 ER 684. Defendant with his hand on his sword said to the plaintiff: '[I]f it were not Assize time, I would not take such language from you.' (In earlier times courts only sat at infrequent intervals, referred to as Assize time. In other words, the defendant

was saying that because the courts are in session I will ignore your remarks.) Held not to be an assault.

3. **Silence as the Voluntary Act**   [42]
Legal commentators are divided over whether repeated harassing silent phone calls can amount to an assault.
R. v Ireland; R. v Burstow [1998] AC 147. The defendant's silence was found to be capable of being a criminal assault. The defendant made repeated silent harassing phone calls to his victim.

4. **Passive Obstruction**   [43]
General rule: Mere passive obstruction is not an assault.
Example: *Innes v Wylie* (1844) 1 Car and K 257. A police officer stood still and barred the plaintiff's way. Held not to be an assault.
Exception: If the defendant takes active steps to block or obstruct the plaintiff this may be an assault.
Example: *Bruce v Dyer* (1966) OR 705 (Canadian). A driver parked his vehicle on the roadway to block another driver. This was held to be an assault.

B. *Apprehension by the plaintiff*

1. **Assault**   [44]
   a. Said to be a *touching* of the *mind* not the body.
   b. *Protects* against purely mental disturbances.
   c. No contact or impact to the plaintiff's person is required.
      (1) An assault may occur without a battery.
      (2) A battery may occur without an assault.

2. **Apprehension**   [45]
   a. Is *not* fear.
      Reasonable apprehension does *not* require the plaintiff to be in fear. The plaintiff must realise or perceive that a battery is imminent.
   b. Must be reasonable.   [46]
      A reasonable person would have the belief that a battery was imminent based upon the defendant's act(s) and the surrounding circumstances.

3. **Imminent battery required**   [47]
Threats of future harm are generally not considered an assault.
Example: *Thomas v National Union of Mineworkers* [1985] 2 All ER. The plaintiff, a miner, refused to join his co-workers on strike. The plaintiff was brought to the pit on a bus through the picket lines of his fellow miners. The striking miners made

violent gestures to the occupants of the bus. These gestures of violence were held not to be an assault. The striking miners were held back by the police and the plaintiff was on the bus with no reasonable grounds that an immediate violent act was going to occur.

C. *Intent or negligence*

1. **Intent** (*See* [16])
   General rule: Assault is *not* dependent on the defendant's intentions: **[48]**
   (1) Toward the plaintiff.
   Example: Henry Hatfield is throwing stones at his enemy Malachi McCoy while Malachi is talking to Sweet Sue. If Sweet Sue is placed in reasonable apprehension of immediate battery, (being hit by a stone), Henry Hatfield has committed an assault to Sweet Sue even though he did not intend to do so and had no quarrel with her.
   (2) To carry out his threat.
   Example: If Conor points a gun in a threatening manner at Michael it does not matter whether the gun is loaded or even able to fire. An assault has occurred if Michael is in reasonable apprehension of being shot. However, there would be no assault if Michael also knew that the gun was not loaded. *R. v St George* (1840) C and P 483.

2. **Negligence**
   Natural and probable consequences — Everyone is deemed to intend the natural and probable consequences of their actions, so if the defendant negligently acts so as to cause the plaintiff to believe that a battery is imminent he is liable for an assault.**[48a]**

D. *Causation*

The plaintiff's reasonable apprehension must have *directly* resulted from the defendant's act(s). See [30]. **[49]**

False imprisonment

A. *Definition: The unlawful and total restraint of the personal liberty of another. Dullaghan v Hillen [1957] IR Jur 10.* **[50]**

Definition by Street: Any act by the defendant that directly, intentionally or negligently causes the confinement of the plaintiff within an area delimited by the defendant. (Definition preferred by most legal commentators.) [51]

B. Required elements of false imprisonment [52]

1. Voluntary act by the defendant
2. Confinement of the plaintiff
3. Intent or negligence
4. Causation.

C. Voluntary act by the defendant

1. **Voluntary** — meaning under the defendant's conscious control. *See* [23] and [39].
2. **Acts** may include the defendant: [53]
    a. *Constraining* the plaintiff.
    b. *Compelling* the plaintiff to go to a particular place.
    c. *Confining* the plaintiff.
    d. *Detaining* the plaintiff against her will.
3. **Physical contact** with the plaintiff's person is *not* required. [54]
4. **Words** alone may be a sufficient act. [55]
    Examples:
    (1) Threats of force. 'If you leave that chair I'll make you sorry you were ever born.'
    (2) Asserting authority. 'You are under arrest. Don't move.'
5. No Act
    Failure to release: If the plaintiff becomes imprisoned on the defendant's land there is *no* false imprisonment if the defendant did not place or induce the plaintiff to become imprisoned. [56]

D. Confinement of the plaintiff

1. **Requires *total restraint* of the plaintiff.** [57]
    (a) The inability of the plaintiff to go in *any* direction.
        (1) Including back the way the plaintiff came.
        (2) However, if the plaintiff is only prevented from going in a certain direction (i.e. north) this is not a total restraint. *Bird v Jones* (1845) 115 ER 668.
    (b) Does *not* require the plaintiff to risk: [58]
        (1) injury, *Sayers v Harlow UDC* (1958) 1 WLR 623
        (2) humiliation,
        (3) property damage.
        Example: Brutus stood in the only door into Olive Oyl's

office and demanded a kiss, otherwise he would not allow her to leave the office. The office is located on the third floor of the Spinach Exchange Building. Olive Oyl is falsely imprisoned because she is totally restrained. The law does not require her to endure a humiliation (Brutus's kiss), or to risk injury or damage her clothing by climbing out of the window onto an adjoining roof.

  (c) **Overt surveillance** is *not* a detention. *Kane v Gov. of Mountjoy Prison* [1988] IR 757 (SC). **[59]**

    (1) So long as the person is free to go where he wants.

2. **Imprisonment** **[60]**

  a. A sentence of imprisonment is *not* a false imprisonment.

  b. Continuation of imprisonment: A person who helps to continue a wrongful detention commits false imprisonment — this is true even if the person is not responsible for the original detention.

3. **Consciousness of confinement** is *not* required. **[61]**

  a. False imprisonment may take place without the plaintiff being aware of being confined.

  b. **Examples:**

    (1) sleeping or unconscious person,

    (2) child,

    (3) mentally handicapped person.

E. *Causation: The defendant's act(s) must be the cause of the plaintiff's false imprisonment.* **[62]**

F. *No consent — See Defences [75].*

II. Intentional infliction of emotional distress

A. *Definition: This is conduct by the defendant that intentionally or recklessly inflicts severe emotional distress to the plaintiff.* **[63]**

B. *Birth of tort* **[64]**

Wilkinson v Downton [1895–9] All ER 267. The defendant told the plaintiff that her husband had been seriously injured in a road accident. He further told the plaintiff that her husband wanted to come home. The plaintiff sent a servant and her son to bring the injured man home. Later, she learned that the story was not true. The story had been intended as a practical joke. The plaintiff suffered trauma to the extent that she suffered serious physical injury with lasting effects.

The defendant in *Wilkinson v Downton* had not committed a recognised trespass to the plaintiff's person, i.e. battery, assault or false imprisonment.

2. Distinguished from trespass   **[65]**
  a. Intentional infliction of emotional distress flows from the ancient principles of trespass to the case rather than trespass.
  b. **Proof of injury** *is* necessary to maintain a cause of action.

C. Required elements of intentional infliction of emotional distress **[66]**
  1. Voluntary act by the defendant
  2. Severe emotional distress to the plaintiff
  3. Intent or recklessness
  4. Causation.

D. Voluntary act by the defendant
  1. **Voluntary** means under the defendant's conscious control. *See* [23] and [39].
     Words — as the voluntary act.   **[67]**
     Unlike assault, words alone may be sufficient.
     Example: *Janvier v Sweeney* [1919] 2KB 316; [1918–19] All ER Rep 1056. The plaintiff was deceived by a private investigator who misrepresented himself as being a policeman. He threatened the plaintiff with criminal proceedings if she did not give information on another matter.

E. Severe emotional distress to the plaintiff
  Proof of injury to the plaintiff is required.   **[68]**
  a. Plaintiff *must* suffer severe emotional distress.
  b. No physical manifestation of the emotional distress is required.
     (1) **Traditionally** a physical injury was required. This requirement was to assure against fraud.
     (2) **Modern approach**: In most jurisdictions a demonstrable physical injury is not required.
        Rationale: There is now a better understanding of mental diseases and illness. Fraud is less of an issue. *See* Nervous Shock [403].

F. Intent or recklessness

1. **Intent:** The defendant must have intended to cause severe emotional distress to the plaintiff. [69]
2. **Recklessness:** The defendant must have acted in disregard of a high probability that his actions would cause severe emotional distress to the plaintiff. [70]

G. Causation

The defendant's act(s) *must* be the cause of the plaintiff's injury. [71]
No Irish cases reported

1. English approach [72]
   McMahon believes that the tort may have been usurped by the statutory tort of harassment.
2. American approach [73]
   a. Tort applies to intentional or reckless infliction of emotional distress through extreme or outrageous conduct.
   b. Extreme or outrageous conduct
      (1) No objective standard but mere rude or offensive behaviour is not sufficient. Restatement 2d, s. 46 describes it as exceeding all bounds of decent behaviour.
      (2) **Example:** *B.N. v K.K.* (1988) 538 A.2d 1175 (Maryland). The defendant doctor had sexual relations with his nurse knowing that he had an active case of herpes. The defendant, as a doctor, was aware that the disease was painful and incurable. The defendant was found liable.

III. Defences to intentional torts to the person [74]

A. Consent
B. Necessity
C. Inevitable accident
D. Parental authority
E. Statutory authority
F. Defence of self and/or property

A. Consent

1. **General rule**: The plaintiff's consent, to the defendant's contact or conduct, renders the contact or conduct lawful. [75]
   Examples:
   (1) *Hegarty v Shine* (1878) 4 LR IR 288. No battery was found to have been committed against a woman who had been

infected with a venereal disease by her partner. The woman had consented to sexual relations with her partner.

(2) *R. v Linekar* [1995] 3 All ER 69. The defendant agreed to pay a prostitute £25 for sex. Afterwards, he refused to pay her. The defendant was charged with rape because the prostitute had consented to the contact for the promise of payment. **Held:** No rape. The prostitute had consented to the act.

2. **May be expressed or implied.**

   a. **Express consent**: A verbal or written agreement to the physical contact or actions of the defendant.   **[76]**

   Examples:

   (a) Verbal — 'Please cut my hair.'

   (b) Written — signing a consent for surgery form.

   b. **Implied consent** by the plaintiff's conduct or act(s) consent is shown.   **[77]**

   (1) **Example:** sitting in a barber's chair implies consent to a haircut.

   (2) **Test for implied consent** is objective.   **[78]**

   Reasonable: From the plaintiff's conduct was it reasonable for the defendant to think that the plaintiff was consenting?

3. **Invalid consent** is consent obtained by *fraud* or *deceit.*

   a. **Exception:** The general rule will not apply if the defendant obtained the plaintiff's consent by fraud or deceit.   **[79]**

   (1) *R. v Case*, 1 Den CC 580. A man told a young girl that the sexual acts that he perpetrated upon her was a surgical operation.

   (2) *R. v Flattery* (1877) 2 QBD 410. A young girl was told that sexual acts would cure her asthma.

   (3) *R. v Williams* (1922) All ER Rep 433. A young girl was told by her singing teacher that his acts (sex) would improve her singing voice by making an air passage.

   b. **Note:** To invalidate the plaintiff's consent, the defendant's fraud or deceit *must* go to the nature of the act.   **[80]**

   Examples:

   (1) **Not to the act.** Joey tells Monica that his name is Chandler, and later he asks Monica for a kiss. If Monica consents to the kiss (i.e. the act) Joey's fraud or deceit (i.e. lying about his name) does not invalidate Monica's consent to the kiss.

(2) **To the act**. However, the fraud or deceit would go to the nature of the act if Joey asked Monica if he could whisper a secret in her ear, but when she leaned toward him he grabbed her and kissed her. Joey's deceit (i.e. lying about his act) invalidates Monica's consent (to allow Joey to whisper in her ear.)

4. **Involuntary consent**

   Undue influence may occur where there is an imbalance of power between the parties making the consent not voluntary.   **[81]**

   Example: *Norberg v Wyannib* (1993) 2 LRC 409 (Canadian). A doctor was engaging in sexual conduct with a patient in exchange for drugs for her addiction. The court held that her consent to the doctor's acts was not voluntary, and therefore invalid.

5. **Consent to medical treatment**

   a. **General rule:** It is a battery to perform any medical treatment or procedures on a patient *without* the patient's consent. *Walsh v Family Planning Services Ltd* [1992] 1 IR 469 (SC) *obiter*   **[82]**

      Example: *Potts v N.W. Regional Health Authority* (1983) (unrep. England). The plaintiff was given a long-acting contraceptive without her consent. Held to be a battery.

   b. **Informed consent** occurs where a patient consented to treatment but:

      (1) his *consent* was *exceeded*, or

      (2) he was *not fully advised* of the risks of the treatment. **[83]**

         (a) **Negligence is the proper tort** (not battery) — *Walsh v Family Planning Services Ltd obiter*   **[84]**

         (b) *See* [312] *et seq.*

   c. **Consent of minor patient**

      Non-Fatal Offences Against the Person Act 1997, s. 23 enables minors aged 16 or older to legally consent to any surgical, medical or dental treatment.   **[85]**

   d. **Right to refuse treatment**

      (1) **Nutrition**: An adult of sound mind has a specific right to refuse food and water. *Sec. of State for the Home Dept. v Robb* [1995] Fam 12   **[86]**

      (2) **Medical treatment**: An adult of sound mind has the right to refuse medical treatment even if her foetus would die. *St. George's Healthcare NHS Trust v S.* [1999] Fam 26   **[87]**

Note: this is an English case, therefore Article 40.3.3 regarding the right to life did not apply.

6. **Sporting events**
   a. **Players**
      (1) **General rule:** players *consent* to physical contact inherent in the particular sport. **[88]**
         (a) *Simms v Leigh Rugby Football Club* [1969] 2 All ER 923. The plaintiff suffered a broken leg when tackled and thrown against the wall. The game had been played according to the rules and the defence of consent was held to be valid.
      (2) **Exception:** A player's consent may be *invalidated* by flagrant, intentional breaches of the game rules resulting in physical injury to the player. *McNamara v Duncan* (1971) 26 ALR 584. **[89]**
         Smolden v Whitworth [1996] unrep. (CA). The defence of consent did not apply where the referee was sued under negligence for failing to apply anti-injury rules in a rugby match.
   b. **Spectators**
      General rule: This states that players voluntarily assume the risk of harm caused by other players, so long as the harm does not result from intentional or reckless behaviour. *Wooldrige v Summer* [1963] 2 QB 43 **[90]**

B. *Necessity*

1. **Definition:** Necessity is defined as the intentional commission of a tortious act to prevent some greater evil where there is no reasonable alternative. **[91]**
   a. Legal commentators wonder if the defence is still valid today.
   b. McMahon notes that the cases are very old, controversial or not on point.
2. **Reasonable alternative** **[92]**
   Lynch v Fitzgerald [1938] IR 382 (SC). The plaintiff claimed damages for the death of his son who was killed by the police when they fired into a mob. It was held that necessity was not a good defence, since shooting *could only be a last resort* to protect lives or property.

C. Inevitable accident

1. **Definition:** An inevitable accident is defined as when the consequences complained of as a wrong were not intended by the defendant and could not have been foreseen and avoided by the exercise of reasonable care and skill. *McBride v Stitt* [1944] NI 7, 10. [93]

2. A person will not be liable for an event over which he had no control and could not have avoided even using the highest skill and care. [94]

   Example: *Stanley v Powell* (1891) 1 QB 86. A bullet ricocheted off of a tree and injured the plaintiff. The injury was held to have been an inevitable accident.

3. **Note:** Many legal commentators believe that inevitable accident has no useful function and according to Winfield 'it is doubtful whether much advantage is gained by the continued use of the phrase'. [95]

D. Parental authority

1. **General rule:** parents may exercise *reasonable* restraint or chastisement on their children without committing intentional torts to the person. [96]

   a. **Example:** If a parent disciplines a child by sending the child to his room for a period of time the parent has not committed false imprisonment.

   b. **Exception:** Art. 3 of the European Convention
   A v United Kingdom [1998] 2 FLR 959. The European Court of Human Rights (ECHR) found that English law violated Art. 3 of the European Convention that prohibits torture, inhumane or degrading treatment or punishment. **Facts:** The stepfather of a nine-year-old hit the boy several times with a garden cane causing bruises. He was charged with causing actual bodily harm to the boy, but a jury acquitted him. The boy appealed to the ECHR arguing that the English law failed to protect him.

2. *Loco parentis:* means acting as a substitute parent i.e. a guardian or teacher: [97]

   a. may exercise reasonable disciplinary measures.

   b. **Exception:** Offences Against the Person Act 1997, s. 24 abolished the criminal immunity teachers had for physical punishment of students.

E. Statutory authority

1. Some statutes authorise acts that would otherwise be the commission of an intentional tort to the person. **[98]**
2. **Lawful arrest**
   a. **Criminal Law Act 1997, s. 4** arrest without a warrant.
      (1) Reasonable cause: Where the police have reasonable cause to suspect an arrestable offence has been committed they may arrest without a warrant any person reasonably believed to be guilty. **[99]**
      Arrestable offence: This is one that is punishable with five or more years imprisonment.
      (2) **Citizen's arrest:** Any person has the right to arrest another person for any arrestable offence where: **[100]**
         (a) The arresting person has reasonable cause to believe the person arrested is in the act of committing an arrestable offence.
         (b) Actual crime must have been committed.
         (c) Person arresting must reasonably suspect that the person arrested was avoiding or likely to avoid arrest by the police.
         (d) Any person arrested must be transferred to the police.
3. **Lawful detention**
   a. A sentence of imprisonment is *not* a false imprisonment.**[101]**
   b. Medical exams and tests
      (1) Health Act 1947, s. 38 — authorises the detention and isolation of persons believed to be the probable source of infectious diseases. **[102]**
      (2) Medical Treatment Act 1945 — authorises the protective confinement of mentally ill persons. **[103]**
   c. Protective custody (unlawful): The arrest and incarceration of a child witness was not lawful even where it was argued that the child's life was in danger. *Connors v Pearson* [1921] 2 IR 51. **[104]**

F. Defence of self and/or property

1. **Self-defence**
   a. **Common law:** A person may use *reasonable force* to protect his/herself or to protect another person. **[105]**
      (1) The degree of force must be *balanced* against the seriousness of the attack. **[106]**

(2) **Example:** *Ross v Curtin* (1989) unrep. (HC). A shop-keeper awoke one night when three men broke into his premises to rob him. When confronted the three men advanced toward the shopkeeper. He fired a warning shot into the air, but one of the intruders was struck in the head by the shot. It was held that the shopkeeper had acted reasonably in the circumstances to defend himself.

b. **Criminal Statutory Reform**

(1) Non-Fatal Offences Against the Person Act 1997, ss 18–20 (known as NFOAPA) mostly restates the common law. **[107]**

(a) **Example:** S. 18(1) — *justifiable use of force* — provides that only *reasonable force* may be used for the protection of oneself or another from injury, assault or detention that is caused by a criminal act.

(b) **Note:** NFOAPA 1997 does *not* apply to fatalities. If the defendant defends himself or another person and kills the attacker the Act is not relevant.

2. **Defence of Property**

a. **Land**

(1) **Right to eject trespassers:** An occupier may use no more force than *is reasonably necessary* to evict a trespasser. *Green v Goddard* (1798) 91 ER 540. **[108]**

Example: *MacKnight v Extravision* (1991) unrep. CC. The plaintiff was preventing the defendants access to their premises. The defendants were entitled to lay hands on the plaintiff to move him aside. When this failed they sought the help of a boxer to remove the plaintiff. Excessive force was used rendering the plaintiff unable to work for several weeks.

(2) If the plaintiff's entry was *without force* he *must* be requested to leave before force may be used. *Green v Goddard* (1798) 91 ER 540. **[109]**

(3) **Criminal statutory reform**: Criminal Justice (Public Order) Act 1994, s. 13(1) provides that an occupier may after a reasonable time, using reasonable force, eject the person who fails or refuses to leave. **[110]**

b. **Chattels**

Common law: A person could use *reasonable force* to defend one's chattels or the chattels of another. **[111]**

(a) Chattels: These are generally goods and personal property such as furniture, jewellery, pets, livestock, vehicles.

(b) **Example:** A person could use reasonable force to stop a pickpocket from taking his watch.

c. **Criminal statutory reform:** NFOAPA 1997 ss 18–20 restate the common law with regard to the use of reasonable force to protect property. (Land and chattels.)   **[112]**

IV. Revision questions

(1) Conor told the drunken man who was annoying him in the pub, 'If it were not for your grey hairs, I would tear your heart out.' Name the tort.

(2) Goliath the Giant noticed David approach swinging his slingshot and preparing to fight him. Goliath was not afraid. Name the tort.

(3) Sam Spade, a private detective, followed Veronica everywhere she went for two weeks. Veronica became afraid and refused to leave her home. Name the tort.

(4) Anthony's girlfriend Big Bertha was angry when she learned that Anthony was seeing another woman. Bertha cornered Anthony in the local pub and sat on his lap until he agreed to give up his other woman. Name the torts.

(5) Peter seduces Anne by telling her that he is a millionaire. Peter is an unemployed actor and Anne states that she would not have consented to sex with Peter had she known the truth. Will Anne's consent to the sexual conduct be a valid defence for Peter if Anne sues him for battery?

(6) Captain Blackbeard agreed to take Grainne in his rowing boat, named the QE 1/2, across the River Suir. Once Grainne got into the rowing boat, Blackbeard rowed to the middle of the river and told Grainne to 'put out or get out'.

(a) Has Blackbeard committed a battery?

(b) Has Blackbeard committed an assault?

(c) If Grainne is a strong swimmer is this a case of false imprisonment?

(7) Little Rotten Ralphie was being very naughty in school. His teacher told him to stand in the corner where he continued to make rude noises. The teacher raised a book as if he was going to hit Rotten Ralphie with it, but decided not to do so. Later, the other students told Rotten Ralphie about the book.

(a) Has Ralphie been falsely imprisoned?

(b) Did the teacher commit an assault when s/he raised the book?

(8) Oliver the Osteopath was treating Sinead, a keen sportswoman for whiplash. Oliver told Sinead that he could cure her condition by 'nerve block tests' that consisted of Oliver spanking Sinead very hard on the buttocks. Sinead agreed to the treatment and attended several sessions until her coach noticed her severe bruising and called the authorities. Medical experts believe that Oliver was spanking Sinead for his own sexual excitement. Sinead is humiliated and seriously upset.

(a) Will Sinead's consent to the treatment be a good defence for Oliver if Sinead brings an action for battery against Oliver?

(b) What other trespass to the person, if any, could Sinead bring against Oliver?

(9) Helen was seated next to an elderly gentleman on a transatlantic flight. Helen reminded the elderly gentleman of his dearly departed wife Jo. During the flight they both fell asleep. However, Helen was rudely awakened when the elderly gent groped her murmuring in his sleep, 'Oh Jo!' Can Helen maintain a cause of action for battery against the elderly gentleman if she was asleep when he touched her?

(10) Lulu saved until she could afford to have plastic surgery. She went to Dr Quack and he agreed to operate to repair her nose, which had been broken in a field hockey accident. While Dr Quack was operating he decided to try out a new technique for removing lines from around the eyes. Although her nose turned out perfect, Lulu is upset that she has two black eyes. Can Lulu bring an action for battery against Dr Quack?

(11) When Santa tried to slide down Liam's chimney on Christmas Eve he got stuck. Santa could not go up, nor could he go down. Has Liam falsely imprisoned Santa?

(12) Mike snatched an elderly lady's handbag from her arm and ran away. Ken saw the incident and chased Mike. As Mike was trying to escape over a wall Ken caught him by the leg. Mike lost his grip and fell onto Bob an innocent bystander.

(a) Identify all the possible intentional torts to the person in the problem.

(b) Are there any valid defences to these torts?

2

INTENTIONAL TORTS
TO PROPERTY

Chapter synopsis

I. Trespass to land
   Modern trespass to land
   Defences to trespass to land
   Remedies for trespass to land
II. Intentional torts to chattels
   Trespass to chattels
   Conversion
   Detinue
   Defences to intentional torts to chattels

I. Trespass to land

A. Historical background — common law trespass to land

1. **General rule:** [113]
   a. Recovery required an invasion which:
      (1) **Interfered** with the right of *exclusive possession* of the land
      (2) Was a *direct* result of some *act* committed by the defendant.
         (a) Dealt with *direct* or *forcible* invasions to land.
         (b) **Examples:** Throwing a stone onto the land of another or forcing your way into the building of another.
   b. Trespass was actionable *per se*. (No proof of damages required.)
2. **Rules** [114]
   a. Were *strict* and *severe* for the common law action of trespass.
   b. Have survived until modern times.
      Until recently this resulted in an *unreasonable* distinction between injuries to persons and injuries to property.

Example: If a tram jumped its tracks and struck a pedestrian on the footpath before destroying a shop front, the pedestrian could only bring an action for negligence. On the other hand, the owners of the tram were absolutely liable to the owner of the damaged shop.

B. *Trespass on the case (Action on the case)*   [115]

1. **General rule:**
   a. Dealt with *indirect* invasions
   b. Required proof of
      (1) negligence or intent
      (2) substantial damage.
         Example: of indirect invasion is obstructing or diverting a stream so that water ultimately flows into a neighbour's premises.
2. **Direct/indirect distinction** between trespass to land and trespass on the case or action on the case has been largely abandoned.
                                                                    [116]
   a. **Example:** Under the common law if a person failed to remove personal property at the end of an agreed period of time from the plaintiff's land an action had to be brought on the case because there was no forcible invasion to sustain an action for trespass to land. *Winterbourne v Morgan* [1809] 103 ER 1056. Today the same situation is simply trespass to land.
   b. Directness distinguishes *trespass* and *nuisance*. See [131] and [140].

C. *What is land?*

1. Under the common law maxim: *quicquid plantatur solo solo cedit*, whatever is affixed to the land belonged to the owner of that land and is regarded as land.   [117]
   Examples: fences, trees, buildings, gates.
2. The common law maxim: *sujus est solum ejus est usque ad coelum*. Roughly translated: He who has the soil owns upward unto heaven and by analogy, downward to hell.   [118]
   Hannabalson v Sessions 116 Iowa 457 (1902), 'The title of the owner of the soil extends not only downward to the centre of the earth, but upward *usque ad coelum*, although it is doubtful whether owners as quarrelsome as the parties in this case will ever enjoy the usufruct of their property in the latter direction.'

3. a. **Exception:** The right to things under the surface of land was qualified.
   b. **Treasure trove:** If an item made of gold or silver was deliberately concealed on land and subsequently found, assuming that its true owner could not be located, at common law the Crown was entitled to the item under the *royal prerogative* of treasure trove.   **[119]**
      (1) Originally items were melted down to make coins.
      (2) Eventually, this became a means of securing and preserving artefacts of archaeological significance.

Modern trespass to land

A. *Definition: Modern trespass to land is the intentional or negligent entering or remaining on, or directly causing anything to come into contact with, land in the possession of another without lawful justification. (Street)*   **[120]**

B. *Required elements of trespass to land*   **[121]**
   1. Voluntary act by the defendant
   2. Intent or negligence
   3. Invasion of land
   4. Plaintiff in possession (or entitled to possession)
   5. Causation
   6. No lawful justification.

C. *Voluntary act by the defendant*   **[122]**
   1. The defendant *must* have voluntarily acted. *See* [15] and [23].
      Example: It is not a trespass to be carried onto the land of another.
   2. Even the most *trivial acts* of trespass are actionable.   **[123]**
      a. **Trespass to land is actionable *per se***
         No damages required: The plaintiff is *not* required to show any damage.   **[124]**
         (a) Illustrates importance — attached from ancient times to the protection of the possession of property.
         (b) Substantial damages: To recover substantial damages the plaintiff must show an appreciable loss.
   3. Acts include:
      a. **Entering on land**   **[125]**
         (1) Slightest crossing of boundary of land will constitute trespass.

(2) Not necessary to cross boundary.

(3) Physical contact with land is enough. **Examples:**

   (a) Striking a door with the intention of breaking it. *Whelan v Madigan* [1978] ILRM 136

   (b) Leaning a ladder against a wall. *Westripp v Baldock* [1939] 2 All ER 799

(4) **Abuse of right of entry** may constitute trespass if the purpose for the entry is outside the scope of authority granted for the entry. **[126]**

   Example: *DPP v McMahon* [1987] ILRM 87. Police entered licenced premises and committed trespass. They had entered without a warrant to investigate possible breaches of the Gaming and Lotteries Act 1956. S. 39 of the Act required a warrant. The police could not claim that they had a public right of entry because they were not there to buy food etc. and they did not have statutory authority to enter.

b. **Remaining on the land**

   (1) Lawfully entered and remained

   (a) Where a person has lawfully entered land in the possession of another he will commit a trespass if he remains there after his right to stay has terminated. *Wood v Leadbitter* (1845) 153 ER 351. **[127]**

   (b) Alternatively, failing to remove property at the end of the agreed time period. **[128]**

   (2) **Refusal to Leave:** It is trespass to refuse or fail to leave after being requested to do so. **[129]**

   (3) **Reasonable Force**: After a reasonable time and using reasonable force the occupier may eject the person who fails or refuses to leave. *See* Defences [108], [109] and [110].

c. **Placing things on land**

   (1) **General rule:** It is a trespass for a person to *place* any chattel on the land of another or to *cause* any object or substance to directly cross the boundary of another person's land, or even to *reach* the boundary. **Examples:** **[130]**

   (a) Animals chased onto the land of another person.

   (b) Tossing litter onto the land of another.

   (c) Placing manure against a boundary wall belonging to a neighbour.

   (d) Causing third person to enter land: by carrying the third person by force, or by leading the third person to enter by making false representations e.g. 'You may hunt in that field.'

(2) **Invasion must be direct** to constitute an actionable trespass for placing things on land. The invasion must be *direct* rather than *consequential*.   **[131]**

    (a) **Note:** *direct* invasions tend to be classified as trespass and *indirect* or *consequential* invasions tend to be classified as nuisance. *See* [140].

    (b) **Example:** A man operates a quarry. During recent blasting his neighbour's land has been invaded by hurled stones and dust. Stones invading the neighbour's airspace and landing on the ground are direct invasions, i.e. trespass. The dust is purely transitory particles and if they do not accumulate they result in an indirect invasion, i.e. nuisance.

D. Intent or negligence   **[132]**

1. It is not necessary for the plaintiff to prove that the defendant intended to invade, injure or harm the plaintiff's land.

    Example: If Goldilocks enters the house of the three bears because she believes it to be her own, she has trespassed even though she did not intend to do so.

2. The defendant must have intended the act(s) that caused the invasion.

    Example: Gary loves to garden. Noticing a healthy crop of weeds in a corner of his garden Gary begins to pull the weeds and tosses them over his shoulder. He thinks that the weeds are landing in a pile in his garden. Unfortunately, most of the weeds are landing in Grouchy Grainne's garden. Gary intended the act, i.e. tossing the weeds over his shoulder, that caused the invasion although he did not intend to invade Grainne's garden. Gary was also negligent in how he carried out his act.

E. Invasion of land

1. **Land**

    Modern statutory provisions: generally follow the common law approach.   **[133]**

    (1) Whatever is affixed to the land is *land*. *See* [117].

    Example: Paragraph 14 of the Schedule to the Interpretation Act 1937, provides that the word *land* when used in an Act of the Oireachtas includes 'messuages, tenements and hereditaments, houses and buildings, or any tenure' unless there is an indication of a contrary intention.

(2) Land stretches 'from heaven to hell'. *See* [118].

2. Direct invasions

This includes anything of substance coming into contact with land.

a. Airspace above land

(1) An encroachment or intrusion into the airspace above land constitutes a trespass to the land even though there is no contact with the surface of the land.   **[134]**

Examples: An advertising sign affixed to an adjoining building overhangs the plaintiff's roof, or the arm of a crane swinging over the plaintiff's land.

(2) **Common law encroachments** for *social necessity* and the *common good* have been recognised for: **[135]**

(a) communication satellites

(b) air travel.

(c) **Example:** *Lord Beirnstein of Leigh v Skyviews and General Ltd* [1978] QB 479. It was held that a balance has to be struck between the rights of an owner to enjoy the use of his land and the interests of the general public in utilising airspace. *The balance was achieved by restricting the rights of an owner in the airspace above the land to such height as is necessary for the ordinary use and enjoyment of the structures on it.* Above that height the owner has no greater rights in the airspace than any other member of the public. The defendant had flown over the plaintiff's land taking aerial photographs.

(3) **Statutory qualification:** S. 55 of the Air Navigation and Transport Act 1936, as amended by s. 47(1) of the Air Navigation and Transport Act 1988, provides that no action in trespass or nuisance will lie by reason only of any flight of any aircraft over any property at a height above the ground which, having regard to the wind, weather and all the circumstances of the case, is reasonable.   **[136]**

b. Under the surface of land

(1) An intrusion into the soil under the surface of land is a trespass, but this rule is qualified.   **[137]**

(a) **Antiquities of importance:** *Webb v Ireland* [1988]
IR 353 (SC). Prerogative of the Crown (treasure
trove, *see* [119]) did not survive the establishment of
the Free State in 1922, but under the 1937
Constitution, with its express reference to the historical origins of the State and the common good, the
Supreme Court held that this carried with it a right
of the State to ownership where antiquities of importance are discovered and there is no known owner.
Majority relied upon Article 10, while the minority
relied upon Article 5 of the Constitution.

(b) *Webb v Ireland.* The plaintiffs were trespassing and
found the Derrynaflan Hoard. A dispute arose as to
who had the better claim, the plaintiffs as the finders
or the landowners.

(2) **Statutes:** The Minerals Development Act 1979, s. 12
gives the Minister for Energy the exclusive right to work
minerals, irrespective of who happens to own the land on
which they are located. (Part II of the Act gives the owner
of the land a right to compensation.)   **[138]**

(3) **Social necessity and the common good** may develop in
the future for underground mass transit. (This has been
recognised in other jurisdictions).   **[139]**
Example: *Boehringer v Montalto* 254 NYS 276 (1931). A
sewer located 150 feet below the surface of the plaintiff's
land was held not to invade the surface owner's rights.

c. **Directness distinguishes trespass from nuisance**   **[140]**

(1) **Nuisance** applies where the invasion or entry on property is *indirect*.
Examples: Where smoke or fumes drift onto neighbouring land, or where tree roots or branches encroach on to
neighbouring land.

(2) **Trespass** applies where the invasion is *direct*.
Examples: Throwing coins in Farmer Fred's stream, or
walking across another person's field.

(3) US approach: *Trespass* is an invasion of the plaintiff's
interest in the exclusive possession of his land, while *nuisance* is an interference with the use and enjoyment of it.

F. *Plaintiff in possession or entitled to possession of land*

1. **General rule:** The plaintiff *must* be in possession of the land invaded. **[141]**
   a. Trespass protects *possession* rather than *ownership*. **[142]**
   b. **De facto possession**
      (1) Any person in *de facto* possession can sue anyone who does not have an immediate right to recover possession of the property. **[143]**
      (2) **Example:** *Petrie v Owners of SS Rostrevor* [1898] 2 IR 556. The plaintiff had no legal entitlement to the foreshore but he placed oysters on it to begin a business. The defendant's boat ran aground damaging the plaintiff's oysters. The court held that, 'the placing of chattels (oysters) on the land allowed the plaintiff to become possessed of it *de facto*'. The defendant only escaped liability because he had authority from the owners of the foreshore.

2. **Occupiers v Owners** **[144]**
   a. **General rule:** If the owner exceeds his lawful authority, the occupier may maintain a trespass action against the owner. **Example:** *Whelan v Madigan* [1978] 1 IR 136. The landlord committed trespass against his tenants by damaging the land, i.e. doors and letterbox.
   b. **Exception: rented rooms**
      Lodgers or hotel guests do *not* have *possession* of the room to maintain an action for trespass. **Examples:** **[145]**
      (a) lodger: *Allan v Liverpool Overseers* (1874) LR 9 QB 180
      (b) hotel guests: *Larkin v Porter* (1828) 1 Hud and Br 524.

G. *Causation*

The defendant's act(s) caused the invasion of the plaintiff's land.

H. *No lawful authority*

The defendant had no legal right to invade the plaintiff's land. *See* rights of entry in 'Defences' below.

Defences to trespass to land

1. License or consent
2. Common law rights of entry
3. Statutory rights of entry — trespass *ab initio*
4. Necessity.

A. *Licence or consent of the plaintiff*

1. **Definition**: A licence is consent from the person in possession to enter land or premises i.e. the person in possession licenses entry by issuing a licence. A licence prevents an entry from being unlawful. [146]

   a. **A bare licence** is one not supported by consideration (e.g. consideration can be a price for entering). [147]
   It can be withdrawn at any time.
   Examples: Shopper in department store or visitor in a hospital.

   b. **Licence with an interest** is a licence with consideration or price for entering or remaining. [148]
   A person can only be removed in accordance with the terms of the licence.
   Example: Swimming pool patron has a right to remain in the pool until the swimming period expires. Cinema patron has a right to remain in the cinema until the film is finished.

B. *Common law*

Rights of entry: People are permitted to enter land in the possession of another in certain circumstances. [149]
Example: The privilege of abatement of a nuisance by self-help is of ancient origin.

C. *Statutory rights of entry*

1. **Statutes allowing entry.** General rule: various statutes grant a number of public officials and others a right of entry on to the land or premises of another. [150]

   a. **Examples:**
      (1) Control of Bulls for Breeding Act 1985
      (2) Misuse of Drugs Act 1977 & 1984.

   b. **The Criminal Law Act 1997** allows for:
      (1) **Entry without warrant**: Section 6 of the Act gives police extensive powers to enter dwellings to arrest with or without a warrant (or committal order). [151]
      (2) **Note**: Constitutional Protection: Art. 40.5 provides that '[t]he dwelling of every citizen is inviolable and shall not be forcibly entered save in accordance with law.'

   c. **Abuse of right of entry** may constitute trespass if the purpose of the entry is outside the scope of the authority granted for the entry. *See* [126]. [152]

2. **Doctrine of trespass *ab initio***
   a. **Common law procedural device** [153]
      (1) **History of doctrine:** Trespass *ab initio* is said to have been first articulated in the *Six Carpenters Case* (1610) 77 ER 695. This case involved the refusal of the six defendants to pay for a quart of wine and a pennyworth of bread that they had ordered and consumed in the plaintiff's inn. The court held that the six were not trespassers ab initio (trespassers from entry).
      (2) Designed to circumvent the general rule.
         General rule: An action for trespass under the common law could not be brought if the original entry was lawful.
   b. **Modern definition:** [154]
      (1) Where a person enters land *under authority of law* and he later abuses or exceeds that authority, he is deemed to become a trespasser *ab initio*, or trespasser from the entry.
      (2) Doctrine usually arises in the exercise of police powers. Doctrine also applies to chattels and persons.
      (3) **Requires:** [155]
         (a) An act of *positive misfeasance* (wrongful act),
         (b) A mere non-feasance such as a failure to pay for goods or services is not trespass *ab initio*.
         (c) **Misfeasance** includes remaining on land longer than is necessary for the purpose of entry.
   c. **Independent reason for entry** [156]
      Where an abuse takes place after entry there is no trespass *ab initio* if there remains an *independent ground* or reason for the entry.
      (1) In other words, a wrongful act will only render the original entry unlawful where it takes away the entire basis of the lawful entry.
      (2) **Example:** *Elias v Pasmore* [1934] 2 KB 164. Police officers lawfully entered property to arrest a man, but then wrongfully seized documents. It was held that the police were trespassers only as to the goods (papers) and not trespassers *ab initio*.
   d. **Criticism**
      (1) English approach [157]
         (a) In *Chic Fashions (West Wales) Ltd v Jones* [1968] 2 QB 299, the English Court of Appeal criticised the very existence of the doctrine. **Rationale**: A subsequent

event cannot make an act unlawful if it was lawful when originally performed.

   (b) Criticism ignored: In later cases such as *Cinnamond v British Airports Authority* (1980) 1 WLR 582.
(2) American approach: The 2nd Restatement rejects the doctrine in all situations.

D. Necessity

Definition: Necessity is the intentional commission of a tortious act to prevent a greater evil, where there is no reasonable alternative. **[158]**

  a. Generally accepted: To avail of defence it must be shown that:
   (1) the trespass was *necessary*, and
   (2) the defendant was *not negligent*.

   Example: *Rigby v Chief Constable of Northamptonshire* [1985] 2 All ER 985. The defence of necessity was successfully used when the defendant caused a fire by firing tear gas into the plaintiff's shop in an attempt to eject a dangerous criminal suspect.

  b. Defence probably only applies when there is a *threat* to life or property. **[159]**

   (1) **Example:** *Cope v Sharpe* [1912] 1 KB 496. The defendant, a gamekeeper, set fire to heather on the plaintiff's land to act as a firebreak to stop the threatened spread of a fire on plaintiff's land onto the land of his employer. The defendant was sued for trespass but necessity was held to be a good defence. There was a real threat of fire and defendant was held to have act reasonably.

  c. The defence applies only if the defendant did not cause the greater evil or peril.

Remedies for trespass to land

A. Injunction   **[160]**

  1. Available where trespass is threatened, or
  2. Where a trespass is of a continuing nature.

B. Action for recovery of land   **[161]**

A lawsuit seeking possession of land to the exclusion of others.

C. Re-entry   **[162]**

  1. A common law remedy of self-help.

Note: All common law self-help actions are fraught with difficulties.

2. Possessor of land may re-enter the land, and expel a trespasser using reasonable force if necessary.

D. *Action for mesne profits* [163]

Enables the plaintiff to claim:
a. the profits taken by the defendant during his occupancy,
b. damages for deterioration, and
c. the reasonable costs of acquiring possession.

E. *Distress damage feasant* [164]

1. Allows any occupier of land to *seize* any chattels that are *unlawfully* on the land, and have done or are doing *damage*.
2. The occupier may *detain* the chattels until the payment of compensation has been made.
3. Originally applied to animals, but now *extends* to all chattels.
   Example: *Ambergate Ry. v Midland Ry.*(1853) 23 LJQB 17. The plaintiff railway was held entitled to seize and detain the defendant railway's locomotive engine that was wrongfully trespassing on the plaintiff's line.

F. *Damages*

1. **For trivial trespasses** damages will be nominal. [165]
2. Beneficial use of land [166]
   a. Where a trespass involves some beneficial use of land the plaintiff is entitled to a reasonable remuneration for the use of land.
   b. Value determined as if made by agreement in a contract, i.e. a fair market value for the use.

II. *Intentional torts to chattels*

General rule:
1. There are three torts recognised today: [167]
   a. **Trespass to chattels** — direct interference with the chattels of another person.
   b. **Conversion** — the wrongful assertion of dominion (ownership) over the chattels of another.
   c. **Detinue** — withholding the chattels of another from the person entitled to their immediate possession.

2. All three protect personal property and goods. **[168]**
   a. **Note:** the same act(s) could give rise to more than one of the torts.
   b. **Example:** *British Wagon Co. Ltd v Shortt* [1961] IR 164 A machine under a hire purchase agreement was *sold* to the defendant. The defendant was not aware of the hire purchase agreement and performed repairs on the machine. The owner sought the return of the machine under theories of detinue and conversion. The defendant refused to return the machine unless compensated for the repairs. It was held that the owner was entitled to succeed on either claim.
3. **Distinction between conversion and detinue** **[169]**
   a. **Conversion** is a *denial* of title by the defendant.
      (1) Conversion is a single act of denial of title.
      (2) Damages are usually awarded to compensate the owner for the loss.
   b. **Detinue** is the *retention* of the chattel(s) by the defendant. **[170]**
      (1) Detinue is a continual denial of possession.
      (2) The central issue is the return of the chattels.
4. **Distinction — between conversion and trespass to chattels** **[171]**
   a. **Conversion** is an *indirect* interference with the chattels.
   b. **Trespass** is a *direct* interference with the chattels.

Trespass to chattels

A. *Definition: Trespass to chattels is the intentional, direct and unlawful injury to, or interference with, chattels in the possession of another.* **[172]**

B. *Historical background*
   1. Developed from the ancient *trespass de bonis asportatis* which applied to cases where chattels were asportated (carried off). **[173]**
      a. Later extended to include chattels damaged but not taken.
         Examples:
         (a) Animals killed — *Wright v Ramscot* (1668) 85 ER 93
         (b) Animals beaten — *Slater v Swann* (1730) 93 ER 906.
      b. Eventually extended to include any *direct* and *immediate intentional interference* with a chattel in the possession of another.
         (1) **Direct and forcible** interference required. *Covell v Laming* (1808) 170 ER 1034, otherwise trespass on the case.

(2) **In possession**: The plaintiff had to be in possession of the chattel at the time of the interference.
Rule relaxed to include plaintiffs entitled to possession.
(3) As *trespass de bonis asportatis* evolved, various remedies developed such as detinue, replevin and trover to deal with other types of interference to chattels.
(4) Over the centuries the various evolving torts dealing with chattels became confused and overlapped.

2. a. **Lack of clarity:** Generally commentators agree that the modern tort of trespass to chattels lacks clarity and consisten cy inIreland.
   b. **Statutory reform:** In England there has been some reform with the enactment of the Torts (Interference with Goods) Act 1977.
   But commentators agree that further reform is needed.

C. *Required elements for trespass to chattels* [174]

1. Voluntary act by the defendant
2. Intent to deal with chattel
3. Injury or interference to chattel
4. Plaintiff in possession or entitled to possession
5. Causation.

D. *Voluntary act by the defendant*

Voluntary i.e. within the defendant's control. *See* [15].
Actual physical contact with the chattel is not required. [175]
Example: Chasing a hen out of the hen house.

E. *Intent to deal with the chattel*

1. Traditionally, as with trespass to land, the *interference* or injury must have been *legally caused* by the defendant's act or a force set in motion by his act. [176]
   At common law all trespass had to be intentional or wilful.
   Example: *McMullan v Bradshaw* (1916) 50 ILTR 205. Deliberate use of a chattel believing it to be his own, still amounted to a trespass.
2. Present status: The injury or interference must be *wilful* or *negligent*.
   a. In Ireland, relying on some English cases decided before the Tort (Interference with Goods) Act 1977, negligence has crept into the traditional intentional torts. [177]

b. **Example:** *E.S.B. v Hastings & Co. Ltd* [1965] IR Jur Rep 51. Liability under trespass to chattels was imposed on the negligent acts of the defendants. The defendants, while resurfacing a road, allowed their digger to damage a high-tension electrical cable in the possession of the plaintiffs. The plaintiffs warned the defendants about the presence of the cable.

c. Some commentators argue that trespass should only apply to deliberate acts. **[178]**

3. The defendant must have intended to deal with the chattel. **[179]**

   a. **Note:** A purely *accidental* interference with chattels is not actionable in trespass, because it is lacking intent and negligence. **[180]**

   b. **Example:** Fred was standing watching a horse race. He did not know that Audrey had removed her new hat to straighten her hair. Audrey set the hat on the seat behind Fred. When Fred suddenly sat on the hat he did not intend to deal with the chattel (hat) in any manner. If Fred performed his act (sitting) negligently he could still be liable.

F. *Injury or interference*

1. **Interference** includes: **[181]**

   a. Removing the chattel from the possession of another, or

   b. Simply moving the chattel from one place to another.
   Example: *Whelan v Madigan* [1978] 1 IR 136. The landlord moved the tenant's chairs.

2. **Injury** includes: **[182]**

   a. Damaging the chattel.

   b. Destroying the chattel.

3. **Actionable *per se*?** **[183]**

   a. Commentators generally write that it is, but:

      (1) Judiciary do not appear to think it is. (McMahon)

      (2) McMahon states that it probably is actionable *per se.*

      (3) Street states that it is actionable *per se,*

         (a) Otherwise people could touch museum objects with impunity.

         (b) It also provides a remedy for instances such as when a person rightfully refuses to use his own toothbrush after another person has used it.

      (4) American approach: not actionable *per se.* (Prosser)

         (a) Trespass remains remedy for minor interference

resulting in some damage, but not serious or important enough to amount to conversion (forced judicial sale of chattel).

(b) Criteria for determining seriousness of interference, discussed in [234].

G. *Plaintiff in possession or entitled to immediate possession*

1. **Possession of chattel** not ownership is the key. *See* [142] re. land.
   a. **Possession includes**:   **[184]**
      (1) **By borrowing**.
          Example: If I borrow my sister's book I am in possession of it.
      (2) **By hiring**.   **[185]**
          Example: If I hire a car I am in possession of it.
      (3) **By creating a bailment**.   **[186]**
          (a) A bailment is generally a contractual relationship where a chattel is delivered to another to hold in trust — with the understanding that the chattel will be returned to the person delivering it.
          (b) **Example of a bailment:** When I leave my clothes at a dry cleaners the cleaner is in possession of my clothes and is expected to return them to me.
          (c) **Note**: Money deposited into an account does not create a bailment. **Rationale:** The depositor does not expect the same coins and notes returned.

2. **Owner v person in possession**
   a. **The owner of the chattels** cannot bring an action for trespass against any person in lawful possession of the chattel. **[187]**
      Example: *Keenan Bros. v CIE* (1962) 97 ILTR 54. The plaintiff's goods were delayed in transit during a labour dispute. The High Court refused to compel the defendant carrier (in lawful possession) to deliver the goods or to allow the plaintiff to remove the goods from the defendants railroad cars. The fact that the goods were plaintiff's did not change the fact that at common law it would be a trespass to chattels for any person to open defendants cars to remove goods without the defendant's consent or some legal right to do so, such as under a contract.

3. **Superior title holder**
   May defeat a plaintiff's claim if the plaintiff's claim to the chattel is based solely on possession. *Webb v Ireland*. See [137]. **[188]**

H. Causation

1. The interference or injury to the plaintiff's chattel must have been caused by the act(s) of the defendant.   **[189]**
2. **For liability interference must be direct.** *See* [173].   **[190]**
   a. **Example of direct interference**: moving jewellery from one room to another. *Kirk v Gregory* (1876) 1 Ex D 55—when the defendant's brother-in-law died she moved his jewellery from one room to another thinking that it would be safer. The jewellery was subsequently stolen, and the deceased's executor successfully sued the defendant for trespass.
   b. **Example of indirect interference**: *McDonagh v West of Ireland Fisheries* Unrep. (HC) 1986. The defendant temporarily removed the plaintiff's boat from its moorings. The boat was damaged, probably due to settling on some unknown obstruction on the seabed. Such an injury was held not to be direct and hence not a trespass.

Conversion

A. *Definition: Conversion is any act to the chattels of another that constitutes an unjustified denial of his title. (This is sometimes expressed as the wrongful assertion of dominion over the chattels of another.)*   **[191]**

Definition by McMahon: Wrongfully and directly interfering with the possession of chattels, cited in *Farrell v Minister for Agriculture and Food* (1995).   **[192]**

B. *Historical background*   **[193]**

1. Trover developed in the late fifteenth century to fill the void between:
   a. Trespass: the wrongful taking of chattels, and
   b. Detinue: the wrongful retention of chattels.
2. Trespass applied if the plaintiff remained the owner of the chattel and his possession was only interrupted or interfered with.
3. Trover applied if the defendant had appropriated (taken possession) of the chattel.
4. Tort of conversion is said to have come about when the basic differences between trespass and trover were highlighted in *Fouldes v Willoughby* (1841) 151 ER 1153.   **[194]**

a. *Fouldes v Willoughby.* Facts: The plaintiff boarded the defendant's ferry. The ferry sailed between Birkenhead and Liverpool. The defendant wrongfully refused to carry the plaintiff's two horses. The defendant told the plaintiff to take the horses ashore, but the plaintiff refused. The defendant then took the horses from the plaintiff and put them ashore. The plaintiff remained on the ferry and was taken across the river: as a result the plaintiff lost his horses. Holding: The mere act of removing the horses from the ferry was wrongful and actionable as a trespass. However, it did not amount to a conversion.

5. Conversion expanded greatly and encroached upon detinue, trespass, and replevin.   **[195]**
   Importance of conversion — expanded to include:
   a. **Appropriation** to one's own use,
   b. **Dispossession** of the chattel to another person,
   c. **Dealing** with the chattel in a manner *adverse* to the plaintiff and *inconsistent* with the plaintiff's right of possession.

C. *Required elements of conversion:*   **[196]**

1. Voluntary act by the defendant
2. Intent to deal with chattel
3. Plaintiff in possession or entitled to possession
4. Causation.

D. *Act by defendant. There must be some voluntary act. See [15].*

1. **By taking possession**   **[197]**
   a. Dealing with chattels in a manner *inconsistent* with rights of true owner.
      Example: Stealing.
   b. Intention to *permanently* deprive is not necessary.   **[198]**
      Example: Taking a car for a joyride.
   c. **Mistaken assumption of ownership**. An innocent purchaser of stolen goods will commit conversion because the mistaken assumption of ownership is a denial of the true owner's title.
                                                                   [199]
   d. **Exception: Rule of commercial convenience.**   **[200]**
      (1) A bailee who merely takes possession of a chattel for storage, safekeeping or transportation, but has no knowledge that the chattel is lost or stolen does not become liable to the true owner for conversion.

(2) However, wrong delivery (giving it or taking it to the wrong person or place) by a carrier or warehouseman will render him liable for conversion. *Lancashire & Yorkshire Ry. v MacNicoll* (1919) 88 LJKB 601.

2. **By detention**   [201]

a. **Required demand and refusal.** Where the defendant has *lawfully gained possession* of a chattel there must be a demand (by the plaintiff) and a refusal to surrender (by the defendant) before conversion arises.

b. **Conclusive evidence of conversion** is a defendant's refusal to return chattels after demand by a person entitled to possession.
                                                                    [202]

Refusal may be reasonable to authenticate claims of ownership. *Poole v Burns* [1944] IR Jur Rep 20.   [203]

3. **By wrongful delivery**

To deprive a person of his chattels by delivering them to someone else.   [204]

Example: Where chattels have been obtained by fraud and the original owner has rescinded the contract — a subsequent purchaser has converted the chattels. *Hollins v Fowler* (1875) LR 7 (HL). The defendant cotton broker brought and resold cotton that was fraudulently acquired by the seller from the plaintiff. The defendant was not aware of the fraud and only received a broker's commission. He was held liable for conversion and paid damages equal to the value of the cotton.

4. **By wrongful disposition**

Where possession has been lawfully acquired it is a conversion to unlawfully give a third party title to the chattels. **Examples:** [205]

a. By pawning the chattels. *Parker v Godin* (1728) 93 ER 866.

b. By selling the chattels. *Hollins v Fowler* (1875) LR 7 HL 757.

5. **By wrongful destruction**

To unlawfully *consume* or *otherwise destroy* a chattel of another is a conversion.   [206]

a. Mere damage is *not* enough for conversion, but it may be a trespass.   [207]

b. **Test for destruction** is whether the identity or character of the chattel has changed. **Examples:**   [208]

(1) taking another person's milk and making cheese.

(2) taking another person's grapes and making wine.

(3) taking another person's corn and grinding it into flour.

c. **Note: Ownership of chattel** is *not* changed because of alteration.   [209]

Example: If clay is wrongfully taken and made into bricks, the bricks belong to the true owner of the clay.

6. **By wrongful use**
   Conversion by forfeiture of chattel. **Examples:** [210]
   a. *Moorgate Mercantile Credit Co. Ltd v Finch* [1962] 1 QN 701. The use of another person's car for the unlawful act of smuggling, which resulted in the car being forfeited, was a conversion.
   b. Infringement of a copyright may be a conversion. *Caxton Publishing Ltd v Sutherland Publishing Co.* [1939] AC 178.

7. **Multiple acts of conversion**
   Note: a person may act in such a way as to commit several conversions with the same chattel. [211]
   Example: The defendant stole the plaintiff's painting and sold it to an unsuspecting third party. Later, the defendant bought back the painting and when discovered by the plaintiff demand was made for its return. The defendant refused plaintiff's demand to return the chattel.

8. **Not act of conversion**
   a. **Mere receipt of chattels**
      (1) **Possession of chattels without title** to them is not a conversion. *See* Finders [219]. [212]
          Only adverse detention from the person entitled to possession of chattel is wrongful.
      (2) **However**, buying or receiving a chattel from a person who did not have the lawful authority to dispose of the chattel is a conversion. [213]
   b. **Redelivery**
      Any person who innocently receives a chattel and returns it to the person who gave it to him, before he has notice of plaintiff's claim to the chattel, is not liable for a conversion. [214]
      Example: Mr A brings a ring to a jeweller for repairs. The jeweller repairs the ring and gives it back to Mr A. before receiving notice from the police that the ring has been stolen from Mrs T. The jeweller has not committed a conversion.

E. Intent or negligence by defendant

1. The plaintiff is not required to prove that the defendant planned to harm or deprive the plaintiff of the chattel. [215]
   Conscious wrongdoer: It is *not* required that the defendant be a conscious wrongdoer.

2. Plaintiff must show that the defendant *intended* to deal with the chattel in the manner in which he actually dealt with it. **[216]**

   a. **Mistaken but honest belief** of the defendant that he had the right to deal with the chattels is generally *not* a valid defence. *Hollins v Fowler* [200]. *See* Non-Valid Defences [268].

   b. **Conversion by negligence:** The defendant breached a duty of care owed to the plaintiff — the breach caused the plaintiff to suffer a direct interference with his/her possession of the chattel. **[217]**
   Shield Life Ins. Co. v Ulster Bank Ltd [1995] 3 IR 225 (HC). The defendant bank accepted for collection, from their own customer (an insurance broker) a £30,000 cheque on which the plaintiffs were the payees. The broker asked the bank to transfer £5,000 to his office account. Court held that the defendant bank should have made inquiries before accepting the cheque. The defendant bank had been negligent in its duty to the plaintiffs.

3. Physical possession *not* required: There is no requirement that the defendant actually takes physical possession of the chattels. **[218]**

   a. As long as s/he has dealt with them in such a way that amounts to an absolute denial and repudiation of the plaintiff's rights. *Douglas Valley Finance Co. Ltd v Hughes* [1969] 1 QB 738.

   b. **Example:** An unjustified levy or attachment under legal process is held to be conversion although the chattel was not taken from the possession of plaintiff. *Tinkler v Poole* (1770) 98 ER 396.

4. Chattels capable of conversion **[219]**

   a. Any corporeal (tangible) personal property.
   Examples: Furniture, vehicles, jewellery, clothing, pets, etc.

   b. Realty when severed.
   Example: A growing tree is land, when cut down the felled tree is a chattel and the act of severance (cutting) is a conversion.

   c. Domestic animals and birds.

   d. Non-domestic animals and birds if they have been reduced into possession.
   Example: Game that has been shot or captured may be converted.

   e. Money, papers, title deeds and negotiable instruments.

F. Plaintiff in possession of or entitled to possession of chattel.
  1. Same requirement as in:
     a. Trespass to land. *See* [142], and
     b. Trespass to chattels. *See* [184].
  2. **Conversion between co-owners**
     a. **General rule:** Each co-owner is entitled to the use and possession of the chattel.   **[220]**
        Neither commits a wrong by taking, restraining, or using the chattel, even if the other co-owner is deprived from using the chattel.
     b. One co-owner cannot sue another in conversion unless: **[221]**
        (1) The acts of the defendant *destroy* the chattel; or
        (2) The acts of the defendant permanently destroy the plaintiff's right to possession.
        Example: Selling the chattel to a third person.
  3. **Entitlement to possession — the battle of titles**
     a. **General rule:** The *true owner* of the chattel *has a better title* to it than either its finder or the occupier of the land where it is found. *Webb v Ireland* [1988] IR 353. *See* [137].   **[222]**
        (1) **Duties of a finder**   **[223]**
            (a) To take reasonable care of the chattel, and
            (b) To return it to the rightful owner.
        (2) **Unknown true owner**: If the true owner cannot be found the finder has a title as against all others *except* the occupier of land where it was found.   **[224]**
            Example: *Quinn v Coleman* (1898). A young girl found a purse containing some money. Later, through fraud she lost possession of the purse. The police recovered it, and it was ultimately returned to the girl when the true owner could not be located within one year and one day.
     b. **Rules from *Webb*:** the battle of titles.   **[225]**
        (1) **True owner of chattel** — has the *best* title and claim.
            (a) Superior to owner of land on which chattel is found.
            (b) Superior to finder of chattel.
        (2) **Attached chattels:** If the chattel is attached to or under the land the owner of the land has a better claim than the finder.   **[226]**
            Exception: unless the owner has *never* been in possession of the land.   **[227]**
        (3) **Not Attached Chattels:** If the chattel is on the land, but not attached to it the owner of the land will have a better

claim to the chattel than the finder — if the owner has *manifested an intention to exert control over* the chattel.

Example: Control may be shown by looking for the lost chattel. In deciding this point the court cited *Parker v British Airways Board* [1982] 1 All ER 834.

c. **Antiquities of Importance:** The State has right of ownership over those that have no known owner. *See* [137].   **[228]**
   (1) Similar to royal prerogative of treasure trove *See* [119].
   (2) In Ireland they are based on constitutional grounds (Art. 10).

d. **Statutory or contractual finders**
   (1) **General rule:** not usually entitled to claim title to found chattels.   **[229]**
   (2) **Statutory finders:** are generally public servants like the police.   **[230]**
       Example: *Crinion v Minister for Justice* [1959] IR Jur Rep 15. A police officer found money on the footpath. He gave the money to his sergeant and after a year and one day he sought the money. When the return of the money was refused he brought an action for conversion. Court held that because he found the money while on duty he was not entitled to it.
   (3) **Contractual finders:** may be employees.   **[231]**
       Example: *Grafstein v Holme* (1958) 12 DLR (2d) 727. The employer is entitled to money found in a box in his basement by one of his employees.

G. Causation

The defendant's act(s) must have resulted in the unjustified denial of the plaintiff's title to the chattel. In other words, the defendant's act(s) must have resulted in the defendant exercising authority or control over the chattels.   **[232]**

H. Remedies for conversion

1. **Damages** for lost chattel; treated like forced sale, or:
   a. The trial court has *discretion* to allow return of chattel: **[233]**
      (1) If it is not injured, and
      (2) There are no special damages as a result of the detention.
   b. **Note:** Recovery of chattel does not bar action for conversion, but it may reduce the damages. *Tucker v Wright* (1826) 130 ER 645.

2. Other approaches [234]

1. English approach
   Adopted the Torts (Interference with Goods) Act 1977. *See* [173].
2. American approach
   a. Conversion has been limited to major interferences with the chattel, or with the plaintiff's right to it, which is so serious or important as to justify a forced judicial sale of the chattel to the defendant. (Prosser)
   b. To determine seriousness of interference all relevant factors are considered. Restatement 2d, s. 222A.
      1. Extent and duration of the defendant's exercise and control over chattels.
      2. Intent of the defendant to assert a right inconsistent with the plaintiff's right to control the chattel.
      3. The defendant's good faith or bad intentions.
      4. The extent and duration of the resulting interference with plaintiff's right of control.
      5. The resulting harm done to the chattel.
      6. The expense and inconvenience caused to the plaintiff.

Detinue

A. Definition: Detinue is the wrongful failure of a person in possession of a chattel to deliver it to the person entitled to immediate possession.
[235]

B. Historical background [236]

1. Common law definition: Detinue is the wrongful detention of another person's chattels.
2. Detinue dates back to the twelfth century.
3. At common law the defendant had the option of:
   a. Returning the chattel, or
   b. Paying for damages.
4. Detinue was not helpful if the chattel was returned but damaged.
5. Detinue was almost completely replaced by *trover* (the forerunner of conversion.)

C. Required elements [237]

1. Defendant in possession of chattel.

2. Plaintiff demands return of chattel.
3. Defendant fails to return chattel.

D. *Defendant is in possession of the chattel*

1. Detinue protects entitlement to possession of chattel. **[238]** Ownership is not essential.
2. Detinue usually arises in bailments. *See* [186]. **[239]**
3. **The finder of chattels:** **[240]**
   a. Will not be liable in *detinue* if he loses possession of the chattel;
   b. But the finder will be liable (in *conversion*) if he wrongfully disposes of chattel.

E. *The plaintiff demands return of the chattel*

1. The defendant must adversely possess the plaintiff's chattel. **[241]**
2. **Establishing adverse possession**
   a. **General rule:** The plaintiff *must* make a *demand* for the possession of the chattel. **[242]**
      Example: *Cullen, Allen & Co. v Barclay* (1881) 10 LR Ir. A potato salesman was held not liable in detinue because the owners of the chattels (potato sacks) failed to demand their return. True: even though the salesman was contractually required to return chattels.
   b. **Exception:** the plaintiff is *not* required to demand return if it would be *futile* to do so. **[243]**
      Examples:
      (1) Chattels destroyed in defendant's possession; or
      (2) The defendant has given or allowed possession of the chattel to go to another person.

F. *The defendant failed or refused to return the chattel*

1. Detinue arises if *after* the plaintiff's demand for possession the defendant *refuses* or *fails* to give the chattel to the plaintiff. **[244]**
2. **Loss of possession during bailment.** If the defendant wrongfully loses possession of a chattel bailed to him, he will still be liable when he cannot return the chattel at the end of the bailment. **[245]**
   Example: Leaving a suit at a dry cleaners and it is either misplaced or given to the wrong customer.

3. **Exception:** The defendant's refusal or failure to return may be excused if the refusal or failure is *reasonable.* **[246]**
   a. **Reasonable failure or refusal**
      (1) A *fair* dispute as to the plaintiff's entitlement to possession. *Poole v Burns* [1944] IR Jur Rep 20. **[247]**
      (2) Where the chattel was destroyed through *no fault* of the defendant, such as an Act of God. **[248]**
   b. **Onus** is on the defendant to prove the absence of fault. *Sheehy v Faughnan* [1991] 1 IR 424. **[249]**

G. Remedies for detinue

1. Usual remedy for detinue is damages: **[250]**
   a. For the value of the chattel, and
   b. For its detention.
2. With the discretion of the court: **[251]**
   a. The return of the chattel may be ordered and also for unique items of special value or interest to the plaintiff.
   b. Damages for its detention.

H. Other approaches: **[252]**

1. Detinue has been abolished in England and replaced by statutory provisions.
2. In the US, detinue is regarded generally as one of the many remedies available under the tort of conversion.

Defences to intentional torts to chattels

A. Consent see *generally [75]* et seq.

1. The plaintiff's consent to the defendant's use or interference with his chattels is a valid defence. **[253]**
   The plaintiff's consent may be expressed or implied.
   Examples:
   (1) Expressly — 'Yes, you may read my book.'
   (2) Implied (by conduct) — Without speaking, offering your opera glasses to the person seated next to you.
2. For consent to be effective, scope cannot be exceeded. **[254]**
   Example: Allowing your brother to drive your car does not give him your consent to his painting the car.
3. Consent to be valid cannot be obtained by: **[255]**
   (a) Fraud; or
   (b) Duress.

B. Volenti non fit injuria — voluntary assumption of the risk

1. The plaintiff agrees to assume the risk of injury to his interests, or damage to his chattel. **[256]**
2. **Example:** *Arthur v Anker* [1996] 2 WLR 602. The defendant, a company, clamped a car parked on private land and was found to have a defence of consent. Notices displayed prominently on the land had warned that anyone parking without authorisation would be clamped. When the plaintiff parked there he was deemed to have accepted that risk.

C. Lawful authority

1. **Judicial authority** — warrants for the search and seizure of chattels. **[257]**
2. **Statutory authority:** Police do not commit a trespass to chattels when they exercise their lawful powers of search and seizure. **[258]**
   a. **Examples:** of statutory powers of seizure:
      (1) Proceeds of Crime Act 1996, s. 15.
      (2) Control of Horses Act 1996, s. 37.
   b. **Power of Seizure**
      (1) **Does not extend** to a general right to interfere with possession in the event of a civil dispute. **[259]**
      (2) **Limited to cases** involving lawful arrest of the person in possession of the chattels. **[260]**
   c. **Leading case of seizure** of chattels *without* a warrant is *Jennings v Quinn* [1968] IR 305. **[261]**
      Public interest requires police, under a lawful arrest, to seize property without a warrant that is in the possession or custody of the arrested person, when the police believe it is necessary because the property is:
      (a) Evidence in support of *the* criminal charge;
      (b) Evidence in support of *any* other criminal charge; or
      (c) Reasonably believed to be *stolen property* not in the lawful possession of that person.

D. Self-help

1. **Common law:** A person could use *reasonable force* to defend one's property or the property of another. **[262]**
   Example: Under the common law a person could chase after and use reasonable force to take back stolen chattels from a pickpocket.

2. **Statutory reform** [263]
Non-Fatal Offences Against the Person Act 1997, ss 18–20, basically restates the common law.
A person may use reasonable force in the defence of his property or the property of another person.

E. Necessity

1. **Definition**: Necessity is the commission of a tortious act to prevent some greater evil where there is no reasonable alternative. *See* [91] and [158]. [264]
2. The degree of interference or damage to plaintiff's chattel must be balanced against the threatened harm to defendant's interests.
    a. **Example:** *Cresswell v Sirl* [1948] 1 KB 241. The defendant shot the plaintiff's dog, which had been worrying the defendant's sheep. The shooting was held justified by the threatened harm.
    b. **Statutory reform**: Control of Dogs Act 1986, s. 23 states that a person who kills a dog he reasonably believes is worrying livestock, or is about to worry livestock, has a defence for any charge for shooting the dog.

F. Contributory negligence

Civil Liability Act 1961, s. 34(2)(d) provides: [265]
That the plaintiff's *failure* to exercise *reasonable care* of his own property will be deemed to be contributory negligence.
Except to the extent the defendant is unjustly enriched.

G. Limitations

The Statute of Limitations 1957, s. 12(11). For detinue and conversion
    a. The limitation period begins to run from the time of the wrongdoing. [266]
    b. Subsequent acts of *detinue* and *conversion* do not give rise to separate periods of limitation. [267]
    c. **Importance:** The running of the limitation period not only will bar a civil case but will lead to extinction of plaintiff's title to the chattel — *see* s. 12(2).

H. Non-valid defences

1. **Mistake**
General rule: A mistake of law or fact is no defence to anyone who intentionally interferes with a chattel in a manner inconsistent with the right of another. [268]

'Persons deal with the property in chattels or exercise acts of ownership over them at their peril.' *Hollins v Fowler* [1874–80] All ER 118. *See* [204] for facts.

2. **Remoteness of damage:** It is no defence that the loss suffered was not intended, or even that it was not the natural or probable result of the act. *Hiort v Bott* (1974) LR 9 Ex 86. **[269]**

3. *Jus tertii*

It is not a valid defence to argue that the chattels belonged to someone other than the plaintiff. **[270]**

Example: Pretty Polly was given her brother's bicycle to go to the shop. While Pretty Polly was in the shop Nasty Nellie took the bicycle so she would not have to walk home. Nasty Nellie cannot claim as a defence that Pretty Polly was not the rightful owner of the bicycle. Pretty Polly was in possession.

III. Revision questions

(1) Henry was having a problem with his garden flooding. He knew that his neighbour Nicola had a drain in her garden, so he moved his chutes to allow the water from his roof to run down into her garden. Name the tort.

(2) Tim was driving fast on a narrow road. On a bend he hit Michael and sent him over the ditch into Farmer Fred's field.
   (a) Did Michael commit a trespass to Farmer Fred's land?
   (b) Did Tim commit a trespass to Farmer Fred's land?

(3) Pauline is eight months pregnant. In the busy bus station there are no empty seats except one next to Naomi. Naomi is reading a novel and her bag is on the seat next to her. If Pauline moves the bag to the floor:
   (a) Has she committed a tort?
   (b) Does she have a valid defence?

(4) Cyril fell asleep during a boring film. When he awoke the cinema was empty and people were entering for another film. Cyril decided to stay and watch the new film.
   (a) What made Cyril's initial entry into the cinema legal?
   (b) Has Cyril committed a trespass to land?

(5) Mai Day was protesting against the opening of a DIY Superstore in Waterford. During the protest she threw a stone that broke two windows which were on special offer near the entrance of the store.
   (a) Has Mai Dai committed a trespass to the DIY's land?

     (b) Has Mai Dai committed a conversion?

(6) I took my pedigree cat Toulouse to the vet for an ear operation. The vet mistakenly neutered Toulouse. Name the tort.

(7) Miss Marbles found an elderly gentleman sitting in her garden enjoying the sun. Before he left the garden he picked a small rose and stuck it in his buttonhole.

     (a) Has the elderly gentleman committed trespass to Miss Marbles land?

     (b) When the gentleman picked the flower what tort did he commit?

(8) Chris grabbed and used her flatmate Fiona's toothbrush by mistake. Name the tort.

(9) Mean Melanie found John's thermos and drank all his tea.

     (a) What act is a conversion?

     (b) What act is a trespass to chattels?

(10) Sean threw a firecracker into his friend Shane's open sitting room window. Unfortunately, it caused a fire. When Shane realised that the sitting room curtains were burning he reached into the window and ripped down the burning curtains.

     (a) Identify the acts that are a trespass to land.

     (b) Is necessity a good defence for Shane to the trespass to land?

     (c) Identify Sean's act of conversion.

(11) Susan is angry that her husband Michael has been having an affair. When Michael comes home from work he finds Susan burning their wedding photos in the fire. Name the tort.

(12) Nicholas is hired by Farmer Finbar to plough a field. While ploughing Nicholas unearths an unusual stone. On closer examination the stone is found to be an important dolman or standing stone. Who has the best title to the stone?

(13) Bob Crachett is very poor. He went to the local shop to buy a Christmas tree and was dismayed to find that he could not afford to buy one. Thinking that if one of the trees was slightly damaged he might be able to purchase it at a reduced rate, he quickly snapped off a couple of limbs. Unfortunately, the shop owner refused to reduce the price, so Bob left the slightly damaged tree and went to the Scrooge farm. Quietly, to avoid detection, Bob chopped down one of Scrooge's ornamental pine trees to use as a Christmas tree. He dragged the tree to his home. Identify all the intentional torts to land and chattels in the situation.

(14) Ziggy was hired as a rat catcher by Limerick Corporation. Under statute he may enter any dwelling in search of rats. Mary saw a rat

in her flat and called for Ziggy. Ziggy arrived and entered the flat. Quickly he began moving furniture away from the walls looking for rats. Mary left the flat in terror. After Mary left Ziggy opened the drawers in Mary's dresser looking for her knickers. He selected a bright red pair with black lace to add to his knicker collection.

(a) Has Ziggy committed trespass *ab initio*?

(b) When Ziggy moved the furniture was he committing a trespass to chattels?

(c) When Ziggy opened the drawer in Mary's dresser was he committing a conversion?

(15) Sean bought a very old desk from an old family friend. He called ABC Antique Restorers to come to his home and give him an estimate on refinishing the desk. Sean agreed to the price quoted for refinishing the desk and helped the men load the desk into their van. After several months Sean contacted ABC and learned that they could not locate his desk. It is believed that the desk may have been destroyed in an accidental fire in one of their workshops.

(a) Can Sean maintain an action for detinue against ABC?

(b) Does ABC have a valid defence because Sean did not make a formal written demand for the return of his desk?

SECTION 2:
FAULT-BASED LIABILITY

3

COMMON LAW NEGLIGENCE

Chapter synopsis

I.   General principles
II.   Common law general duty of care
III.   Special duty issues
IV.   Duty may be limited by type of harm
V.   Breach of the duty of care by defendant
VI.   Causation
VII.   Defences
VIII. Damages

I. General principles

A.   Historical background
B.   Basic present requirements for negligence
C.   Influencing policies

A. Historical background — liability based on fault

1. Prior to the development of the tort of negligence a plaintiff had to establish provisions of the appropriate writ.   **[271]**
   a. The two writs used:
      (1) Trespass, and
      (2) Trespass on the case.
   b. **Direct and immediate harms:** The writ of trespass was used with liability being strict. *See* [2].
   c. **Indirect harms:** Plaintiffs were required to use trespass on the case:
      (1) Because trespass on the case was the proper writ for fault-based liability,
      (2) It was the forerunner to negligence.
      Therefore, negligence is *not* actionable *per se*.
2. **Before duty:** While negligence liability existed for centuries there was no concept of duty until the nineteenth century.   **[272]**

a. Generally, the word *negligence* was used to describe *inadventure or indifference* by a person while entering into the commission of other torts.

b. Liability existed within defined contractual relationships of those who held themselves out to the public as being competent.

(1) **Examples:** Doctors, innkeepers, blacksmiths.

c. If the case fell outside the recognised relationships there was *no* liability.

3. **The Industrial Revolution** is credited with bringing about social, industrial and technological changes including the need for a *test* to determine whether liability existed *outside* the recognised relationships.

a. The economic view was that a duty should not be imposed unless:

(1) The person *agreed* to it, and **[273]**

(2) That by requiring persons injured by industry to prove fault, (as opposed to direct harm under the trespass writ), defendants were much more likely to avoid liability.

b. 'Perhaps one of the chief agencies in the growth ... is industrial machinery. Early railway trains, in particular, ... killed any object from a Minister of State to a wandering cow, and this naturally reacted on the law.' (Winfield)

4. **Denial of negligence:** Many commentators in the early part of the twentieth century, such as Salmond (*Law of Torts*, 6th edn. 1924), continued to argue that negligence was not a separate tort but merely one way of committing other torts. **[274]**

a. Negligence was seen as having no legal significance.

b. These assertions were laid to rest in England with the famous case of *Donoghue v Stevenson*, [1932] AC 562 (HL). *See* [315] for facts.

Importance of *Donoghue*: **[275]**

(a) **Destroyed** the privity of contract requirement.

(b) **Created a new category of duty**: Manufacturers of dangerous products owe a duty to their ultimate consumers.

(c) **Birth of neighbour principle:** Lord Atkin stated his famous neighbour principle as a *general test* for determining whether a duty of care existed.

b. *Donoghue v Stephenson* was accepted into Irish law by *Kirby v Burke* [1944] IR 207 (HC).

Quill — Interestingly Gavin Duffy J indicated that *Donoghue* alone would not be sufficiently convincing authority, but accepted the neighbour principle as it conformed to the views expressed by the American jurist Oliver Wendell Holmes. *See* [285].

B. *Basic present requirements for negligence* [276]

1. Duty of care
2. Breach of the duty of care
3. Causation
4. Damage, loss or injury

1. The defendant *owed* the plaintiff a *legal duty of care*. [277]
   a. **Duty** is a legally recognised relationship between the parties.
   b. There are two types of duties owed:
      (1) **General duty — to act as a reasonable person.**
      (2) **Special duties — imposed by statute or case law**.
   c. **Special duties**
      (1) May be in addition to, or
      (2) In place of the general duty to act as a reasonable person.
   d. Duties imposed by statute are covered in Chapter 4.
2. The defendant *breached* the legal duty of care owed. [278]
   a. By *failing* to achieve the standard of care required;
      Standard of care — the required level of conduct expected.
      Most common standard — *reasonable person.*
   b. By performing:
      (1) An **act**, or
      (2) An **omission** (failure to perform a required act).
3. **Causation:** The defendant breached the duty of care that he owed to the plaintiff and caused the plaintiff's injury, loss or damage. [279]
   a. **Actual cause** (cause in fact): Plaintiff's harm *must* have the required nexus to the defendant's breach of duty.
   b. **Proximate cause** (legal cause): There are *no* policy reasons to relieve the defendant of liability.
4. The plaintiff suffered an *injury, damage* or *loss* as a result of the defendant's act or omission. [280]
   Note: Negligence is not actionable *per se.*

C. Influencing policies

Whether a duty exists is largely a policy-based determination. Some of the various policies that influence duty include: **[281]**
a. Foreseeability of the harm to the plaintiff.
b. The degree of certainty that the plaintiff would suffer harm.
c. The closeness of the connection between the defendant's conduct and the injury suffered by the plaintiff.
d. The moral blame attached to the defendant's conduct.
e. The policy of preventing future harm.
f. The burden to the defendant.
g. The consequences to society for imposing a duty.
Note: Negligence is the *most* important area of tort law. To successfully approach a negligence problem you should always systematically start with duty of care. Only after concluding that the defendant owed the plaintiff a duty of care should you analyse breach etc. NEVER ASSUME that the defendant owed a duty of care to the plaintiff. (For more helpful hints *see* Chapter 9.) **[282]**

II. Common law general duty of care

Duty of care — owed to the plaintiff
A. Reasonable person standard
B. Standard of care for professionals
C. Standard of care for solicitors
D. Standard of care for doctors
E. Foreseeable plaintiffs

A. Reasonable person standard [283]

1. General rule — this model or standard:
   a. Applies to *all* persons.
   b. Is used to *test* the defendant's act or conduct for conformity with what is required at any given time and place to avoid unnecessary danger.
   c. Is based on a fictitious person 'who never existed on land or sea'. (Prosser)
   d. Was first articulated as the 'man of ordinary prudence' in *Vaughan v Menlove* (1837) 132 ER 490, and continued to be known as reasonable man standard until recently.
   'Instead, therefore, of saying that the liability for negligence should be co-extensive with the judgment of each individual, which would be as variable as the length of the foot of each

individual, we ought rather to adhere to the rule which requires in all cases a regard to caution such as a man of ordinary prudence would observe.'

    e. Most commentators generally agree that the standard should now be known as the *reasonable person*.

2. **Objective standard:** The defendant's good faith belief is *not* material.   **[284]**

    a. **Reasonable person standard** serves as a *goal* to be worked toward.

    b. Is *not* based on how any specific person would have acted, rather how the reasonable person would have acted.

    c. **Flexible** — although situations and circumstances change the standard remains the same, *the reasonable person*, under the same or similar circumstances.

3. **Rationale** — for use of objective standard   **[285]**

    a. Subjective standard would be difficult to use.

    b. Oliver Wendell Holmes Jr in *The Common Law* (1881) reasoned:

        (1) 'The impossibility of nicely measuring a man's powers and limitations is far clearer than that of ascertaining his knowledge of law.'

        (2) Further, society members should be able to expect a certain level of behaviour from others.
        'If a man is born hasty and awkward, and is always hurting himself or his neighbours … his slips are no less troublesome than if they sprang from guilty neglect. His neighbours accordingly require him, at his peril, to come up to their standard, and the courts which they establish decline to take his *personal equation* into account.'

    c. **Criticism:** A person can be negligent for failing to meet some standard that he cannot meet.
    McMahon alleges that to 'eliminate the *personal equation* completely and apply an objective standard would result in considerable injustice and hardship.'

4. **Characteristics of the reasonable person**
   Knowledge   **[286]**

    (1) Expected to know *facts* of *common experience*.
        Example: Laws of nature, normal incidents of weather, characteristics of common animals etc.

    (2) Expected to know *personal limitations* and act accordingly.
        Example: A reasonable person coming into contact with an

unfamiliar breed of snake will not handle the snake.

(3) **Physically** [287]

    (a) Reasonable person is the same as the defendant. Standard becomes reasonable person afflicted with same physical limitation.

    Example: A blind person is not required to see.

    (b) But, a physically challenged person must be reasonable in light of his/her impairment.

    Example: A blind person would be negligent in driving a car.

    (c) **Voluntary intoxication:** If physical impairment results from voluntary intoxication, impairment is not taken into account. Intoxicated persons are held to the *same standard of care* as a sober and reasonable person. [288]

5. **Standard for children** — very few Irish cases.

  a. Appears to be *subjective* standard taking into account the child's:

    (1) age, [289]

    (2) intelligence, and

    (3) experiences.

  b. Adult activity exception

    In the US, Canada, New Zealand and Australia a child engaging in adult activities such as driving cars, motorcycles, motorboats or flying aeroplanes is held to the adult standard.

6. **Mentally disabled persons** [290]

  a. **General rule:** The objective reasonable person standard applies.

    In other words, a mentally disabled person is held to the same standard (reasonable person standard) as persons who are not mentally disabled.

  b. **Rationale** — for disparity of treatment between physical and mental disabilities: [291]

    (1) Difficulty in determining what types of mental disabilities will reduce the duty of care owed, and

    (2) Fear of complicating tort law in much the same way that the insanity defence has complicated criminal trials in some jurisdictions.

  c. **Law reform commission** (LRC 18–1985) recommended a single rule for negligence and contributory negligence, i.e. the ordinary standard of care (reasonable person) would apply to a person unless:

(1) At the time of the act the person was suffering from a serious mental disability which affected that person in the performance of the act, and

(2) The disability rendered the person unable to behave according to the standard of care appropriate to the reasonable person.

   d. **US approach:** 2nd Restatement. The ordinary standard of care should be applied to mentally disabled persons unless they are children.

7. **Standard of care for learners**   **[292]**

   a. **General rule:** A person who engages in an activity with known risks is held to same standard of care as an experienced reasonable person.
   Classic example: Driving a car on a public road.

   b. **Rationale:** Learners who engage in such activities should bear the risk of harm rather than the person injured.

B. Standard of care for professionals   **[293]**

1. **General rule:** A person holding themselves out to the public as being *skilled* must have the standard of care customarily exercised by the members of that profession. *O'Donovan v Cork Co. Council* [1967] IR 173 (SC).

   a. **Profession:** There is much debate about what is a profession.

     (1) *Nursing* is held *not* to be a profession for professional negligence purposes. *Kelly v St Laurence's Hospital* [1989] ILRM 437.

     (2) *Mechanics* are held to be professionals because they exercise and profess special skills.

   b. The professional standard of care *only* applies if the defendant is acting in her professional capacity.
   Example: A solicitor driving a vehicle is held to the same standard as all other drivers.

   c. **Duty of care:** A professional owes a general duty of care to his clients/patients/customers to exercise the skills of a reasonable mechanic/doctor/solicitor/accountant etc.   **[294]**

2. **Exception to the general rule — advocate immunity**

   a. **Established** by *Rondel v Worsley* [1969] 1 AC 191 — which generally held that barristers cannot be sued for negligently conducting a client's case in court or for work closely connected with the conduct of the case in court.   **[295]**

Rationale for immunity: While barristers owe a duty to their clients, they owe a broader duty to assist in the administration of justice. To achieve the broader duty, activities in court need to be protected.

  b. **Application in Ireland**

    To actions of the attorney general (AG).   **[296]**

    HMW v Ireland [1997] 2 IR 141 (HC). The plaintiff was the victim of a convicted paedophile. She sued the AG in negligence for the injuries she sustained as a result of the delay in extraditing the paedophile. The court held that the AG did not owe the plaintiff a duty of care. It also rejected arguments that the plaintiff's constitutional right to bodily integrity had been infringed. Constitutional rights are not absolute.

  c. **Advocate immunity abolished** by the House of Lords. *Hall (Arthur J.J.) & Co. v Simons* [2000] 3 All ER 673.   **[297]**

    (1) Abolished 'under the shadow of the European Convention on Human Rights.'(McMahon)

    (2) McMahon recommends that Ireland also abolish advocate immunity.

3. **Concurrent liability** may arise because most clients have entered into a contractual relationship with the professional, liability may be based in contract or tort.   **[298]**

  Note: Relationship between professional and client is *not* required to be contractual.

  Example: Relationship could arise in a gratuitous situation such as free legal aid.

C. Standard of care for solicitors

1. **Traditionally** no negligence actions were allowed because the relationship between a solicitor and his client was based on contract.   **[299]**

2. **Modern view:** *Finaly v Murtagh* [1979] IR 249 (SC).   **[300]**

  a. **Negligence applies** if the negligence arises due to a breach of a general professional duty of care.

  b. **Negligence does not apply** if the breach *is* due to a special term in a contract.

    The Test: Would a solicitor be liable if the contract had not contained the term?

3. **Giving incorrect advice:** *Roche v Peilow* [1985] IR 232 (SC).   **[301]**

If the law being advised upon:
(1) Is clear — there will be negligence.
(2) Not clear (or difficult) — the advice may be reasonable.
4. **Failure to advise**: *See* [348] *et seq.* Solicitors' Duties to Third Parties.

D. *Standard of care for doctors (medical malpractice)*   [302]

1. **General rule:** A doctor must exercise the skills of a reasonable doctor.
   a. **Specialist** must exercise the skills of a reasonable specialist in that particular area of medicine.
   b. **General practitioner (GP)** must exercise skills of a reasonable GP.
   Knowledge of limitations: A reasonable GP realises and refers patients to specialists when speciality care is needed.
   c. Malpractice allegations usually arise in:
   (1) Diagnosis, and/or
   (2) Treatment.

2. **Fast-changing technology**   [303]
   a. The actions of a doctor will be judged according to the standards accepted at the time of the actions. *Roe v Minister of Health* [1954] 2 QB 66.
   b. However, once a risk becomes known a doctor may be under a duty to investigate the suspected risk.
   N. v UK Medical Research Council [1996] 7 Med LR 309 QB. In 1959, the defendant began a medical trial of human growth hormone for children with growth problems. In 1976, the defendants were warned that the hormone could cause Creutzfeld-Jacob Disease (CJD) — the deadly human form of mad cow disease. In 1977, the defendants were told that two of the four methods of giving the hormone carried the risk of transmitting CJD. Several children in the trial died of CJD. The court held that the failure to investigate the risks in 1976 was negligent.

3. **Standard of care**   [304]
   a. Perfection is *not* the duty owed by a doctor to her patient.
   b. Traditional approach: *Bolam* rule — 'custom of the profession.' *Bolam v Frien Barnet Hospital Management Committee* [1957] 1 WLR 582. The plaintiff suffered broken bones as the result of drugs given to him before electric shock treatments. Doctors were split over the use of such drugs in the procedure.

It was found that the *doctor was not negligent because he acted in accordance with the accepted practice.*

Important effect of *Bolam*: So long as a doctor could find a medical expert to state that his actions were within the bounds of a responsible body of medical opinion there would *never* be a finding of negligence.

c. **The Irish Supreme Court has *not* followed *Bolam*:** *Dunne v National Maternity Hospital* [1989] IR 91. The Supreme Court set forth general principles: **[305]**

   (1) **Diagnosis and treatment test:** A doctor will be negligent if no practitioner of *equal status* (specialist or GP) and *skill*, acting with *ordinary care*, would have done the same.

   (2) **Deviations from general and approved practice** will not be negligent unless *no* doctor of *equal status* and *skill*, acting with *ordinary care*, would have done the same.

   (3) **Inherent defects:** It is not a defence for a doctor to allege that he followed an established practice of conduct, if the practice has *inherent defects* that should be obvious to any person giving due consideration to the matter.

d. **Recent erosion of *Bolam* in England** **[306]**

   (1) *Bolitho v City and Hackney Health Authority* [1997] 3 WLR 1151. This was a typical battle of the experts: each party presented an expert to testify concerning correct medical treatment. While *Bolam* was not rejected outright, the court held that it was not required to find a doctor not liable in negligence because a medical expert had testified that the doctor had acted within accepted practices. Yet, no recovery for the plaintiff. *See* [483] for facts.

   (2) **Bolitho test**
      (a) **Reasonable:** Was the medical experts opinion reasonable?
      (b) **Properly balanced:** Had the medical expert weighed up the associated risks and benefits?
      (c) **Logical basis:** Was there a logical basis for the expert's conclusion?

   (3) **Bolitho applied:** *Wisniewski v Central Manchester Health Authority* [1998] PIQR P. 324. A trace during labour revealed that the baby was under stress. The midwife negligently failed to bring the trace to the attention of the doctor. The baby was born with cerebral palsy. The plaintiff

claimed that had any reasonable doctor been shown the trace the baby would have been delivered by a caesarian section and thereby avoided injury. Experts for the defendant said that a reasonable doctor may have delayed and the harm would have occurred anyway. When the doctor on duty at the birth declined to testify the judge applied adverse inferences to this fact, upholding the plaintiff's expert that no reasonable doctor would have delayed. **Court of appeal:** This is *not* the type of case outlined in Bolitho for special treatment. The appeal was dismissed on other grounds upholding the defendant's liability. **[307]**

e. **Onus**: The plaintiff *must establish* that the doctor did not meet the applicable standard of care that resulted in injury to the plaintiff.

f. **Alternative treatments:** If there are two or more accepted medical treatments it is *well settled* that the doctor is protected from liability if he follows one of the accepted medical treatments. *Dunne v National Maternity Hospital (see* [305]*)* and *Daniels v Heskin* [1954] IR 73 (*see* [450] for facts).**[308]** Unless treatment has an *inherent defect* that should be obvious to anyone using due consideration.

Example: *Collins v Mid-Western Board* [1991] (SC). A system that vested all hospital admission to one senior house officer was found inherently defective.

4. **Duty to disclose medical information**

a. **Debate** has endured over whether battery or negligence is the correct tort for a doctor treating a patient without their consent. *See* [83]. **[309]**

(1) **Example:** *Wells v Surrey Area Health Authority* (1978) *The Times* 20 July. The plaintiff, while in distress during a long labour, was seen by a consultant who recommended a caesarean section and sterilisation. The plaintiff signed the consent form agreeing to both procedures. Later, she alleged that had she not been in distress she would never have agreed to sterilisation on religious grounds. Her claim for trespass failed — she had consented to procedure. Her claim for negligence succeeded because she was not properly counselled before the operation.

(2) **Negligence** is the proper tort if the plaintiff was not fully advised concerning the risks and/or side effects. *Walsh v Family Planning. See* [82]. **[310]**

b. Traditional approach — *Bolam*: The decision of what to tell a patient is a medical decision determined by the doctor(s). **[311]**

c. McMahon outlines three approaches regarding informed consent:
  (1) The *Bolam* — traditional approach
  (2) The disclosure of *all* material risks approach — used in the US. The doctor has a duty to give all information concerning risks, so that the patient can make an informed choice concerning treatment.
  (3) Middle-of-the-road approach — *Bolam* applies except where a particular risk must be disclosed for the patient to make an informed choice: such that *no* reasonably prudent medical person would fail to make it. *Sidaway v Gov. of the Bethlem Royal Hospital* [1985] AC 871.

d. Australia has limited *Bolam* to treatment and diagnosis, but not to the decision to inform a patient of the inherent risks of a procedure. *Rogers v Witiker* (1992) ATR 81.

e. **Irish approach — elective surgeries:** The Irish courts have toyed with the principle that information regarding risks is different for elective and non-elective procedures.   **[312]**
  (1) *Walsh v Family Planning Services Ltd* [1992] 1 IR 496 (SC). The plaintiff suffered a serious but rare injury following a vasectomy. The Supreme Court held that there was a duty to warn of the risks, but doctors had given sufficient warnings in this case.
  (2) *Bolton v Blackrock Clinic Ltd* (1997) (SC) unrep. The plaintiff had two surgeries, both resulting in further injuries. The court held that sufficient warnings had been given.

E. Foreseeable plaintiffs: To whom is the duty of care owed?   **[313]**

1. **General rule:** Not everyone who is careless will be liable in negligence.
   Liability is *limited* to: **[314]**
   (1) Circumstances where the *law imposes a duty of care*, and
   (2) The duty of care is owed to any person *reasonably foreseen* to be injured by defendant's acts or omissions.

2. **Foreseeable plaintiffs:** First articulated in England in *Donoghue v Stevenson* (1932) — a famous case which introduced the *neighbour principle*. See [275].

a. **Neighbour principle:** 'The rule that you are to love your neighbour becomes in law you must not injure your neighbour ... [or] persons who are so closely and directly affected by [your] act that [you] ought *reasonably to have them in contemplation as being so affected...*' [315]

b. *Donoghue v Stevenson*. **Facts:** The plaintiff's friend purchased a bottle of ginger beer from a retailer and gave it to the plaintiff to drink. The bottle was opaque (not clear glass). The plaintiff drank some of the ginger beer and when she poured the rest of the bottle into a glass the remains of a small snail allegedly came out of the bottle. The plaintiff became seriously ill and sued the defendant manufacturer in negligence. The defendant argued that he did not owe a duty of care to the plaintiff as she had not purchased the bottle of ginger beer. (No privity of contract.)

c. **Reasoning:** The defendant had prepared the product in such a way as to show that he intended it to reach the ultimate consumer in the form in which it left his control. He could reasonably foresee that someone other than the original purchaser might consume the product. Thus, he was held liable to the plaintiff.

3. Accepted into Irish law in *Kirby v Burke* [1944]. *See* [275].

4. Legal commentators often use the famous US case, *Palsgraf v Long Island Railway* 248 NY 339 (1928), to illustrate issues concerning foreseeability that are still debated today. [316]

Facts: A passenger was running to catch one of the defendant's trains. The train was beginning to pull away from the platform when one of the defendant's employees helped the passenger onto the train. In helping the employee knocked an innocent-looking parcel from the passenger. It contained explosives and when it hit the ground an explosion occurred. It shook the platform causing a heavy scale at the end to fall on Helen Palsgraf and injuring her.

Majority opinion — written by Justice Cardozo: The defendant owes a duty of care only to those persons that the reasonable person would have foreseen as at risk of harm under the circumstances. The plaintiff must be a *foreseeable plaintiff* located in a *foreseeable zone of danger*.

Dissenting opinion — written by Justice Andrews is much broader. The defendant railroad did owe Helen Palsgraf a duty of care. Andrews reasoned that if a duty was owed to passengers on the train then it was owed to everyone who suffered injuries as a proximate result of the defendant's breach of that duty regardless if the injured were *foreseeable plaintiffs*.

5. **Special forseeability issues** [317]
   a. **Rescuers:** Traditionally injuries sustained to rescuers, during rescues, were not allowed.
      The courts used a number of theories to disallow the claims:
      (1) Rescuer voluntarily assumed the risks.
      (2) The rescuer was not a foreseeable plaintiff.
      (3) Rescuer was contributorily negligent.
   b. **Present status** [318]
      (1) Within the scope of the defendant's duty is the rescuer who comes to the aid of the defendant or others placed in peril because of the defendant's conduct.
          Example: *Phillips v Durgan* [1991] ILRM 321 (SC). The defendant hired his sister to paint his house. The kitchen was a greasy mess. The sister tripped or slipped and started a fire — it spread quickly. Her husband rescued her and they both sustained personal injuries. **Held:** The defendant failed to warn his sister of the risks and the rescue efforts of her husband were foreseeable and provoked by the defendant's negligence.
      (2) **Rationale:** 'Danger invites rescue.' (Cardozo in *Wagner v Intern'l Railroad Co.* (1921) 232 NYS 176.) [319]
          Foreseeability: If the defendant unreasonably acts so as to put him/herself or another in peril it is foreseeable that a rescue attempt could take place.
      (3) The rescuer *must* exercise reasonable care. [320]
          (a) If a rescuer is contributorily negligent his damages will be reduced.
          (b) If a rescuer is foolhardy under the circumstances — no damages.
          (c) **Note:** No distinction is made between professional and non-professional rescuers. Thus, a lifeguard does not assume the risk when rescuing a swimmer although it is part of his/her job. *See* Defences to Negligence [537] *et seq.*
      (4) The rescuer must be *provoked* into action by the defendant's negligence that created the peril. [321]

III. Special duty issues

A. Affirmative duties
B. Duty owed to third parties
C. Duty to control third parties
D. The common law duties owed by an employer to employees
   Note: Duties imposed by statute are covered in Chapter 4.

A. Affirmative duties

1. The law *distinguishes* between misfeasance and nonfeasance.**[322]**
   a. **Misfeasance** — doing a lawful act in a wrongful manner.
      (1) Due care is required.
      (2) Do not confuse *mis*feasance with *mal*feasance (doing an unlawful act).
   b. **Nonfeasance** — not acting. Generally, no duty is owed.
   c. 'There is no distinction more deeply rooted in the common law and more fundamental than that between misfeasance and non-feasance, between active conduct working positive injury to others and passive inaction, a failure to take positive steps to benefit others, or to protect them from harm not created by any wrongful act of the defendant … In the case of active misfeasance the victim is positively worse off as a result of the wrongful act. In cases of passive inaction plaintiff is in reality no worse off at all. His situation is unchanged; he is merely deprived of a protection which, had it been afforded to him, would have benefited him.' Francis H. Bohlen, *The Moral Duty to Aid Others as a Basis of Tort Liability*, 56 U.Pa.L.Rev. 217, 219–220 (1908).

2. **Misfeasance**
   a. **General rule:** Tort liability is normally based on the defendant doing a lawful act in a wrongful manner.   **[323]**
      (1) Generally, a person is liable for positive acts that create an unreasonable risk of harm, but not for nonfeasance.
         Example of affirmative misfeasance: Operating a motorboat at a high rate of speed through a group of swimmers.
      (2) **Note:** Generally, a person is always liable for malfeasance. **Example:** *Kennedy et al v Ireland and the AG* [1988] ILRM 472 (HC). The plaintiff's constitutional rights were infringed deliberately, when the plaintiff's phone was tapped without justification.
   b. **Exception:** Misfeasance can also be by a negligent omission.
         [324]

(1) **Negligent omission:** Failing to do something that a reasonable person would do while engaged in other activity. **Example:** Not paying attention while driving a car.

(2) Rationale: because a negligent omission is a risk-creating failure to act, liability may be imposed.

3. **Nonfeasance** [325]

a. **General rule:** A person does not owe a duty for *not* acting.

(1) Nonfeasance usually arises when the plaintiff asserts that the defendant should have acted or intervened in order to prevent harm to the plaintiff. **Examples:**

(a) Failed to prevent harm to the plaintiff by controlling a third party.

(b) Failed to take steps to protect the plaintiff from injury.

(c) Failed to rescue the plaintiff.

(2) **Note:** Unlike omissions [324] and acts [323] constituting misfeasance, the defendant that took no action did not create the risks that injured the plaintiff.

(3) **Example:** P fell while rollerblading. D saw the accident but walked past P. P suffered extensive brain injuries because he was not found — he therefore did not receive medical treatment for several hours. P alleges that if D had summoned help at the time of the accident P would not have suffered his brain injury. D does not owe P a duty of care.

b. **Exception — negligent omissions:** Failing to do something that a reasonable person would do while engaged in other activity. [326]

(1) Negligent omissions are a type of nonfeasance for which liability may be imposed.

(2) **Example:** Not paying attention while driving a car. *See* [324].

c. **Exception — affirmative duties:** There are other nonfeasance situations where liability may be imposed: [327]

(1) **Special relationship** between the parties may give rise to a legal duty for the defendant to act. **Examples:** [328]

(a) occupier to entrant (*See* [585] *et seq.*)

(b) parent and child

(c) employer/employee.

(2) **Assumption of duty by acting:** If the defendant gratuitously acts for the benefit of the plaintiff, he must act like a reasonable person. [329]

Gratuitous act: The defendant was not required to act, but elected or chose to act.

> *i*   **Example:** A road authority does not have a duty to keep roads in repair, but if it elects to repair the road it must meet the duty, i.e. not be negligent by leaving the road in a dangerous condition. *Phelan v Kilkenny Co. Council* [1943] IR Jur 1 (SC).
>
> *ii* **Example:** Coastguard responding to an emergency at sea. *OLL Ltd v Sec. of State for Transport* [1997] 2 All ER 897 (QB).

(3) **Assumption of duty by promise:** If the defendant gratuitously undertakes to perform an act and causes the plaintiff to rely on it to her detriment, liability may be imposed.   **[330]**

Example: The defendant promised to send an ambulance, but did not. Liability was imposed. *Kent v Griffiths* [2000] 2WLR 1158 (CA).

4. Examples of affirmative duties   **[331]**
   a. **Duty to warn**
      (1) *McKenna v Best Travel* (1997) (SC). Travel companies are generally found to owe a duty to warn customers of known dangers at destinations. Plaintiff lost — dangers were not known to the defendant.
      (2) Regarding defective products. *See* [754].
      (3) Regarding risks. *See Phillips v Durgan* [318].
   b. **Duty to protect**
      (1) General rule: *See* [378].
      (2) Exception: *Osman v UK* [379].
   c. **Duty to control.** *See* [358] *et seq.*
   d. **Duty to investigate.** *See N. v UK* [303].
   e. **Duty to disclose.** *Doolan v Murray* [338] *et seq.*
   f. **Duty to advise third party.** *See* [349].
5. **No duty to rescue**
   a. **General rule:** In common law jurisdictions there is no general duty to rescue or go to the aid of others in danger.   **[332]**
      (1) **Example:** A person may witness a neighbour's toddler drowning in a small fountain in the park: he has no duty to go to the aid of the toddler even if he is in no risk of injury.
      (2) **Rationale:** Tort law is not concerned with purely moral obligations.

b. **Exceptions to general rule:**
   (1) **Special relationship:** The defendant will owe a duty to go to the aid of another where some *special relationship* exists between defendant and victim. **Examples:** **[333]**
      (a) parent/child,
      (b) jailer/prisoner,
         McKevitt v Ireland [1987] ILRM 541 (SC). The police owed a duty of care to an intoxicated person in custody to take all reasonable steps to keep the person from injuring himself.
      (c) employer/employee.
   (2) **Responsible for peril:** If defendant is responsible for the injury or peril, the defendant is under a duty to aid (and *must* exercise reasonable care in aiding). **[334]**
      Example: *Adderly v Great Northern Railway Co.* [1905] 2 IR 378 (CA): The plaintiff was injured by the acts of an intoxicated passenger. The defendant railway was held liable as it chose to accept the intoxicated passenger. It owed a duty to take reasonable care to prevent injuries to other passengers.

6. **US statutory exceptions to affirmative duties** **[335]**
   a. **Motor vehicle codes:** In some common law jurisdictions in the US, it is a criminal offence to fail to go to the aid of another motorist involved in a car accident even though the defendant was not at fault for the accident. (Civil liability may be imposed.)
   b. **Good samaritan statutes:** This is where the defendant did *not* owe a duty of care. If s/he *voluntarily* undertakes to come to the aid of the plaintiff s/he must exercise reasonable care.
      In other words, the defendant is not required to act, but s/he does act — s/he then owes a duty to act with reasonable care.
   c. **Limitation of liability for doctors:** Every state in US has adopted legislation shielding doctors from negligence liability when they render aid in an emergency.
      Rationale: To encourage doctors to go to the aid of injured persons without fear of malpractice claims.
   d. **Duty to rescue statutes:** A few states (Vermont and Minnesota) have passed statutes requiring all persons to render reasonable aid to anyone exposed to grave physical injury.
      Exception: If acting to aid another would endanger the person offering aid or interfere with important duties that person

owes to others. **Examples:** A parent responsible for a small child, a teacher on a school trip responsible for young students.

B. Duty owed to third parties [336]

1. Negligent infliction of emotional distress
2. Negligent misstatements
3. Solicitors' duties to third parties
4. Doctors' duties to third parties

1. **Negligent infliction of emotional distress** [337]
   See Nervous Shock, [403] *et seq.*
2. **Negligent misstatements** [338]
   a. **Traditional common law rule:** A duty of care was *only* imposed for negligent statements *causing* economic loss where:
      (1) There was a fiduciary relationship between the parties or fiduciary relationship, e.g. X holding property in trust for the use and benefit of Y.
      (2) Where the statement was prepared pursuant to a contract between the parties.
   b. **Expansion to third parties — the Hedley Byrne Principle**
      (1) Approved in Ireland. *Securities Trust Ltd v Hugh Moore & Alexander Ltd* [1964] IR 417 (HC). *See* [343]. [339]
      (2) *Hedley Byrne v Heller* [1964] AC 465 (HL). The plaintiff was asked by a firm to buy advertising for them. To check the firm's credit the plaintiff asked its own bank to check on the firm. The plaintiff's bank contacted the defendant (the firm's bank) twice to make credit inquiries. Both times the defendant gave favourable references, with a disclaimer of liability for the statement. Relying on the advice the plaintiff entered into a contract, but the firm went into liquidation leaving the plaintiff with £17,000 in unpaid advertising fees. The defendant escaped liability because of the express disclaimers. **Holding:** a duty exists where there is a *special relationship* between the parties and the person making the statement can *foresee* the person receiving the statement *relying* on it to his detriment. **Important elements:**
      (a) Special relationship between the parties.
      (b) The defendant can foresee the plaintiff relying on the statement.
      (c) The plaintiff relied on the statement to his detriment.

c. Irish approach: *Hedley* principle interpreted broadly.   **[340]**
   (1) *Hedley* principle has merged with the broader concept of the *Donoghue* duty of care.
   (2) **Duty of care:** Requirements from *Ward v McMaster* [1988] IR 337 (SC).   **[341]**
       (a) Proximity of the parties
       (b) Foreseeability of the damage
       (c) Absence of any compelling public policy.
d. **Proximity of the parties (special relationship)**
   (1) Generally, the defendant owes a duty of care only to the persons he *made* the negligent statement to, or to those persons he could foresee would rely on it.   **[342]**
       There is *no duty* owed to the *world at large*.   **[343]**
       i   *Securities Trust. See* [339]. It was because of a printing error in the Art. of Association that the plaintiff invested to its detriment in the defendant company. The action failed because the defendant did not owe a duty to the world at large to avoid mistakes and printing errors. However, the court found that the relationship between a limited company and its shareholders is close enough to be considered special.
       ii *Bank of Ireland v Smith* [1966] IL 646 (HC). The defendant auctioneer published an ad incorrectly stating that land was in pasture. The plaintiff bought it relying on the statement. No special relationship found.
   (2) Made statement to: **[344]**
       (a) *Treston v Mayo Co. Council* (1998) unrep. (HC). The defendant found liable for negligent misrepresenting to the plaintiff that it intended to upgrade houses in an estate. In reliance, the plaintiff bought a house then the defendant gave the neighbouring house to known troublemakers.
       (b) *Doolan v Murry* (1993) unrep. (HC). The owner of land negotiated and executed deeds representing an intended right of way as being for pedestrians. In fact, under planning permission vehicular access was necessary. Owner found liable.
   (3) Should foresee reliance on statement.   **[345]**
       (a) *Potterton Ltd v Northern Bank* [1993] ILRM (HC). The defendant deliberately put a false statement on cheque where the plaintiff was payee.

(b) *McCullogh v PB Gunne* (1997) unrep. (HC). A couple relied heavily on the defendant's employee, an auctioneer. Court found that auctioneer had taken a proactive role with the couple and knew they relied on his statements.

(c) *Grayson v AIB* (2000) (HC). The plaintiff, a customer of the defendant, had a bogus foreign account. The plaintiff alleged that the defendant's employee told the plaintiff, during a brief exchange, not to avail of the 1988 tax amnesty. Case dismissed: remarks by employee did not show assumption of responsibility.

e. **Foreseeability of damage**

(1) The damage *must* be caused by the plaintiff's reliance on the statement.   **[346]**

(a) *Kelly v Haughey Boland & Co.* [1989] ILRM 373. The defendants were negligent in the performance of yearly audits of a company. The plaintiff relied upon the audits in a takeover and then sustained heavy losses. While a duty was recognised, the plaintiff failed because the accounts did not give a misleading account of the company's financial status.

(b) **Causation:** The incorrectness of the statement must lead to the plaintiff's damage. *Potterton Ltd v Northern Bank Ltd* [1993] ILRM 225 (HC).

(2) Purpose of statement: In weighing foreseeability a court may look to the purpose of the statement.   **[347]**

(a) *Caparo Industries v Dickman* [1990] 2 AC 650 (HL). The plaintiff took over a company relying on statements prepared by the defendant auditors pursuant to the Companies Act. No liability was imposed for the negligent statements as they were not designed to guide potential investors.

(b) *Reeman v Department of Transport* [1997] 2 Lloyd's Rep 648. The defendant department issued an annual certificate of seaworthiness for a fishing boat later bought by the plaintiff. Plaintiff relied on the certificate when he bought it and sued when it was found that the inspector had been negligent. No liability: the object of the certificate was to promote safety, not to establish commercial value. When the certificate was issued it was not foreseeable that plaintiff would rely on the statement.

3. **Solicitors' duties to third parties.** *See* [299] Professional Duty of Care.
   a. **Advice or information**
      The Supreme Court drew up *general terms* regarding the solicitor's duty for advice or information supplied to third parties in *Doran v Delaney* [1998] 2 ILRM 1 (SC).   **[348]**
      (1) **Solicitor** must have *expressly* or by *implication* led the third party to believe that he had the required skill or knowledge to advise or give information.
      (2) **Detrimental reliance:** The third party must have relied on the advice or information to his detriment.
      (3) **Solicitor aware** that the third party was likely to rely on the advice or information.
   b. **Expanded — affirmative duty to advise third party [349]**
      While a solicitor's primary duty is to his client he may also have a duty to advise others in certain circumstances.
      Doran v Delaney. See [348] Duty found to exist between the defendant solicitor (for vendor) and the plaintiff buyer, where defendant was aware of a boundary dispute but answered inquiry concerning whether litigation was pending or threatened with 'vendor says none'.
   c. **Negligent acts or work** (not statements)   **[350]**
      (1) **Wills:** A solicitor drawing up a will has a duty of care to the *intended beneficiaries,* but his *primary duty is to his client. Wall v Hegarty* [1980] ILRM 124.
          (a) *Ross v Caunters* [1979] 3 All ER 580. A solicitor negligently drafted a will breaking the probate law. The intended beneficiary successfully sued for the value of her lost inheritance.
          (b) *White v Jones* [1995] 1 All ER 691. A father disowned two of his daughters and later instructed his solicitor to reinstate his original legacies to the two. After a long period of the time the father dies, and the solicitor had failed to make the necessary changes. The daughters successfully sued the solicitor for his negligent work.
      (2) **No extension** of the duty to other transactions affecting the value of assets the beneficiary is to receive.   **[351]**
          Clarke v Bruce Lance & Co. [1998] 1 All ER 364. The plaintiff was not entitled to have the value of a potential benefit preserved during the lifetime of the testator by solicitor.

d. **Voluntary assumption of responsibility**
   (1) **General rule:** A solicitor does not owe a duty to the opposing party in contested litigation.   **[352]**
   (2) **Exception:** When the solicitor voluntarily assumes responsibility toward the opposing party.   **[353]**
       al-Kandari v J.R. Browne & Co. [1988] QB 655. The defendant solicitors represented the plaintiff's husband in a divorce. The defendant solicitors agreed to hold the husband's passport to prevent him from taking the children out of the jurisdiction. The defendants sent the passport to the Kuwaiti embassy and it was returned to the husband who took the children and fled. The defendant solicitors were found to owe a duty to plaintiff because they had voluntarily assumed a responsibility toward her.

4. **Doctors' duties to third parties**
   a. General rule arises in cases involving: **[354]**
      (1) Injury to unborn,
      (2) Contraceptive failures, and
      (3) Patient's condition is a danger to third parties.
   b. **Injury to unborn**   **[355]**
      (1) A duty is owed by a doctor treating a pregnant woman to her unborn child. *Dunne v National Maternity Hospital* [1989] IR 91.
      (2) English approach: The right to refuse medical treatment is paramount even if the refusal results in the death of the patient's unborn child. *See* [87].
   c. **Failed contraceptives** — no Irish cases.   **[356]**
      (1) A duty may be owed by a doctor performing a failed sterilisation procedure resulting in an unwanted pregnancy for the cost of raising the child. The decision not to abort did not break the chain of causation. *Emeh v Kensington & Chelsea & Westminister Area Health Authority* [1985] QB 1012.
      (2) **Limited duty:** No duty owed to unknown partners.
          (a) *Goodwill v British Pregnancy Advisory Service* [1996] 1 WLR 1392. A man had a vasectomy and was assured that he was sterile. Several years later the plaintiff became pregnant. No duty owed to the plaintiff. However, *obiter* if a partner was known to the doctor the procedure would have benefited both and doctor would have owed her a duty.

(b) *McFarlane v Tayside Health Board* (1998) BMLR (Scottish). Where it was assumed that a duty was owed to the wife of a man who had a vasectomy and was negligently advised that that he was sterile.

(3) **Public policy** — debates have raged over:

   (a) Whether a healthy child conceived after a failed contraceptive surgery should be regarded as a blessing or damages.

   (b) Whether a woman having the child suffers damages as a result of the *natural process* etc.

   (c) Public policy arguments rejected by the House of Lords in *McFarlane*. Question involved law, not social policy.

d. **Patient's condition a danger to third parties**   **[357]**

   (1) (a) In the US where a doctor has reason to know that a patient is likely to harm a specific third party, the doctor owes a duty of care to that person to warn the intended victim or the police. *Tarsoff v Regents of the University of California,* 17 Cal.3d 425 (1976).

   (b) *Hammon v County of Maricipa,* (775 P.2d 1122 (AR 1989)). A psychiatrist who knew, or should have known, of the risk of violence to others owed a duty to the violent child's parents even though no specific threat of violence was made against them by the child.

   (2) *Urbanski v Patel* (1978) 84 DLR 3d 650. A doctor, who negligently removed a patient's only kidney leaving her in a very dangerous position, was found to have owed a duty of care to the patient's father who donated one of his kidneys to her.

C. Duty to control third parties   **[358]**

1. General principles
2. Vicarious liability
3. Doctrine of *respondeat superior*
4. Liability of parents for torts of child
5. Publican liability
6. Police

1. General principles

   a. A defendant may be held liable for *nonfeasance* in the failure to control the conduct of third persons where the defendant had the power of control.   **[359]**

b. **Direct liability:** Where the *defendant is present* at the time of the third person's wrongful conduct, his failure to exercise control to stop such conduct may be an act of negligence.

[360]

Examples:
(1) A driver may have a duty to control passengers so they do not injure other road users. *Curley v Manion. See* [677].
(2) A publican may have a duty to protect a patron against a battery by another patron. *Hall & Kennedy v Routledge* (1993) unrep. (HC).

d. **Indirect liability:** Where the *defendant is not present* he may be liable for the acts of third persons in limited situations such as vicarious liability.

[361]

2. **Vicarious liability.** *See* Chapter 5 — Strict liability.

a. **Definition**: Vicarious liability is where one person is held liable for the acts of another person.

[362]

b. May be imposed by:
(1) Common law, or
(2) By statute.

c. Arises in:
(1) **Formal legal relationships** such as: **[363]**
    (a) Employer/employee. *See* [365],
    (b) Principal/agent,
    (c) Firm/partner imposed by liability of partners under the Partnership Act 1961.
(2) **Informal relationships** where one person has control over another person.   **[364]**
    (a) Driver/passenger — *Curly v Manion. See* [677]
    (b) Social host/guest — *Moynihan v Moynihan. See* [683].
    (c) Owner of vehicle/driver — s. 118, Road Traffic Act.

3. **Doctrine of *respondeat superior*** — employer vicarious liability

[365]

a. **General rule:** An employer may be liable for the tortious acts committed by employees within the scope of employment.

b. **Crucial requirement:** The act must be within the *scope of employment.*
(1) **Scope of employment:** Vicarious liability will not apply if the tort is committed outside the scope of employment.

[366]

    (a) Scope does *not* include travel to and from primary place of employment.

(b) **Examples:** After reaching primary place of employment (shop, office, farm etc.), travelling to see clients or being sent to run errands for employer would be within scope of employment.

(2) **General rule:** Leaving the place of employment on private or personal business is usually outside scope of employment.

  (a) **Example:** *O'Connell v Bateman* [1932] LJ IR 160. A man borrowed his employer's lorry to visit his family. **Held:** The employer was not liable for the damage caused when the lorry crashed.

  (b) **Example: Detour** — *Jameson v Byrne & Maguire* (1926) 60 ILTR 11. An employee made a detour on his route for personal reasons and crashed. **Held:** There was no evidence to infer that the employee was acting within the scope of his employment.

c. **Intentional torts** committed by employees

  (1) **General rule:** An employer may be vicariously liable for the intentional torts (such as batteries) committed by his employees within the scope of their employment. **[367]**

    (a) Where the employee's duties involve the use of physical force on others, such as bodyguards and bouncers, or

    (b) Where force is used to further the employer's interests. **Example:** *Farry v Great Northern Railway Co.* [1898] 2 IR 352. A stationmaster detained the plaintiff to force the plaintiff to surrender his ticket after a dispute arose over his trip. The employer railway was held vicariously liable for false imprisonment of the plaintiff. **Rationale:** the stationmaster had been acting to protect the interests of his employer.

  (2) **Criminal conduct** by employee **[368]**

    (a) **Irish approach:** *Johnson & Johnson (Ireland) Ltd v C.P. Security Ltd* [1985] IR 362. A security guard employed by the defendant to protect the plaintiff's premises assisted others in stealing plaintiff's goods. The *employer was held vicariously liable because it was specifically engaged to safeguard plaintiff's property.*

    (b) **English approach:** *Trotman v North Yorkshire Co. Council* (1998) *The Times* Sept 10. A mentally handicapped teenager suffering from epilepsy required attendance during the night because of his seizures. During a school trip, the deputy headmaster sexually assaulted the teenager in the room they shared and was convicted of sexual assault. *Where an employee performs an act that actually negates the employer's duty (to take care of the teenager), the employer cannot be held vicariously liable.*

d. **Independent contractors:** An employer may be vicariously liable for torts committed by independent contractors if the employer's degree of control was comparable to that of an employee. **[369]**

  (1) *Phelan v Coillte Teo* [1993] 1 IR 18. The plaintiff was injured due to the negligence of an independent contractor — a welder/fitter with whom the plaintiff was working.

  (2) Test of control is not settled.

  (3) English approach regarding issue of control:

    (a) Was the wrongful act authorised by the employer? Or

    (b) Was the act authorised by the employer, but the method of performance was not authorised?

4. **Liability of parents for torts of child**

  a. **Common law rule:** No vicarious liability. **[370]**

    (1) Generally, a parent is *not* vicariously liable for torts committed by his child.

    (2) **Rationale**: Parents do not have sufficient control to justify imputing liability where parent was not otherwise negligent.

  b. **Liability based on parent's own negligence.** A parent or any one else having care or custody of a child may be liable for injuries caused by a child where the parent was negligent by: **[371]**

    (1) *Failing to control* the acts of a child committed in the presence of the parent. **[372]**
    Example: *Curley v Manion. See* [677].

    (2) *Failing to exercise* reasonable care to protect against the child's known dangerous tendencies. **[373]**
    Example: Allowing a child previously caught setting fires to have access to matches.

    (3) *Failing to warn* others who are likely to come into contact with the child of the child's dangerous tendencies. **[374]**
    Example: *Ellis v D'Angelo* 116 Cal App 2d 310 (1953). Childminder injured by violent four-year-old.

(4) *Failing to prevent* the child's foreseeable use of inherently dangerous things. **[375]**

Examples: Leaving loaded shotgun within reach of the child or leaving the child in vehicle with keys.

5. **Publican liability**
   a. **General rule:** Under the common law a publican is not liable for injuries to third parties resulting from a patron's intoxication. **[376]**
   b. **Exception**: A publican has a duty to protect a patron on his premises from a battery by another patron. *Hall & Kennedy v Routledge* (1993) unrep. (HC). **[377]**

   Note: A publican may owe other duties such as in his capacity as an occupier. *See* [585] *et seq.*

6. **Police**
   a. **General rule:** The police are typically not liable for failing to protect individual persons. **[378]**
      (1) **Public policy rationale**
          (a) To impose such a duty would determine how the limited police resources should be allocated.
          (b) Floodgate concerns
      (2) *Hill v Chief Constable of West Yorkshire Police* [1993] 4 All ER 344. The plaintiff's daughter was the last victim of the Yorkshire Ripper. He sued the police for negligently conducting the investigation of the previous murders. The plaintiff contended that had a proper investigation taken place the killer would have been caught sooner. Case dismissed: public policy grounds.
   b. **Exception:** An individual may be owed a duty of protection from the police where there is a specific, increased risk of harm. **[379]**
      (1) *Osman v UK* [1999] 1 FLR 193 (ECHR) 1998. A teacher harassed the plaintiff's family for over ten months. Armed with a shotgun the teacher shot two members of the family. The plaintiffs sued the police for negligently failing to protect. After being dismissed in the English courts the case was appealed to the European Court of Human Rights (ECHR).
          (a) ECHR found relationship of proximity to police and harm caused was foreseeable. Blanket immunity for police violated Art. 6 — right to a court.
          (b) Distinguished from *Hill* — Osman family members

were identified. The Ripper's next victim was not identified.

(2) Blanket immunities questioned. *See also Hall (Arthur JJ) & Co. v Simons* [297].

(3) Regarding state omissions, *see also A v UK* [96].

D. Common law duties owed by an employer to employees

1. Historical background   **[380]**
   a. During the nineteenth century with increased industrialisation injured employees sought redress for their injuries through the courts. The response of most courts in the majority of jurisdictions was hostile.
   (a) Liability generally rested on the terms of employment.
   (b) Terms of Employment tended to be dictated by the employer.
   b. The judicial response to workers seeking redress included:
                                                             [381]
   (1) The Doctrine of Common Employment,
   (2) *Volenti Non Fit Injuria*, and
   (3) Contributory negligence.
   c. **The Doctrine of Common Employment:**
   (1) Excluded claims for injuries caused by co-workers, even if the co-worker was performing an activity on the employer's behalf.
   (2) Was abolished by s. 1, Law Reform (Personal Injuries) Act 1958.
   d. ***Volenti Non Fit Injuria*** (voluntary assumption of the risk):
   (1) Excluded claims for injuries caused by the place, system, method or lack of safety equipment on the job.
   (2) In agreeing to work, the injured employee agreed to assume the risk of injury. Application of this doctrine has been greatly curtailed by:
   (a) Various work safety acts, *see* [392], and the
   (b) Civil Liabilities Act 1961.
   e. **Contributory negligence**
   Total bar: Before the Civil Liabilities Act 1961, contributory negligence was a total bar to any recovery by an injured employee.
2. Employers also owe common law duties to third parties: **[382]**
   a. As occupiers. *See* occupiers' liability [585] *et seq.*
   b. If manufacturing. *See* products' liability [705] *et seq.*

c. If professional. *See* professional negligence [293] *et seq.*

d. Under the doctrine of vicarious liability. *See* [362] and [670].

3. **Present status of law — employers common law duty of reasonable care to employees**

   a. Four primary duties, to provide: **[383]**

      (1) **Safe place of work,**

      (2) **Safe system of work,**

      (3) **Safe work equipment,** and

      (4) **Competent co-workers.**

      Note: In most cases the various duties owed overlap.

   b. **Safe place of work**

      (1) **General rule:** An employer must take reasonable steps to ensure that employees have a safe place to work. **[384]** Physical environment must be safe. *Kielthy v Ascon* [1970] IR 122. One of the methods of access to the employer's premises was not safe.

      Gallagher v Mogul of Ireland Ltd [1975] IR 204 (SC). The roof of the employer's mine collapsed due to insufficient support.

      (2) **Extended** to a place where the employee is *sent* by the employer to work. **[385]**

         (a) *Dunne v Honeywell Control Systems Ltd & Virginia Milk Products Ltd* [1991] ILRM 595 (HC). The plaintiff was injured when he fell off a ladder after repairing equipment at Virginia Milk Products' premises. His employer could not control the premises where the employee was sent, but he could inspect and warn the employee of dangers.

         (b) **No duty to inspect.** *Mulcare v Southern Health Board* [1988] ILRM 689. The plaintiff was employed to provide home care to elderly patients. She injured an ankle on an uneven floor in one of the homes she visited and alleged that her employer was negligent for failing to inspect the premises and warn her. Recovery denied: the house was not sufficiently unsafe and the plaintiff had been in the house numerous times over seven years.

   c. **Safe system of work**

      (1) **General rule:** The employer has a duty to provide a safe system of work. **[386]**

         (a) Proper training and supervision, and

    (b) Suitable methods of operation including:
        i   Design, and
        ii Operation of work practices.

(2) **Proper training and supervision**

    (a) *Heeney v Dublin Corp.* (1991) unrep. (SC). The plaintiff's decedent died while employed as a fire fighter — as a result of injuries suffered while fighting a fire without a suitable breathing apparatus. Besides the obvious failure to provide equipment the defendants were held liable for failing to implement a Labour Court recommendation to assign tasks pursuant to medical exams, as well as the failure to supervise by failing to give instructions for fire fighters not to enter burning buildings without proper breathing apparatus.

    (b) *General Cleaning Contractors v Christmas* [1953] AC 180 (HL). The plaintiff window cleaner was told by his employer to hold onto the window sash while cleaning. A window fell on the plaintiff's fingers, and the plaintiff fell to the ground. The employer was held liable for failing to have a safe system of work because he failed to tell the plaintiff to test the sashes and wedge all loose sashes.

    (c) *Dunne v Honeywell. See* [385]. The employer was also found negligent for failing to warn the employee concerning the danger of the handheld tool case on ladders. In order to improve image the employer had replaced the employee's shoulder satchel for carrying tools, with a case that had to be held in the hand.

(3) **Suitable methods of operation**

    (a) **High-risk activities** require every precaution to be taken.   **[387]**
        Walsh v Securicor (Ireland) [1993] 2 IR 507 (HC). The plaintiff was the driver of a security van being escorted by police when he was injured by armed raiders. The employer was held liable for negligently failing to alter the delivery route for over seven years.

    (b) Design of a safe system of work requires more than provision of safety equipment.   **[388]**
        Barry v Nitrigin Eireann Teo [1994] 2 ILRM 523 (HC). An unsuitable work system was found to exist

due to incompatible equipment. The protective earmuffs had to be removed for the plaintiff to use his
communication system.

(4) **Unsafe design of operation**
McDermid v Nash Dredging & Reclamaiton Co. [1987]
AC 906 (HL). The plaintiff's employer failed to operate
a safe system of work. The plaintiff was injured when a
tugboat captain failed to wait for the double knock of the
plaintiff on the door of the bridge. That was the means of
communicating that it was safe to proceed. The plaintiff
was seriously injured when he was tangled in ropes and
dragged into the sea.

d. **Safe equipment**
(1) **General rule:** The employer must provide and maintain
suitable equipment.   **[389]**
Note: Duty is *not* limited to safety equipment.

(2) **Incompatible safety equipment**   **[390]**
Barry v Nitrigin Eireann Teo, see [388]. The plaintiff's
safety goggles and earmuffs were not compatible. The
goggles pushed the earmuffs slightly out of place.

(3) **Inferior quality equipment**   **[391]**
Deegan v Langan [1966] IR 373. The plaintiff carpenter
was injured due to the inferior quality of the nails provided by the employer.

(4) **Failure to maintain**   **[392]**
(a) *Burke v John Paul & Co. Ltd* [1967] IR 277, *see*
Causation [519]. The plaintiff was cutting steel rods
and complained to his employer that the blades were
dull. Liability was imposed on the employer for negligently failing to maintain the blades for the hernia
the plaintiff suffered.
(b) Duty has been bolstered by statutory protections:
i   Factories Act 1955
ii Mines and Quarries Act 1965
iii Safety, Health, Welfare at Work Act 1989

(5) **Building material may be equipment**   **[393]**
Knowles v Liverpool City Council [1993] ICR 21. The plain-
tiff was injured when a flagstone he was handling broke.
The court of appeal held that the flagstone was equipment.

e. **Competent co-workers**
General rule: The employer has a duty to exercise reasonable
care to provide competent staff.   **[394]**

Note: This provision is less important since the abolition of the Doctrine of Common Employment.

a. **Qualifications and experience** must be properly considered when hiring someone to work in a position that carries the potential to put others at risk. **[395]**
Black v Fife Coal Co. Ltd [1912] AC 149. The employer was held to have negligently hired a colliery manager who was without experience with carbon monoxide that was a known hazard at the work site.

b. **Monitoring staff**: It may be negligent to continue to employ a person who continually engages in practical jokes and/or horseplay resulting in injuries to co-workers. *Hudson v Ridge Manufacturing Co.* [1957] 2 QB 348. **[396]**
Hough v Irish Base Metal Ltd (1967) unrep. (SC). It was held that the employer was not negligent for failure to provide competent staff when the plaintiff was injured by a prank. The prank was not reasonably capable of detection, it was of recent origin and there was no failure to supervise staff.

IV. Duty may be limited by type of harm

A. Pure economic loss
B. Nervous shock
C. Death

A. Pure economic loss

1. **Traditional common law approach — exclusionary rule**: This did not allow any recovery for negligently inflicted *pure* economic loss. **[397]**

a. **Definition**: Pure economic loss is economic loss without property or protected personal interests being affected, i.e. no property damage or injuries to the person. **[398]**
Example: Captain Marvel negligently sailed his ship into the Waterford Bridge damaging it to the extent that it had to remain closed to vehicle and ship traffic for one week. Pauline Plaintiff owns a shop on the quay in Waterford that caters to tourists. The ship damaged neither her shop nor her person. However, due to the bridge closure Pauline's business suffers heavy losses. Pauline has suffered a pure economic loss.

b. **Rationale for traditional common law approach:** No duty
of care was found because of public policy concerns about
potential crushing liability being out of proportion to the
defendant's fault.
Criticism: Persons with similar losses are not treated the
same.
Example: Herbie ran into an ESB pole late on Friday night.
The pole hit the corner of the ABC frozen fish factory and
various wires disconnected from the pole. All of the frozen
food businesses on the street were without electricity all week-
end. All suffered similar economic losses, but only ABC (that
also suffered a physical injury) would be able to recover for
the economic losses sustained.
2. **Direct or restrictive approach** — favoured in England   **[399]**
a. **Recovery** is allowed only where the loss is a *direct* result of the
defendant's conduct and the plaintiff is the *immediate* victim.
b. **Damage to property** is allowed only for persons with a proprietary interest in the property.
c. **Pure economic loss** is allowed only when there is a high
degree of proximity between defendant's act and the plaintiff's
pure economic injury.
Leigh & Sillavan Ltd v Aliakmon Shipping Co. Ltd [1986] AC
785. Goods were damaged in transit by the defendant's negligence. At the time of the injury the plaintiff had no proprietary interest in the goods, just a financial risk because it covered the risk of damage to the goods. The House of Lords
denied a recovery — plaintiff had no proprietary interest in
goods nor the required proximity.
d. Approach has been used in Ireland:
(1) *Irish Paper Sacks Ltd v John Sisk & Son* (Dublin) Ltd
unrep. (1972) (HC). The defendants cut a cable that supplied electricity to the plaintiff's factory while digging.
They suffered economic loss but no property loss — no
recovery allowed.
(2) **Criticism:** This approach is inherently uncertain in
dimensions, i.e. when will it apply?
(3) **Benefit** of restrictive approach — it limits potentially
crushing liability or floodgates.
3. **Broad approach** — *favoured* in Ireland.   **[400]**
a. Treats economic loss with the same principles as physical damage.
Approach accepted in Ireland in *Ward v McMaster* [1985] IR

29 (SC). The case involved a house with dangerous and non-dangerous defects.

b. **Requirements:** from *Ward v McMaster* **[401]**
   (1) **Proximity:** There must be sufficient proximity between the parties.
   (2) **Reasonable foreseeable damage:** The damage must be a reasonable foreseeable consequence of the defendant's conduct.
   (3) **No adverse public policy considerations.**
       Same approach — negligent misstatements. *See* [338].

c. **Applied in:** *McShane Wholesale & Vegetable Ltd v Johnston Haulage Co. Ltd* [1997] I ILRM 86 (HC). The defendant's premises suffered a fire and the fire caused the plaintiff's factory to lose electricity.

d. **Criticism** of approach
   Problems with determining foreseeability.
   Madden v Irish Turf Club [1997] 2 ILRM 148 (SC). The plaintiff bet on a horse that came in second to a horse that was not eligible to run in the race. The plaintiff sued the defendant for failing to stop the ineligible horse from running. Case dismissed: the defendant's function was to regulate and control racing not betting.

4. **Vulnerability approach** — favoured in Australia. **[402]**
   a. **Vulnerability** is the relevant criterion for determining whether a duty of care exists.
      (1) Where a person knows or ought to know that his act(s) or omissions may cause the loss or impairment of legal rights possessed, enjoyed or exercised by another, whether as an individual or as a member of a class, where *the latter person is in no position to protect his interest*, there is a relationship such that the law should impose a duty of care on the actor to take reasonable steps to avoid foreseeable risk of economic loss resulting from the loss or impairment of those rights. (Gaudron J.) *Perre and Others v Apand Pty Ltd* [1999] 164 ALR 606 (HC)
      (2) *Perre* Facts: Potato farmers in a rural locality were prohibited from exporting their crops after the defendant negligently supplied diseased seed that introduced potato wilt onto neighbouring lands. The potato farmers were placed by the government in a five-year exclusion zone that prohibited exporting their crops. **Held:** A duty of care was owed to all the farmers affected.

b. Detrimental reliance and assumption of responsibility are indicators of the plaintiff's vulnerability to harm from the defendant's conduct.

B. *Nervous shock — sometimes referred to as psychological, psychiatric, mental or emotional distress or injury.* **[403]**

1. **Definition**: Psychiatric harm caused by the plaintiff suffering a sudden or unexpected shock.
2. **Historical development**
   a. **Traditional general rule:** If a defendant acted negligently causing a mental injury (nervous shock) to the plaintiff, there was no liability. **[404]**
      (1) However, if the defendant acted negligently causing a *physical* and *mental* injury (nervous shock) to the plaintiff, the plaintiff could generally recover for both.
      (2) Dependent nervous shock is usually called 'pain and suffering'.
   b. **Criticism** of nervous shock. *See* Intentional Infliction of Emotional Distress, [68]. **[405]**
      (1) Fear of fraudulent claims.
      (2) Floodgates: potentially limitless claims from a single negligent act.
   c. Erosion of traditional rule — said to be due to railway development of the nineteenth century.
3. Earliest recognition of nervous shock:
   a. **For person in *fear* of his *own* safety**
      (1) With *resulting physical injury.* **[406]**
      Byrne v Southern & Western Railway Co. (1884) unrep. (CA). The plaintiff was in a building struck by a train. Plaintiff suffered no physical injuries (at time of the crash), but the resulting shock led to a deterioration of his health.
      (2) With *resulting mental injuries,* but no physical injury. **[407]**
      Bell v Great Northern Railway Co. (1890) 26 LR 428. The plaintiff was a passenger in a train carriage that detached from the train and careered backward down a hill. Plaintiff's mental health suffered.
      (3) With *resulting physical harm* to *unborn child.* **[408]**
         (a) *Dulieu v White & Sons* [1901] 2 KB 669. Often cited as the first successful nervous shock case. A publican's wife who suffered a severe fright when a horse-drawn vehicle crashed through the window of

the pub where she was working. Soon after the event her child was born prematurely and died. (Court relied upon *Bell* and *Byrne*.)

(b) **Kennedy limitation**: The shock must be a *reasonable* fear of *immediate* personal injury to oneself.

(c) Limitation was used for some time to *limit* the scope of liability for nervous shock.

4. **Expansion** to include:

a. **Parent in fear for safety of child.** [409]

(1) Parent *must* perceive the injury or near miss with their own *unaided senses*.

(a) *Hambrook v Stokes Bros.* [1925] 1 KB 141. The plaintiff saw a lorry out of control heading for her four children. She suffered nervous shock, suffered a miscarriage and died. Although the mother herself was never in harm's way the court extended liability to include the experience she witnessed with her own *unaided senses*. Reasoning: It was absurdity to deny remedy, whereas had the mother feared for her own safety the claim would have succeeded.

(b) *Kralj v McGrath* [1986] 1 All ER 907. Recovery allowed for a mother who suffered nervous shock when she saw the condition of her baby who was the victim of a negligent delivery.

b. **Person in fear for safety of family member** but where the person did not witness the accident or occurrence. [410]

(1) *McLoughlin v O'Brian* [1982] 2 All ER 298. The plaintiff recovered for the severe psychological injuries she suffered, including a personality change, after seeing the injuries of her spouse and children (in hospital) caused by the defendant's negligent driving.

(2) *Mullally v Bus Eireann* [1992] ILRM 722 (HC). The plaintiff recovered for post-traumatic stress disorder she suffered as a result of searching for her family members in two different hospitals, and viewing her family members and victims immediately after a bus crash caused by the defendant's negligence.

(3) *Broomfield v The Midland Health Board* (1990) (HC). The defendant's hospital gave the plaintiff another person's baby. After nine days the mistake was ratified. The defendant refused or failed to give the plaintiff documents concerning her child until a year after the event.

c. **Person in fear of safety of friend.** [411]

Dooley v Cammell Laird & Co. Ltd [1951] 1 Lloyd's Rep. 271.
The plaintiff, a crane operator, witnessed a load dropping into
the hold of a ship and feared injury to his workmates. A duty
was held to be owed to the plaintiff.

5. **No expansion** [412]

a. **Person in fear of injury to property**: This is generally not
recognised.

(1) *Attia v British Gas* [1988] QB 304. The defendant negligently installed central heating in the plaintiff's home causing a fire. When the plaintiff returned home and found her
home on fire she suffered nervous shock. Claim allowed.

(2) *Campbell v Animal Quarantine Station*, 632 P.2d 1066
(Haw. 1981). The plaintiffs recovered for *emotional distress* where their nine-year-old pet dog died of heat stroke
after being negligently put into a van with no ventilation
by the defendants

b. **Non-sudden shock** [413]

Sion v Hampstead Health Authority (1994) unrep. The plaintiff was denied recovery for his stress-related psychiatric illness
caused from watching his son slowly die in intensive care
because of negligent medical treatment. Recovery denied
because the illness was not caused by a sudden shock.

c. **Person in fear for safety of a stranger** [414]

(1) *Bourhill v Young* [1943] AC 92. A woman exiting a tram
heard a serious accident outside her field of vision. She
went to the scene of the accident and suffered nervous
shock — her child was stillborn shortly thereafter. Claim
for nervous shock failed. Reasoning:

(a) Plaintiff outside **area of impact**.

(b) Person injured was a total **stranger.**

(c) Plaintiff outside **foresight of shock.**

(2) **Rescuers exception** — **general rule:** a rescuer may
recover for nervous shock if he comes upon an accident
and assists and also exposes himself to potential physical
injury. [415]

Chadwick v British Railways Board [1967] 2 All ER 945.
The plaintiff helped the official rescue teams at the scene
train crash. He suffered nervous shock and eventually
committed suicide. Recovery allowed. **Note:** the rescuer
in *Chadwick* was distinguished in *White* [417] because he

was foreseeably exposed to physical injury in entering the damaged railroad cars.

6. **Present status of nervous shock in Ireland.** *Kelly v Hennessy* [1995] 3 IR 253. The plaintiff's husband and daughters were involved in a car crash. The husband and one daughter suffered brain injuries. The *Supreme Court set out six principles* to determine whether a plaintiff, suffering nervous shock, comes within the defendant's duty of care. **[416]**

   (1) Plaintiff *must* suffer a *recognised psychiatric illness.*
   Note: Post-traumatic stress disorder *is* a recognised psychiatric illness.

   (2) Plaintiff's illness *must* arise from *shock.*

   (3) It must be *foreseeable* that the defendant's act or the event *could cause* psychiatric injury.

   (4) The illness must result from the *perception of actual injury*, or a *risk of injury* to oneself or another person.
   Curran v Cadbury Ltd [2000] 2 ILRM 343 (CC). The plaintiff sustained injury when she turned on a machine at work and thought that she had killed a co-worker who unknown to the plaintiff was working inside the machine.

   (5) If harm results from exposure to *aftermath*, there must be a *close personal relationship* between victim and plaintiff.
   Aftermath continues as long as the victim remains in the state caused by the accident, i.e. until s/he receives immediate post-accident treatment. *Jaensch v Coffey* (1984) 54 ALR 417, *(dicta)*.

   (6) There are *no public policy limits* on the recovery where the plaintiff establishes sufficient proximity and foreseeability by fulfilling the five criteria above.

7. **Present English approach:** e.g. the Hillsborough football stadium disaster cases. (Retraction from previous liability expansion for nervous shock and generally more restrictive than the Irish approach.) **[417]**

   a. *Alcock v Chief Constable of South Yorkshire* [1991] 4 All ER 907. In 1989, ninety-five people were crushed to death and 400 were injured at a football match when police negligently allowed too many people into the stadium. The 150 plaintiffs were friends and family of the dead and suffered nervous shock.

      (1) Categories of perception by plaintiffs:
         (a) Direct — at stadium and saw disaster occur.
         (b) TV — saw disaster on television.

(c) Went to stadium — to look for family member or friend.

(d) News — told to them by third party.

(e) Morgue identification — had to identify family member or friend in temporary morgue at the stadium.

(2) **Reasonable foreseeability test:** Secondary victims must prove that psychiatric injury was a *reasonably foreseeable* consequence of the defendant's negligence.

(3) Psychological damage must be caused by the plaintiff suffering a sudden and unexpected shock. Excludes:

(a) Psychiatric illness as a result of grief, or

(b) Stress from looking after someone injured by the negligence of the defendant.

b. **White & Others v Chief Constable of South Yorkshire** [1999] 1 All ER 1. This is the same event as outlined above in *Alcock*, but this case dealt with the rescuers, i.e. secondary victims — required to meet *Alcock* test of reasonable foreseeability. Rescuers not in a special position regarding psychiatric damage, i.e. must show objectively that s/he had been exposed to physical danger.

(1) **Alcock test explained:** For a bystander, foreseeability would occur when a person of *reasonable fortitude* would be likely to suffer psychiatric injuries.

(2) **Susceptibility to shock:** If a person suffers psychiatric injury because s/he is unusually susceptible to shock, reasonable foreseeability is *not* proved.

(a) **Eggshell psyche:** If a bystander of normal fortitude would be likely to suffer psychiatric injury it does not matter that the psychiatric injury is made *more serious* by the personal characteristics of the plaintiff.

(b) **Note:** This is *not* the same as the general eggshell rule that a defendant takes his victim as he finds him.

(3) **Psychological damage** must be a *recognised* psychiatric illness.

(a) **Primary victim defined**: Where a person is put in danger of physical harm but actually suffers only psychiatric injuries.

(b) **Secondary victim defined**: Where a person is not in danger of physical injury but suffers psychiatric harm as a result of witnessing injury to another.

(c) *Chadwick v British Railways Board* [1967] 2 All ER 945. The plaintiff, a passer-by, helped the official rescue teams at the scene of a serious rail crash. He suffered nervous shock and eventually committed suicide. Recovery allowed.

Note: the rescuer in *Chadwick* was distinguished in *White* because he was foreseeably exposed to physical injury in entering damaged railroad cars.

   c. **Rescuer as a primary victim**: A rescuer that witnesses an accident is a primary victim and may recover for nervous shock even though he suffered no physical injury during the rescue. *Hale v London Underground* (1992) 11 BMLR 81.

8. **American approach** — General rule: **[418]**

   a. For tort of negligent infliction of emotional distress the plaintiff must suffer some physical manifestation of emotional distress.

Recognised physical manifestations vary from:

(1) Miscarriages and heart attacks, to

(2) *Panic attacks* with extreme abdominal pain. *Olson v Connerly,* 445 NE2d 706 (Wis. 1989).

(3) Must be shown by objective symptoms, e.g. weight loss, loss of sleep, general physical deterioration. *Corrigal v Ball & Dodd Funeral Home Inc.,* 577 P.2d 580 (Wash. 1978).

   b. Some jurisdictions allow recovery without any *physical manifestation of emotional distress.*

(1) Erroneously reporting a close relative's death.
Johnson v State, 37 NY2d 375 (1975). Plaintiff recovered where a hospital advised her that her mother had died, when in fact she had not died.

(2) Mishandling the corpse of a relative.
Cohen v Groman Mortuary, 231 Cal.App.2d 1 (1964). The defendants negligently caused the corpse of the plaintiff's husband to be mutilated in public.

(3) **Rationale**: These cases involve a high likelihood of genuine and serious distress.

   c. **Fear of future harm**
Used primarily in the context of toxic or environmental exposure resulting in the plaintiff seeking damages for the mental anguish suffered for fear of contracting a disease in the future. Often referred to as *cancerphobia.*

(1) Most jurisdictions are wary of permitting recovery because of:

    (a) Difficulty in measuring damages,

    (b) The potential of crushing liability (floodgates), and

    (c) The serious proof difficulties.

  (2) Two types of approaches are used:

    (a) *Without* physical injury, recovery of damages for fear of cancer in a negligence action is *limited* to cases where the plaintiff proves that it is probable that s/he will develop cancer in the future due to exposure. *Potter v Firestone Tire & Rubber Co.*, 863 P.2d 795 (Calf. 1993).

    (b) The plaintiff may recover for serious mental distress arising from the fear of developing cancer where the fear is *reasonable* and *casually related* to the defendant's negligence. *Hagerty v L. & L. Marine Services Inc.*, 788 F.2d 315 (1986).

C. Death

1. Death of a party

  a. **Traditionally:** Under the common law the death of one of the parties ended all actions in personal torts. **[419]**

  b. **Statutory exceptions** to the common law rule allowed actions for personal torts to continue.

    (1) **Examples:**

      (a) S. 117, Road Traffic Act 1961 — regarding personal liability for negligent driving.

      (b) S. 23, Air Navigation & Transport Act 1936 — for damages caused by aircraft to persons or property.

  c. **Civil Liability Act 1961 (CLA) — abolished the common law rule**.

    (1) **General rule**: The death of either party does not extinguish the action. **[420]**

      (a) **S. 7** — All tort actions are transferred to the estate of the deceased.

      (b) **Exception**: S. 6 excludes defamation, seduction and claims for worker's compensation.

      (c) **S. 7(2)** — *Damages* are confined to economic losses and property damage. All personal damages (pain and suffering etc.) died with the plaintiff. **[421]**

    (2) Limitations with regard to death

      (a) **General rule: S. 4** of the CLA provides that the ordinary limitation period applies. *See* [522] *et seq.* for limitations. **[422]**

   (b) **Exception:** If the action was not pending at the time of death, it must be brought within the normal period or within two years of death, *whichever* is shorter. **[423]**

2. **Wrongful death:** The defendant wrongfully caused the death of another

   a. **Common law rule:** The death of a human being could not be the basis of a cause of action. **[424]**

     It was cheaper to kill than to injure.

   b. **Statutory reform: Civil Liability Act 1961 (as amended)** **[425]**

     (1) **S. 48(1)** — An action may be brought for the benefit of the dependants of the deceased against the person causing the death. (The plaintiff is the dependent of the deceased.)

     (2) The defendant's conduct must have been an actionable wrong against the deceased.

      In other words, if the decedent had lived s/he must have had an action against the defendant.

   c. **S. 48(2)** — Only *one action* is allowed. **[426]**

     Example: If a man is injured and dies because of the negligent acts of another, the deceased's four dependent children cannot each bring an action separately.

   d. **S. 47(1)** — A dependent is any member of the family of the deceased suffering injury or mental distress because of the death. **[427]**

     Expansion: This relates to dependent classes of persons by the *Civil Liability (Amendment) Act 1996.*

     (a) S. 47(1)(b) — A former spouse may be a dependent.

     (b) S. 47(1)(c) — A person in cohabitation with the deceased for three years prior to his death.

   e. **Special period of limitation** **[428]**

     The action must be brought within *three years* of the death — statute of Limitations (Amendment) Act 1991 *s. 6 (1).*

   f. **Damages for wrongful death** — s. 49 **[429]**

     (1) **Emotional distress:**

      (a) Has a recovery cap of £20,000 (1996 Act).

      (b) Not available to former spouses.

      (c) **Note:** A family member may still maintain their own action for nervous shock under proper circumstances. *See* [403].

(2) **Expenses**
   (a) Costs of funeral.
   (b) Medical bills related to death.
(3) **Injury suffered**
   (a) Loss of financial support due to the death. *Gallagher v ESB* [1933] IR 558.
   (b) Loss of services for work in the home. *Cooper v Egan* (1990) unrep. (HC). Financial valuation made for work performed in the family home.
(4) **Damages calculated**
   Without reference to the gain (e.g. insurance) or loss (except funeral costs) caused by the death.

V. Breach of the duty of care by defendant

A. General rule
B. Act or omission
C. Determining unreasonable conduct
D. *Res ipsa loquitur*

A. General rule [430]

Once it is found that the defendant *owed a duty of care* to the plaintiff, then:
a. It must be shown that the *defendant breached this duty* through an act or omission (failure to act).
b. The *breach must be unreasonable* under the circumstances.

B. Act or omission (failure to act) by defendant [431]

1. **Act** must be a *voluntary* act by defendant. *See* [15].
   Voluntary — meaning under the defendant's conscious control.
   Example: A person whose hand is physically forced by another person to pull down a lever, allowing the escape of a dangerous substance, did not act voluntarily.
2. **Omission** (or a failure to act) may be the basis for liability in negligence.
   Note: Only when the defendant is under a duty to perform an act. *See* Affirmative Duties [322] *et seq.* [432]
3. **Negligent act** is said to be: [433]
   a. An act or omission (failure to act) by the defendant,
   b. With a duty of care owed to the plaintiff, and
   c. A breach of that duty by the defendant's unreasonable conduct.

C. *Determining unreasonable conduct*

1. **Balancing test**: The defendant's act or conduct is not considered unreasonable if the *magnitude of the risk* involved to the plaintiff is less than the *utility of the defendant's conduct.*   **[434]**

Magnitude of risk to plaintiff act(s)	Utility of the defendant's act(s)
— likelihood of harm	— social value of the defendant's act(s)
— gravity of threatened harm	— cost of eliminating the risk

2. **Magnitude of risk**
   a. **Likelihood of harm**: Generally, the less the risk of injury the less the likelihood of liability.   **[435]**
      (1) **Example:** *O'Gorman v Ritz (Clonmel)* [1947] Ir. Jur. Rep. 35. The plaintiff stretched her legs under the seat in front of her. The occupant caused the plaintiff's leg to be cut by the seat. At trial, evidence heard that in the previous seven years nearly one million people had used the seats without injury or complaints. The trial court dismissed the action.
      (2) **Injury not foreseeable**
         (a) *Plunkett v St. Lawrence Hospital* [1952] 86 ILTR 157. It was not foreseeable that a quiet patient, barely able to move due to a suspected spinal injury, would fall off an X-ray table.
         (b) *Walsh v Dublin Corp.* (1998) (HC). The plaintiff, a visitor to a flat owned by the defendant, suffered an injury to her thumb when a door slammed on it due to *wind tunnel effect* in the flat. Case dismissed — injury could happen to anyone at anytime.
      (3) **Injury foreseeable**
         a. Possibility of harm need *not* be *probable* — just *possble.*   **[436]**
         b. *Kelly v Governors of St. Lawrence Hospital* [1988] IR 402. Liability imposed where a patient admitted to hospital was taken off all drugs for epilepsy and was allowed to go to the toilet unattended. The patient jumped from a window.
   b. **Gravity of threatened harm**
      (1) Where potential harm is great, the *creation* of the slightest *risk* to the plaintiff may constitute negligence. **[437]**

(2) To be reasonable — the defendant's duty of care must meet the risk created. **[438]**

Classic example: *Paris v Stepney Borough Council* [1951] 1 All ER 42. The plaintiff (with only one good eye) was working as a welder for the defendant when he was blinded by a welding injury to that eye. Precaution expected for the plaintiff was higher than that expected for persons with normal vision.

(3) The *nature* and *extent* of the *threatened harm* significantly impacts on determining standard of care. **[439]**
Fitzsimmons v Bord Telecom Eireann & the ESB [1991] 1 IR 536. The plaintiff's spouse was electrocuted when he attempted to move a fallen telephone cable that came into contact with an electric cable.

3. Utility of the defendant's conduct

a. A social value of defendant's conduct

(1) An act of high social utility or value will be regarded as reasonable. **[440]**

(2) **Example:** *Whooley v Dublin Corporation* [1961] IR 60 (HC). The plaintiff was injured when she stepped into an open fire hydrant box. She alleged the defendant was negligent in the easy access design. **Held:** social purpose of easy access (quick response to fires) outweighed the protection of the public against malicious interference with the hydrants.

b. A social value is not absolute

Police driving in course of employment must still exercise reasonable care in the circumstances. **[441]**

(1) *Marshall v Osmond* [1983] 2 All ER 225. Police officer caused injury while in pursuit of a joyrider. While the officer's driving was held not to be negligent the court noted that similar driving by a civilian would be negligent.

(2) *Strick v Tracey* (1993) (HC). While escorting a civil defence fire tender to a fire, the police entered an intersection well in front of the fire tender. A collision occurred between the tender and another vehicle. All three drivers were held negligent. Police allowed too much space between emergency vehicles. Fire tender failed to take steps to halt traffic in intersection. Motorist negligent in assuming the emergency had passed.

   c. **No social value or utility** is regarded as unreasonable even if the risk of injury is small. **[442]**

   Classic example: There is a big difference between throwing a burning object from a house onto the street below for fun and throwing it in order to save the house from fire. (Fleming)

   d. **Cost of eliminating the risk.** A slight risk is reasonable if the cost of eliminating it is high. **[443]**

   Example: *O'Gormon v Ritz* above. All cinema seats could be made completely safe, but at what cost?

D. Res ipsa loquitur *(the thing speaks for itself)* **[444]**

  1. Types of evidence: There are two basic forms of evidence that a plaintiff can use in attempting to establish negligence by the defendant.

    a. Direct evidence: this is evidence that comes from personal knowledge or observation, e.g. from an eyewitness.

    Example: A security camera captures a car crash on film.

    b. Circumstantial evidence: this is proof that requires inferences to be drawn from other facts. **Examples:**

      (1) Hoofprints in the sand indicate that a horse walked across the beach earlier.

      (2) Skid marks at the scene of a car crash indicate that the driver braked.

  2. History of phrase: **Byrne v Boadle** [1863] 159 ER 299. Chief Baron Pollock stated 'There are certain cases of which it may be said *res ipsa loquitur* and this seems one of them.' … 'A barrel could not roll out of a warehouse without some negligence and to say that the plaintiff, who is injured by it, must call witnesses from the warehouse to prove negligence seems to me preposterous.' *See* [450] for facts.

  3. The fact that a particular harm occurs may tend to establish a breach of the duty of care. **[445]**

  4. **Required elements for *res ipsa loquitur*** are articulated *in Scott v London & St. Katherine Docks Co.* (1865) 159 ER 665. **[446]**

    a. Incident or injury must be of a type that normally does not occur in the absence of negligence, and

    b. The *source* of negligence must be *within the scope of a duty* that the defendant owes to the plaintiff.

  5. The plaintiff must prove:

    a. That the defendant had *sole control* of the incident. **[447]**

      (1) **Examples:**

(a) Operation of vehicle — *Corcoran v West* [1933] IR 210 (HC).

(b) Operation of aircraft — *Fosbroke-Hobbes v Airwork Ltd* [1937] 1 All ER 108.

(2) Sole control expanded to management of the incident. *Mullen v Quinnsworth* [1990] IR 59 (SC). Clear cooking oil on the defendant's store floor was held to be under the management of the defendant.

(3) No control: If the defendant did not have the *right* to control at the time of the injury. **[448]** *Tracey v Hagen* (1973) unrep. (SC). The plaintiff was injured by a machine six months after it left the defendant's control. *Res ipsa* denied.

b. That the defendant had *knowledge denied* to the plaintiff. **[449]**

Note: This does not relieve the plaintiff of the onus of proving that the thing causing the injury was under the defendant's control.

(a) *Hanrahan v Merck Sharp & Dohme* [1988] ILRM 629 (SC). The plaintiffs bought a nuisance action premised on negligence claiming that emissions from the defendant's factory was damaging their field and killing their cattle. *Res ipsa* denied: it does not apply only when the evidence is more accessible to the defendant. *Plaintiff must prove* that the thing that caused injury was under the defendant's control.

(b) *O'Mahony v Tyndale* 2000 (HC). The plaintiff's injuries at birth alleged to have occurred because of the negligence of the defendant. While the defendant hospital had been found wanting, the plaintiff did not prove that disabilities were caused by it.

c. That the *damage* would *not normally happen* without some element of negligence by the defendant. **[450]**

(1) *Byrne v Boadle* [444]. A barrel of flour fell out of an upper storey window of the defendant's warehouse — it landed on the plaintiff causing serious injuries.

(2) *Collen Bros. Ltd v Scaffolding Ltd* [1959] IR 245. Scaffolding was erected inside a giant silo by the defendants. It collapsed causing the plaintiff, a workman, to fall sixty feet.

(3) *Daniels v Heskin* [1954] IR 73 (SC). A needle broke while the defendant doctor was stitching the plaintiff. The court held that *res ipsa* did not apply. Evidence showed that while surgical needles usually break because of the doctor's technique, evidence also showed that the needle could have broken due to a flaw not detectable to the defendant.

6. **Procedural effect**: The onus or burden of proof *shifts* from the plaintiff to the defendant. [451]
   a. The *defendant has the onus of proving that he did not act negligently.* [452]
   b. However, the defendant is not required to prove what injured the plaintiff. [453]
   Lindsay v Mid-Western Health Board [1993] 2 IR 147 (SC). A child suffered seizures after surgery and lapsed into a coma. The court ruled that the defendant, to avoid liability, had to show that he exercised reasonable care. *Not required to show what caused the injury.*

7. **Medical malpractice cases** — cause difficulties
   a. Sometimes *experts are needed* to determine whether negligence can be inferred from the event. [454]
   Reasoning: The finder of fact is not competent to infer negligence from the injury in the course of complicated medical treatment. *Lindsay v Mid-Western Health Board* [1993] 2 IR 147 (HC).
   b. **Exception:** Even in medical malpractice, expert testimony is not required where negligence is obvious. **Examples:** [455]
      (1) *Mahon v Osborne,* [1939] 1 All ER 535. The plaintiff had a swab left in him after surgery.
      (2) *Ybarra v Spangard,* 154 P.2d 687 (Cal. 1944). The plaintiff's shoulder was injured while he was unconscious and undergoing an appendectomy. The plaintiff sued everyone who might be responsible and all defendants denied liability or knowledge of the cause of the injury. The court held all defendants jointly liable.

8. **Factual Defences to *Res Ipsa Locquitur***
   Defendant may defeat *res ipsa licquitur* by showing: [456]
   a. That he exercised reasonable care, or
   b. There was no causal link between his act or conduct and the plaintiff's injury. *See Lindsay* [454].

9. **Criticism** [457]
   a. Circumstancial evidence is treated differently than it would normally be treated.
   b. Other courts, such as Canada (SC) and Australia (HC) have announced the demise of the doctrine of *res ipsa loquitur*. Negligence litigation is to be resolved on the weight of the evidence.

   McMahon — such a trend would clarify Irish law.
   c. In the US: The doctrine has been used as a means of assuring that the case gets before a jury.

   However, with modern rules of discovery there is less need for the doctrine than when *Ybarra* [455] was decided.

VI. Causation

A. General principles
B. Actual cause
C. Proximate cause
   – Remoteness
   – *Novus actus interveniens*
   – Eggshell skull rule
D. Limitations

A. In general — causation is:

1. Concerned with the link between defendant's *act* and the *harm* suffered by the plaintiff. [458]
2. The two types of *required* causation are: [459]
   a. **Actual cause** (sometimes called *cause in fact*), and
   b. **Proximate cause** (sometimes called *legal cause*).

B. Actual cause — cause in fact

1. **General rule**: The defendant's negligent act *must* have been the *factual cause* of the harm suffered by plaintiff. [460]
   a. If the negligent act is not the cause in fact, of the harm suffered, there is no liability.
   b. **Note:** Negligence is not actionable *per se*. [461]
   If the plaintiff did not suffer any harm (injury, loss or damage) she cannot maintain a cause of action in negligence against the defendant regardless of how negligent the conduct of the defendant.

2. **Traditional approach:** *But for* test requires the plaintiff to prove by a preponderance of the evidence, that more likely than not, the defendant's conduct was the cause of the harm suffered by plaintiff. **Examples:** [462]

   a. *Barnett v Chelsea Kensington Management Committee* [1969] 1 QB 428. The plaintiff's husband, a night watchman, went to the hospital after drinking a cup of tea and becoming ill. He died shortly after leaving the casualty ward where he was seen by a nurse who consulted with a doctor over the phone. The decedent died of arsenic poisoning. The court concluded that the doctor had negligently failed to see the decedent, but since the decedent would have died anyway the harm was not *but for* the doctor's negligence.

   b. *Kenny v O'Rourke* [1972] IR 339. The plaintiff was injured when he fell off a defective ladder. The jury found that plaintiff fell due to leaning over too far on the ladder rather than due to the ladder's defect. Could not say that *but for* the defect in the ladder the plaintiff would not have been injured.

3. **Criticism** of the *but for* test [463]

   The test is *not* able to adequately deal with:

   (1) Successive causes of harm,
       Dillon v Twin State Gas & Electric Co. See [474].

   (2) Simultaneous causes of harm, or
       Summers v Tice. See [473].

   (3) Uncertain causes of harm.

4. **Concurrent liability** addresses some of the problems [464]

   a. Section 11(3) of the Civil Liability Act 1961:

      (1) **Definition — concurrent wrongdoers:** This is where two or more persons may be responsible for the plaintiff's damage, but it is not possible to establish which caused the damage, both are concurrent wrongdoers. [465]

      (2) The Act allows total recovery against any of the defendants leaving it to the defendants to work out liability under rules of contribution per Part III of the Act.

   b. **Person may become concurrent wrongdoer** by: [466]

      (1) Vicarious liability of another,

      (2) Breach of a joint duty,

      (3) Conspiracy or a concerted action to a common end, and

      (4) If independent acts cause the same damage.

   c. **Cause of action**

      (1) **General rule:** Bringing an action against one concurrent

wrongdoer does not bar the plaintiff from bringing a
cause of action against the others. **[467]**

(2) **Exception**: The plaintiff cannot recover more damages
than what he suffered.

d. **Liability**

(1) **General rule**: Each concurrent wrongdoer is *liable* for the
entire amount of damages. **[468]**

(2) **Exception**: Where one person caused independent items
of damage the court may apportion the damages.

e. **Contribution**: Section 5, Joint Tortfeasors Act 1951 **[469]**
No contribution is allowed to be made to a concurrent
wrongdoer from a person who is entitled to be indemnified.
Example: An employer will not be able to claim contribution
from an employee who would be entitled to indemnification.

f. **Release** — satisfaction of judgment **[470]**

(1) Under the common law the release of one joint tortfeasor
released *all* the joint tortfeasors.

(2) Sections 17 and 18 of the Civil Liability Act 1961 abolished the common law rule.
Release or accord (agreement on settlement) with one
concurrent wrongdoer does not discharge the others
unless the release and accord reflects such an intention to
release all of them.

5. **Introduction of material and substantial factor test** **[471]**
The defendant's acts will be treated as a cause of an injury if the
act is a *material* element and *substantial* factor in bringing about
the injury. Laffory J. in *Superquinn Ltd v Bray Urban District
Council & Others* (1998) unrep. (HC).

6. American approaches

a. **Substantial factor test** — General rule: **[472]**

(1) Jeremiah Smith is credited with proposing this approach
in 'Legal Cause in Actions of Tort', 25 Harv. L. Rev. 102
(1911).

(2) Used in the US as a *supplement* to the *but for* test where
multiple causes would preclude a recovery for a plaintiff
under the traditional rule.

(3) **Definition**: The defendant's conduct will only be treated
as a cause of an injury if it is a *material* element and *substantial* factor in bringing about the injury.

b. **Expansion: Simultaneous causes of harm — shifting onus
of proof** **[473]**

(1) *Summers v Tice*, 33 Cal.2d 80 (1948) — The two defendants negligently fired shotguns in the plaintiff's direction. Plaintiff was hit in the eye by one pellet, but could not tell which defendant fired the shot. Under the traditional *but for* analysis, the plaintiff could not prove that *either* of the defendants caused her injury. The court shifted the onus to the defendants to prove that they were not the cause of the plaintiff's injury. Both defendants were unable to exculpate themselves, thus both were found liable as joint tortfeasors. **Note**: Neither defendant was innocent of wrongdoing, but only one caused the injury.

Summers shifting onus — adopted by 2nd Restatement s. 433B.

(2) **Expansion of *Summers*** — *Haft v Lone Palm Hotel*, 478 P.2d 465 (Calif. 1970). The onus of proof of causation was shifted to the defendant where a father and his child drowned in the defendant's swimming pool. The plaintiff was able to prove that the defendant breached a Californian safety statute requiring lifeguards, or warning signs indicating no lifeguard service provided. Because the statute was violated and the violation made it difficult for the plaintiff to prove the cause of the drownings, the court shifted the onus onto the defendant.

c. **Successive causes of harm** [474]

Dillon v Twin State Gas & Electric Co., 163 A 111 (NH 1932). The defendant electric company's liability was limited to the value of the pain suffered by a boy electrocuted after falling from a bridge. The court held that the boy's life expectancy was negligible due to the fact his death was inevitable from the high fall. **Note:** Under the traditional *but for* test the plaintiff would not have been able to recover.

d. **Uncertain causes** — often arises in medical malpractice [475]

(1) **Reduction of chance of survival.** *Herskovitz v Group Health Co-operative of Puget Sound*, 664 P.2d 474 (Wash. 1983). The court allowed the plaintiff to recover for the wrongful death of the decedent against the doctor whose malpractice significantly reduced the decedent's chance of survival — e.g. thirty-nine per cent dropped to twenty-five per cent. It was held that the reduction of the chance of survival was sufficient evidence to allow the jury to determine whether the increased risk to the decedent was

a *substantial factor* in causing the death.

Case seen as a relaxing of causation requirement.

(2) **New cause of action for loss of opportunity to survive.** *Falcon v Memorial Hospital,* 462 N.W.2d 44 (Mich. 1990) — *But for* the doctor's negligence the chance of survival for the decedent of the plaintiff would have risen from nil to 37·5%. The court awarded the plaintiff 37·5% of the wrongful death damages on the theory that the decedent had lost a *substantial* opportunity for survival. **[476]**

(a) No relaxing of causation requirement.

(b) New cause of action developed.

e. **Criticism** of statistical approach: Use of statistics in trials is subject to criticism as being unreliable, misleading, easily manipulated and confusing to a jury. *Fennell v Southern Maryland Hospital Center Inc,* 580 A.2d 206 (Md. 1990). **[477]**

f. **Market share liability** is imposed on industry groups when it is impossible to know which defendant was responsible for the plaintiff's injury. **[478]**

(1) **Example:** *Sindell v Abbott Labs,* 26 Cal.3d 588, cert. denied 449 US 912 (1980). The daughters of women who took an anti-miscarriage drug (DES) developed reproductive diseases, including ovarian cancer, as a result of the defendant drug manufacturer's negligence. Because the health problems developed years after DES was taken, it was usually impossible to determine which manufacturer had supplied the drug taken by the particular woman. Several courts required all producers of DES unable to prove non-involvement to pay a proportion of their percentage of the market share.

(2) Rejection of approach — for asbestos cases *Goldman v John Mansville Sales Corp.,* 514 NE2d 691 (OH 1987). The court found some asbestos products distinguishable from other asbestos products.

(3) Approach used in blood clotting protein for haemophiliacs in *Smith v Cutter Biological Inc.,* 823 P.2d 717 (Hawaii 1991).

7. English approaches: **Substantial contribution test** **[479]**

a. **Simultaneous causes of harm:** *McGee v National Coal Board* [1972] 3 All ER 1008. The plaintiff suffered dermatitis and alleged that it was caused by his exposure to brick dust at work. The work he performed did carry the risk of dermatitis. His employers were found negligent in failing to provides showers which would have lessened the risk, but not eliminate the risk, of dermatitis. The House of Lords held that where a defendant's negligence made a *substantial contribution* to the harm suffered they could be liable. It is not necessary to show that the defendant's negligence was the sole cause.

Page v Smith II [1996] 1 WLR 855. The Court of Appeal upheld the trial courts use of the McGhee test allowing the plaintiff to recover. The plaintiff was not physically injured in the car crash, but argued that the disease of chronic fatigue syndrome was reactivated and made worse by the mental shock he suffered as a result of the crash. *See* nervous shock.

(1) **No onus shifting.** Onus remains on the plaintiff to prove causation.   **[480]**

Pickford v Imperial Chemical Industries [1998] 1 WLR 1189. The plaintiff, a secretary, suffered repetitive strain injury after her employers increased her amount of typing. Evidence concluded that condition could be caused by physical factors, psychological factors or both. The plaintiff was held required to prove the condition resulted from typing. The court did not shift the burden onto the defendant to prove that the cause was psychological.

(2) **Uncertain causes:** The plaintiff must prove that the defendant's act was a *material* cause of injury suffered. Material cause requires that on the *balance of probabilities* the defendant's *act caused the harm.*

b.   **House of Lords decisions — causation requires:**   **[481]**

(1) **Preponderance of evidence** or 51%.

Hotson v East Berkshire Health Authority [1987] AC 750. A child was released from hospital without proper diagnosis and treatment, then developed serious complications. Experts concluded the child had a 75% chance of developing complications if proper diagnosis and treatment had taken place.

(2) **More than mere fact that defendant increased the risk of injury.**   **[482]**

Wilsher v Essex Area Health Authority [1988] 1 All ER 871. The plaintiff was born three months premature and suffered several medical problems. A treating doctor negligently gave twice the required amount of oxygen. The child suffered permanent blindness that could have been caused by the overdose of oxygen or any one of five separate medical conditions. It was held that the plaintiff had to prove that the defendant's breach of duty was on the balance of probabilities a *material* cause of the injury.

(3) ***Bolitho* test** [483]

Bolitho v City & Hackney Health Authority [1997] 3 WLR 1151. A two-year-old was taken to the hospital with breathing problems. The child was not seen by a doctor, suffered a heart attack and died. The mother sued alleging that the doctor was negligent in not seeing the child and failing to intubate (placing a tube down the throat to aid breathing). The doctor countered that even if she had seen the child she would not have intubated because it was not the proper procedure, therefore her alleged negligence was not the cause of the child's death. Under *Bolem* (*see* Medical Malpractice [302] *et seq.*) the doctor would have won, but the House of Lords held that the plaintiff could prove causation if:

(a) The plaintiff proved that the defendant would have intubated if she had attended, or

(b) That she should have intubated if she had attended because she had a duty to do so.

c. **Rejection of House of Lords decisions by the Court of Appeal**

Following *Hotson*, the Court of Appeal has generally failed to follow the House of Lords decisions and continues to treat the *evidence* as being *relevant to damages* and not relevant to causation. **Examples:**

(1) *Stovold v Barlows* [1995] NPC 154. The plaintiff claimed that the defendant's negligence caused him to lose the sale of his house. The Court of Appeal decided that there was a 50% chance that the sale would have gone ahead had the defendant not been negligent. The court upheld the plaintiff's claim, but awarded him 50% of the damages he would have normally been awarded.

(2) *Allied Maples Group v Simmons & Simmons* [1995] 1 WLR 1602. The plaintiff alleged that he was prevented

from entering into a business deal due to the defendant's negligence. The Court of Appeal found that where damage depends on the possible action of a third party the plaintiff must prove that the chance was a substantial one, as opposed to pure speculation. **Held:** the action could succeed on causation and the evaluation of the change taken into account when calculating damages.

C. Proximate cause (legal cause)

1. **General rule:**
   a. **After** *proving* actual cause the plaintiff *must establish* that the defendant's act or conduct was the *proximate* or legal cause of the harm.　　　　　　　　　　　　　　　　　　　　　　**[484]**
   b. **Proximate cause** is seldom a factor in intentional torts.
   　　　　　　　　　　　　　　　　　　　　　　　　　　　[485]
   Example: If I throw a stone at you, I am liable if I hit you, even if there is little chance of the stone actually hitting you.
   c. Scholars argue that the proximate cause requirement is a *policy question* rather than the application of legal rules. *See* [281].
   d. Variety of factors influence this policy issue including: **[486]**
      (1) Foreseeability of injury,
      (2) Intervening acts,
      (3) Acts of God, and
      (4) General social and economic policy goals.
2. **Remoteness**: Even when actual cause is proven the court may not hold a defendant liable if the *causal relationship* between the defendant's conduct and the plaintiff's injury is remote.　**[487]**
   a. Generally, problems arise in three areas:
      (1) **Unforeseeable manner** in which damage occurred,
      (2) **Unforeseeable results** where the damage is different than anticipated,
      (3) **Unforeseeable plaintiffs**.
   b. Common law — two approaches are used for remoteness:
      (1) **Direct consequence rule:** This is usually associated with the case of *Re Polemis* [1921] 3 KB 560. *See* [496].**[488]**
      Rule: The defendant is liable for all the direct consequences of his actions.
      (2) **Reasonable foreseeability rule:** This was established in the famous case of *Wagon Mound I* [1961] AC 388. *See* [497].　　　　　　　　　　　　　　　　　　　　　　　　**[489]**
         (a) Rule fine-tuned by *Wagon Mound II*.

(b) *Wagon Mound I* approved in Ireland in *Burke v John Paul and Co. Ltd* [1967] IR 277.

(c) *Wagon Mound II* approved in Ireland in *Wall v Morressey* [1969] IR 10 (SC).

c. **Present foreseeability test:** focuses on whether the defendant should have reasonably foreseen as a risk of his conduct the harm suffered by the plaintiff. **[490]**

(1) **Foreseeable result:** Even if the result was foreseeable there will be no liability if there is an intervening act or force which takes place after defendant's act. **[491]**

(a) **Intervening force:** This is a new force that joins with the defendant's act(s) to cause the plaintiff's injury.

(b) Intervening force: Can be human, animal, mechanical or natural (e.g. a change of wind). *See* [499].

(2) **Unforeseeable**

(a) **Results:** The defendant is not liable for unforeseeable harm. *Wagon Mound I. See* [497]. **[492]**

(b) **Extent:** So long as the type of harm or general consequence is reasonably foreseeable, the extent of the harm need not be foreseeable. **[493]**
Condon v Cie (1984) unrep. (HC). The plaintiff was employed by the defendant and suspected of being responsible for a train crash. After a statutory inquiry the plaintiff sought damages from the defendant and costs for being represented at the inquiry. **Held:** The plaintiff's damages were a reasonably foreseeable result of the defendant's negligence.

(c) **Manner:** While the consequences or type of harm must be reasonably foreseeable, the precise manner in which the harm occurs is not required to be foreseeable. **[494]**
Egan v Sisk [1986] ILRM 283. The plaintiff's warehouse was flooded, ruining business brochures due to the defendant's negligence. Damages were sought for lost profits — could not reprint in time. Claim allowed.

(d) **Plaintiffs:** A duty of care is owed to any person reasonably foreseen to be injured by defendant's acts or omissions (failure to act). *See Donoghue v Stevenson* [315] and *Palsgraf v Long Island Railway* [316]. **[495]**
Turner v Irish Rail (1996)(HC). The defendant's fence near houses was not maintained. The plaintiff

was injured when she went through a hole in the fence to look for her child.

d. Important remoteness cases:

(1) ***Polemis:*** *the defendant is liable for all direct consequences of his actions.*   **[496]**

***Polemis* facts**: While unloading plaintiff's ship, the defendant's employee negligently knocked a plank into the hold. Unknown to the defendant's employee gas fumes were in the hold, the plank created a spark that ignited an unforeseeable fire which destroyed the ship. Defendant was liable on the theory that he should be responsible for all harm directly caused. Fact: the explosion and fire was different from what could reasonably be anticipated from dropping plank into a hold —it was not material.

(2) ***Wagon Mound I*** [1961] AC 388. *Introduced requirement for foreseeability to proximate cause.*   **[497]**

Facts: The defendant negligently spilled oil into Sydney harbour. A large amount of oil settled near the plaintiff's wharf. The plaintiff's employees were using welding equipment on the wharf and stopped welding to make inquiries about the safety of continuing work. After inquiries they resumed work and some hot molten metal ignited the oil damaging the wharf. The Privy Council held that the consequence (damage to the wharf) was not reasonably foreseeable.

(3) ***Wagon Mound II*** [1967] 1 AC 617. The court attempted to define *foreseeable* and *reasonably foreseeable.* **[498]**

Facts: The owner of another ship destroyed in the fire sued the same defendant for the negligent discharge of the oil. The plaintiff argued that the fire was a foreseeable risk of the spilled oil. Court held that while probability of fire was relatively remote, *foreseeable* means that the likelihood need not be great if the magnitude of the risk would be significant. Especially true if there was no justification to incur the risk. **Held:** If it is clear that the *reasonable man* would have *realised* or *foreseen* or *prevented the risk*, then the defendant is liable.

3. ***Novus actus interveniens*** — new intervening act

a. **Definition**: New forces join with the defendant's negligence to injure the plaintiff.   **[499]**

(1) Intervening forces can be human, animal, mechanical or natural.

(2) Intervening occurs after the defendant has acted.

b. **General rule:** The defendant will not be liable if the intervening act or force is the sole cause of the plaintiff's harm. **[500]**

    (1) The intervening force becomes the legal cause of the plaintiff's injuries.

    Example: *Conole v Redbank Oyster Co.* [1976] IR 191 (SC). The defendants were testing a boat and it was found that it was not safe. Despite orders to tie up the boat, one of the defendant's employees took fifty children out on the boat — the boat sank. It was held that the decision to use the boat after the defect was discovered was the legal cause of the injuries. The *reckless* decision broke the causal connection between the alleged negligence of the manufacturer for the defect and the injuries.

    (2) The new intervening force could be: **[501]**

        (a) **The act of a third party,**

        (b) **The act of the plaintiff,**

        (c) **An independent physical force** (like a hurricane).

c. **The act of a third party** **[502]**

    (1) May be an independent sole cause — making the defendant not liable, or

    (2) May combine with the defendant's wrongful act making the defendant and third party concurrent wrongdoers. *See* [464].

d. **The act of the plaintiff**

Contributory negligence occurs if the plaintiff's act adds to or joins with the wrongful act of the defendant to cause the plaintiff's injuries. *See* [537]. **[503]**

    (1) **Exception to general rule:** Where the defendant causes the new intervening force he will be liable. **[504]**

    (2) **Example:** *Doran v Dublin Plant Hire* [1990] 1 IR 88 (HC). If the plaintiff acts and injures himself or another, the defendant will not escape liability for his prior negligence if the defendant caused the plaintiff's act to be dangerous.

e. **Exception to general rule:** Where the defendant could reasonably foresee the new intervening act he may still be liable.

    (1) The intervening person will not be liable if: **[505]**

        (a) The defendant intended for him to act, or

        (b) He acted as an inevitable response to the defendant's unlawful act, or

      (c) It was likely that he would act in response to the defendant's unlawful act.

          Example: *Smyth v Industrial Gases* (1950) 40 ILTR 1 (SC). The plaintiff was seriously injured when another child threw lime putty in his eyes. Other child found the putty on the road after it leaked from the defendant's cart — it looked like snow. **Held:** The defendant should have reasonably foreseen the intervention, i.e. child throwing it.

  (2) **Note:** If the intervening force is human, foreseeability is not the sole test. Court will examine the: **[506]**

      (a) Nature of the *act*,

      (b) Character of the *act*, and

      (c) Mental state of the intervening person.

  (3) The intervening person may be liable if his actions were foreseeable, but not probable or likely. The court will look at the nature of his act. **[507]**

      (a) If intentional, criminal or reckless his act will be a *novus actus interveniens*. (Breaks the chain.)

      (b) Gross negligence by the intervening person is not enough to break the chain of causation to relieve the defendant of liability. **[508]**

          Connolly v South of Ireland Asphalt Co. [1977] IR 99 (SC). While driving C hit and killed a man. The asphalt company had made potholes next to the road. The holes filled with water and splashed onto the road rendering it dangerous. **Held:** The gross negligence of C was not a *novus actus* extinguishing the negligence of the asphalt company in failing to maintain the road. Gross negligence (objective recklessness) alone is not enough to break the causal chain.

f. **Factors not *novus actus interveniens*** — General rule: **[509]**

  (1) **Pre-existing conditions:** If the plaintiff's condition *combines* with the defendant's negligence to cause an unexpected injury, this is not a *novus actus interveniens*. Defendant takes the plaintiff as he finds him. *See* Eggshell Skull Rule [516]. **[510]**

  (2) **Force set in motion** by the defendant's conduct is not an intervening act. **[511]**

      Example: A motorist driving negligently runs into a parked lorry loaded with watermelons, causing the melons to fall off the lorry onto a pedestrian. The melons are set in motion by the motorist.

(3) **Omission (failure) to act**: Generally, a third person's failure to act may contribute to the plaintiff's injury and this is not considered an intervening act. **[512]**

    (a) **Example:** The defendant strikes a swimmer while negligently operating a motor boat. A fisherman sees the incident, but stands idly by watching the swimmer drown. The fisherman's refusal or failure to act, i.e. attempt to save the swimmer or summon help, is not an intervening act.

    (b) Exception: When the third party was required to act. **[513]**

        (i) Crowley v AIB & O'Flynn [1988] 1 ILRM 225 (SC). The plaintiff was injured when he fell from the roof of a bank. He sued the architect that designed the flat roof without a rail. **Held:** No nexus between the architect and the injury. The link was broken by the fact that boys played on the roof and bank failed to stop them. Omission of bank as *novus actus interveniens.*

        (ii) But see, *Daly v Guinness Peat Aviation Ltd et al* 1998 (HC) unrep. The plaintiff was injured through the negligence of two of the defendants. The third (medical) defendant failed to render proper medical treatment and this attributed to the plaintiff's injuries. Held: All three defendants were concurrent wrongdoers and the third defendant's negligence did not constitute *novus actus interveniens.*

g. English approach: Where a force, event or act breaks the chain of causation, the defendant will only be liable for such damage as occurred *up to* the intervening force, event or act. **[514]**

(1) *Baker v Willoughby* [1969] 3 All ER 1528. The plaintiff injured his left leg because of the defendant's negligence. Later, he was shot by an armed robber and his left leg was amputated. The defendant successfully argued that his liability only extended to the time of the armed robbery.

(2) *Jobling v Associated Dairies* [1982] AC 794. The plaintiff was injured at work in 1973, rendering him fifty per cent disabled. In 1976, the plaintiff was diagnosed with a

medical condition that had no connection with the work injury. Due to the new condition he was rendered 100 per cent disabled. The House of Lords applied the *but for* test strictly. The risk of unrelated medical conditions is habitually taken into account when calculating damages for future loss of earnings — it should not be ignored when it is already present.

(3) *Thompson v Blake-Jones* [1998] Lloyd's Rep Med 197. The defendant doctor advised the parents of a six-month-old child not to immunise the child against measles. The parents talked to other doctors and when the child was eighteen months old they decided not to have her immunised. The child caught the measles and developed a rare condition that caused brain damage. The Court of Appeal held that the advice given by the other doctors was an intervening event that broke the chain of causation. It showed the parents were not relying on the defendant's advice.

h. American approach   **[515]**
   (1) General rule: The courts characterise intervening forces as:
       (a) Dependent — or stimulated by the defendant's negligence, or
       (b) Independent — not stimulated by the defendant's negligence.
       (c) **Example:** If X negligently knocks Y onto a high ledge, a rescuer's efforts to save Y is stimulated by X's earlier negligence and therefore is a dependent intervening force. If a mountain climber collides with Y on the ledge, the climber's actions were not stimulated by X's actions, and would be characterised as an independent intervening force.
   (2) Whether an intervening force or act will supersede the original negligence depends on how improbable the intervening force is.
       Superseding allows the earlier tortfeasor to be relieved of further responsibility.
   (3) **Intervening natural forces**: Storms may be superseding, but if an extraordinarily violent storm could be anticipated then the storm is foreseeable and not superseding. *See* 2nd Restatement [451].
   (4) **Exception**: Car accidents and medical malpractice have been held not to be superseding *although* the odds of their occurring may be slight.

Pridham v Casy & Carry, 359 A.2d 193 (1976). The plaintiff suffered a serious injury due to the defendant's negligence. The plaintiff died when the driver of the ambulance suffered a heart attack and drove into a tree while rushing the plaintiff to hospital. The defendant was held liable.

4. **Eggshell skull rule:** (also known as the **thin skull rule**) [516]
   a. **General rule**: The defendant takes the plaintiff as s/he finds him/her.
      (1) Usually, the type of injury is foreseeable but the extent of the injury is not. [517]
      (2) **Classic example**: A negligently hits B on the head. Normally B would only suffer a minor bump or bruise, but B has an eggshell-like head and the knock to the head results in a catastrophic brain injury. A is liable for all B's brain injuries.
   b. Rule alleged to have originated in *Dulieu v White* 2 KB 669 (1901). *See* nervous shock [403].
   c. This rule has *survived Polemis* and the *Wagon Mound* cases. [518]
      (1) **Importance** has reduced the practical differences between:
         (a) *Polemis* — defendant liable for all consequences of his act, also
         (b) *Wagon Mound I* — defendant liable for the damages that are reasonably foreseeable.
   d. **Once any personal injury is foreseeable** the particular type of harm need not be foreseeable. [519]
      (1) **Physical injuries**
         Burke v John Paul & Co. Ltd [1967] IR 277 (SC). The plaintiff suffered a hernia while cutting steel bars. The plaintiff had complained without success about the dullness of the cutting machine, to his employer the defendant. The defendant argued that it could not reasonably foresee the plaintiff might develop a hernia. Medical evidence showed that to develop a hernia a person must have some congenital weakness. **Held:** The tortfeasor has to take his victim as he finds him.
      (2) **Psychological injuries** [520]
         (a) Controversial — courts and jurisdictions divided on this issue. *See* nervous shock [403] *et seq.*

    (b) *Malcolm v Brodhurst* [1970] 3 All. ER 508. No difference in principle between eggshell skull and eggshell psyche.

    (c) *McCarthy v Murphy* (1998) (HC). The plaintiff suffered whiplash in a minor car accident and developed a depressive reaction which was due in part to an underlying depressive condition. The Eggshell Skull Rule was applied.

e. **Criticism** of the eggshell skull rule   **[521]**
Many legal commentators believe that the application of the rule can be very harsh. A defendant can be held liable for injuries that were not foreseeable.

D. Limitations of action

1. The **Statute of Limitations 1957** (as amended) sets forth time limits within which all tort actions must be brought.   **[522]**
Statute barred: If a tort action is not brought within the specified time frame it can never be brought.

2. **General rule:** S. 11(2)(a) provides that tort actions shall be brought within *six years* of the date on which the cause of action accrued.   **[523]**

    a. **Cause of action accrues:**
        (1) Once the tort is complete, or
        (2) When all elements required to be established have come into existence.

    b. **Examples:**
        (1) If the tort is actionable *per se* — at the time of the act.
        (2) If the tort is continuing in nature — a new cause of action accrues every day, e.g. continuing trespass.
        (3) If the tort is not actionable *per se* — it accrues when the damages occur.
        Example: *Hegarty v O'Loughran* [1990] 1 IR 148 (SC). Cause of action accrued only when the personal injury manifested itself. The statute begins to run at that time.

3. **Exception: Statute of Limitations (Amendment) Act 1991**
    a. **Section 3**
        (1) **Personal injury**: The limitation period is *three years* from the date of the accrual of the cause of action.   **[524]**
        (2) **OR later:** Where *relevant information* is not known to the plaintiff, the statute begins to run from the date of knowledge. *See* s. 2(1).

    (a) **Note:** The extension for late discovery of vital knowledge *only* applies to personal injuries.

    (b) Extension does *not* apply to property damage or economic loss. *Touhy v Courney* [1994] 2 ILRM 503.

b. **Date of knowledge** is when a person has knowledge: **[525]**

  (1) **Of his injury.** **[526]**

Behan v Bank of Ireland [1998] 2 ILRM 507 (SC). The plaintiff alleged that he had received bad advice from his bank. The plaintiff suffered a nervous breakdown because of the advice. The court held that the statute began to run on the date on which he suffered the nervous breakdown.

  (2) **That his injury was significant.** **[527]**

Reasonable belief that it was significant — subjective test. *Gallagher v Minister for Defence* (1998) (HC) — army deafness claims.

  (3) **That the injury was attributable to the defendant's act or omission.** **[528]**

  (4) **Of the identity of the defendant.** **[529]**

  (5) **Of the identity of any other person** who performed the act or omission, along with any additional facts supporting the action against the defendant. **[530]**

Example: Vicarious liability, *see* [362].

c. **Presumed knowledge:** The statute presumes that a person: **[531]**

  (1) Will have knowledge of fact observable or ascertainable.

  (2) Will have knowledge from facts ascertainable with the help of medical or other expert advice that is reasonable to seek.

4. **Exception: Fatal injuries** **[532]**

a. **S. 6(1)** of the Statute of Limitations (Amendment) Act 1991, requires any actions for fatal injuries must be brought within three years of the later of:

  (1) the date of death, or

  (2) the date of knowledge of the plaintiff (representative of the deceased, or dependent person etc.). *See* Death [419].

  (3) **S. 2** of the Statute of Limitations (Amendment) Act 1991 sets forth the criteria for determining the date of knowledge.

S. 8 of the Civil Liability Act 1961 provides that no causes of action can be maintained against the estate of a deceased, unless the action was brought within the period of limitation and were pending at the time of his death, or **[533]**

S. 9 the action was brought within the first to expire of:

(a) Two years from the date of his/her death, or

(b) Within the required limitation period.

5. **Exception: Disabilities**

   a. S. 48(1) provides that the limitation period does not begin to run until the end of the disability or the death of the disabled party.

   b. Disabilities may include: **[534]**

     (1) Persons under 21,

     (2) Persons of unsound mind, and

       Example: A person suffering brain damage in an accident. *Rohan v Bord na Mona* [1991] ILRM 123.

     (3) A convict without an administrator or curator.

     (4) **Statute of Limitations (Amendment) Act 2000. S. 2** added a fourth disability, i.e. a victim of sexual abuse who is suffering from consequent psychological injury. **[535]** However, **S. 3** allows the court to dismiss the action on the grounds that the interests of justice would not be served due to the delay.

6. **Exception: Fraud**

   a. **S. 71 (1)** provides that the period does not begin to run until the plaintiff has, or with reasonable diligence could have discovered, the fraud. **[536]**

   b. Could arise from:

     (a) A right of action based on defendant's fraud, or

     (b) Essential facts may have been concealed by the defendant from the plaintiff.

VII. Defences

A. Contributory negligence

1. **Definition**: Contributory negligence is an act or failure to act by a plaintiff that is a contributing cause to his/her damage, injury or harm; also the act or failure to act falls below the required standard of reasonable care. **[537]**

   a. The same act can be negligence and contributory negligence. **Example:** *See* rescuers [415].

   b. Distinguished from negligence **[538]**

     (1) Negligence — the defendant owes a duty of care to others.

(2) Contributory negligence — the plaintiff owes a duty to exercise reasonable care for his own protection.

2. **Prior to the Civil Liability Act 1961**, contributory negligence afforded a complete defence to the defendant. **[539]**

3. **Section 34(1) of the Civil Liability Act 1961**
   a. **General rule:** Damages must be *apportioned* between the parties where the damage suffered by the plaintiff results partly from the defendants' wrongful act and partly from the plaintiff's own negligence. **[540]**
   Apportionment based on fault is deep rooted in civil law jurisdictions and admiralty law.
   b. **Exceptions** **[541]**
      (1) Equal apportionment is made if it is not possible to establish the different degrees of fault.
      (2) Contributory negligence will not apply if the plaintiff agreed to waive his legal rights prior to the act. *See* [549].
      (3) Limitations still apply any limitations imposed by contract or legislative enactments apply.
      Example: If P agreed to waive his rights before he got into D's rally car, he cannot defeat the defence of assumption of the risk by relying on contributory negligence apportionment.
   c. **Defendant's onus:** The defendant must show that the plaintiff was negligent. **[542]**
   Plaintiff's negligence caused some of the plaintiff's loss.

4. **Negligence of the plaintiff**
   a. **Principles of standard of care** are the same as those in negligence. **[543]**
      (1) Did the plaintiff exercise reasonable care?
      Contributory negligence is concerned with the plaintiff's contribution to his injury, *not* to the incident that caused the injury. **[544]**
      (2) **Test** for reasonable care is objective — reasonable person standard. **[545]**
      Would a reasonable person, under the same or similar circumstances, behave like the plaintiff?
      (3) **Causation:** The defendant's negligence must be at least part of the factual and legal cause of the plaintiff's injuries. **[546]**
         (a) **Dilemma principle**: The defendant's negligence placed the plaintiff in such a position, so that to

avoid a greater inconvenience he chose to run a slight risk of injury or damage.

 (b) McMahon — since apportionment, contributory negligence applies.

 Sayers v Harlow UDC [1958] 2 All ER 342 (CA). A woman locked in a lavatory was injured while trying to escape.

 b. **Duty to mitigate damages**: The plaintiff has a duty to take reasonable steps to reduce the loss resulting from the injury suffered.   **[547]**

  (1) **Failure to mitigate damages** will lead to apportionment of the additional loss suffered. *See* s. 34(2)(b). **[548]**

  (2) **Examples:**

   (a) Failure or refusal to return to work.

   (b) Failure or refusal to undergo necessary medical treatment.

B. *Volenti non fit injuria (voluntary assumption of the risk)* **[549]**

 1. **Traditional general rule**: If the plaintiff consented to the defendant's actions or conduct, the defendant may have the defence of consent (or as it was called in negligence — voluntary assumption of the risk.)

 2. **After the Civil Liability Act 1961, s. 34(1)(b)**

  a. The plaintiff's consent to the risk created by the defendant's act(s) will not automatically evoke contributory negligence.   **[550]**

  b. However, the action *must* be dismissed if the defendant can show that: **[551]**

   (1) The parties entered into a contract to exempt, or

   (2) The plaintiff agreed to waive his legal rights. *O'Hanlon v ESB* [1969} IR 75 (SC).

 3. **Waiver of legal rights** requires some sort of communication. *See O'Hanlon.*

Communication requires more than mere notice. **[552]**

Example: *McComsikey v McDermott* [1974] IR 75(SC). The parties were together in a rally car. The plaintiff was navigating and the defendant was the driver. The plaintiff was injured when the rally car crashed. The issue of waiver was raised because of a notice on the dash that stated that passengers travelled at their own risk. The notice was in the car when the defendant bought it and the parties joked about it. The court held that there was no real communication regarding the waiver. The defence was not available.

C. *Illegality — wrongful conduct*

1. *Ex turpi causa non oritur actio* defence — no action can be founded upon a wicked act.   **[553]**

   a. The defence of illegality is based on the public policy objection to allowing a person engaged in an illegal activity from maintaining a lawsuit when injured during the course of the illegal activity.   **[554]**

      Example: *Ashton v Turner* [1981] QB 137. The plaintiff was injured while a passenger in a getaway car speeding away from a burglary he committed. The plaintiff sued the driver of the getaway car but his claim was dismissed. English law refuses to recognise the existence of a duty of care owed by one participant in a crime to another in respect of an act done in furtherance of the crime.

   b. **Scope of defence in Ireland** — is not clear.

      Except: S. 57(1) of the Civil Liability Act 1961 provides that it is *not* a defence to *merely* show that the plaintiff was in breach of a civil or criminal law.

2. **Note:** Not every illegal act will bar the claimant from recovering in negligence.   **[555]**

   Example: Dan is driving to work. Dan is not aware that the fuse that controls his brake lights has failed. Dan is driving in violation of the traffic regulations. If Sandra negligently drives into the side of Dan's car his illegal act — driving with non-functioning brake lights — will not bar him from seeking damages from Sandra.

3. **Joint illegal enterprise:** One criminal claims against another criminal.   **[556]**

   Courts have had great difficulty in assessing when illegality will act as a bar.

   (1) **Public conscience test.** Would it shock the public conscience if the plaintiff were allowed to recover?

      Test rejected by *Tinsley v Milligan* [1994] 1 AC 340.

   (2) **Australian approach**: This considers whether there would have been a cause of action had there not been a joint enterprise. *Jackson v Harrison* (1978) 138 CLR 438.

4. **Illegality by the plaintiff**   **[557]**

   a. **General rule**: *Ex turpi* bar will apply to those situations where the plaintiff (while engaged in a crime) is negligently injured by the defendant (who was not engaged in the crime).

b. **Exception: Trespassers** [558]

Revill v Newberry [1996] QB 567. R, an elderly man, slept in his garden shed to safeguard his possessions. N with another man tried to break into the shed while on a crime spree. R shot N with his shotgun through the door of the garden shed. R was acquitted of wounding N. N sued R and was awarded damages. Court relied on duties imposed by occupiers' liability statute.

c. **No expansion — for failure to care cases** [559]

(1) *Clunis v Camden and Islington Health Authority* [1998] 3 All ER 180 (CA). The plaintiff stabbed a man to death on the platform of the underground. The plaintiff had a long history of mental illness and was convicted of manslaughter on the grounds of diminished responsibility. He sued the defendant alleging that it failed to care for him and this failure caused him to kill. His claim was dismissed.

(2) *Worral v British Railways Board* (1999) unrep. (CA). The plaintiff alleged that he committed a number of sexual assaults because he had suffered a personality change due to the defendant's negligence. He sought damages for his imprisonment. Dismissed.

D. Not defences in negligence

1. **Necessity:** (*see* [91]) only applies to intentional damage. It does not apply in negligence. [560]

2. **Mistake:** does not generally apply because of the emphasis on the standard of the reasonable person. [561]

3. **Inevitable accident:** (*see* [93]) is not relevant in negligence.
   In negligence the burden is on the plaintiff to prove the defendant's fault. [562]
   However, Winfield argues that it should apply in *res ipsa loquitur* because the defendant bears the burden of proof regarding whether s/he acted negligently.

VIII. Damages

A. Negligence is not actionable per se. [563]

The plaintiff must prove an injury, loss or damage to his person or property.

a. Person: includes both physical and/or mental injuries. *See* nervous shock [403] *et seq.*

b. Property: includes chattels and land.
Expansion: for foreseeable pure economic losses. *See* [397].

B. *Basic purpose of damages in negligence is compensatory.* **[564]**

Purpose: is to restore the plaintiff, as far as possible, to the condition the *plaintiff was in prior to injury.*

C. *Types of damages*

1. **Special damages**: The plaintiff is entitled to all economic losses and expenses incurred as a result of the injury. **[565]**
   a. Medical costs
   b. Lost wages
   c. Business profits.
   Exception: for impecunious (penniless) plaintiff. While a person acts reasonably in mitigating damages by taking out a loan to repair a car, the cost of the loan may not be recoverable unless the plaintiff's impecuniosity is itself foreseeable. *Doran v Delaney II* [1999] 1 ILRM 225. **[566]**
2. **General damages** or damages inherent to the injury itself.
   a. pain and suffering (past, present, future) **[567]**
   b. disfigurement
   c. disability.
3. **Property damages** for destruction of personal property. Generally measured by the: **[568]**
   a. Fair market value;
   b. Cost of reproduction or replacement, or
   c. Value to owner, excluding unusual sentimental value.

IX. *Revision questions*

(1) Peter negligently drove his petrol tanker too fast around a bend. The tanker toppled over sending hundreds of gallons of petrol down the main street of Ballyrose. The street is closed for three days while the clean-up takes place. Margaret has a café in Ballyrose, and due to the spill no-one can enter her café. Nicola was crushed to death in the tanker crash. Andy, an ambulance driver, has suffered recurring nightmares after removing Nicola's mangled body from under the tanker. Nicola is survived by her husband and three adult children.
   (a) What type of damage, if any, has Margaret suffered?
   (b) Will Margaret be able to maintain a negligence suit against Peter for her losses?

    (c) Assuming that Andy is suffering from post-traumatic stress can he maintain a cause of action against Peter?

    (d) Under what statute can Nicola's husband bring a cause of action against Peter?

    (e) What is the name of the type of action Nicola's husband can bring for her death?

    (f) When will Nicola's husband be statute-barred from bringing a cause of action?

    (g) Can each of Nicola's children, if dependent, bring a cause of action against Peter?

(2) Tony negligently drove his car into the side of Mary's car. Mary has an unusual medical condition that makes her bones very brittle. Mary suffered two broken legs, a broken arm, a fractured skull and a broken neck in the minor crash. The impact from the crash caused Mary's boot to fly open and her suitcase was thrown onto Paul, who was out riding his new motorcycle. Neither Paul nor his motorcycle were injured when hit by the suitcase, but his passenger Shelly was injured by it. David witnessed the crash. He was standing on the corner talking to his friend on his mobile and he saw the entire incident. When Tony rushed over to David and asked to use the mobile phone to call an ambulance, David refused.

    (a) Is Tony liable in negligence for all the injuries suffered by Mary in the minor crash?

    (b) Is Tony liable in negligence to Paul?

    (c) If Mary suffers further injuries because of the delay in being transported to the hospital, can she maintain a cause of action in negligence against David?

    (d) Can Tony claim *novus actus interveniens* with regard to the injuries suffered by Shelly?

    (e) Assuming that Mary's boot was securely shut, can Shelly maintain a cause of action in negligence against Mary for the injuries she suffered?

(3) Tom is being bullied by other students at his school. One day, while walking home from school he notices that Elmer Fudd's window is open. He climbs through the open window and begins to search the house. Tom knows that Elmer Fudd is an avid rabbit hunter. Eventually, Tom locates Elmer's gun safe and continues searching until he finds the key to the safe hidden in another room. Tom steals one of Elmer's shotguns and shells for the gun. Tom hides the gun in the garden and retrieves it after dark. Once

he has it home he saws off the barrel so it can easily be hidden under his coat. The following day at school Tom shoots Richard, one of the students who has made Tom's life a living hell. Richard is severely injured. Richard's parents want to bring a negligence action against Elmer Fudd because they believe that any person who owns a gun should be legally responsible for injuries caused by that gun.

(a) To bring a successful negligence action what are Richard's parents required to prove?

(b) Will Elmer have the defence of contributory negligence because Richard bullied Tom?

(c) Richard's parents believe that Elmer Fudd was negligent in (i) leaving his window open and (ii) leaving the keys to the gun safe in his home. For each allegation determine if there is actual causation.

(d) Assume that Tom is also injured due to the poor job he performed in sawing off the gun barrel. Can he maintain a cause of action against Elmer Fudd?

(4) Stephen had a terrible toothache while on holiday. He went to the local dentist who informed Stephen that he had an impacted wisdom tooth that needed to be removed immediately. Stephen agreed to the removal of the tooth and was put under anaesthetic. When Stephen awoke the wisdom tooth had been pulled but his chest was very sore. Stephen went to the local doctor the following morning because he was having difficulty in breathing. When the doctor removed Stephen's shirt he was amazed to find a fresh bruise, in the shape of a foot, on Stephen's chest. The doctor informed Stephen that he had two broken ribs at the exact location of the bruise. Stephen was not bruised prior to his visit to the dentist and he incurred no injuries after his visit.

(a) What duty of care, if any, did the local dentist owe to Stephen?

(b) Assume that impacted wisdom teeth are difficult to remove and that most dentists refer such patients to oral surgeons. Has the local dentist breached the duty of care he owed to Stephen merely because he did not send him to an oral surgeon?

(c) Will the doctrine of *res ipsa loquitur* apply to the injuries Stephen sustained to his chest?

(5) Anthony is a television producer. He has just come up with an idea for a new programme based on real Dublin crimes. He employs Daniel to act in the programme. Anthony gives Daniel

his costume and an authentic-looking handgun prop. On the day of the filming Daniel decides to have a little fun. In the taxi on the way to the filming Daniel takes the handgun out of his briefcase and begins to polish it. Daniel never says a word even though he knows that the taxi driver has seen the gun in the mirror and he is frightened. The taxi driver is sweating profusely and shaking when Daniel exits the taxi and pays the fare.

(a) Has Daniel committed an assault?

(b) Can the taxi driver bring an action against Anthony as Daniel's employer?

(c) Assume that Daniel first went to the wardrobe department and was travelling in the taxi from wardrobe to the location of the filming on a back street in Dublin. Can the taxi driver bring an action against Anthony as Daniel's employer?

4

STATUTORY-BASED TORTS

Chapter synopsis

Statutory standard of care
Occupiers' Liability Act 1995

I. Statutory Standard of Care

A. General principles

1. **Duty:** Some statutes impose a duty, and   **[569]**
2. **Liability** may be imposed for breach of that duty.
   a. **Note:** Not all statutory duties can be enforced through a tort action.
   b. A statute may: **[570]**
      (1) Contain *all* elements necessary for action.
          Example: Occupiers' Liability Act 1995.
      (2) Contains *provisions* governing actionability,
          (a) either allowing, (Data Protection Act 1988), or
          (b) refusing to allow.
      (3) Have *no express* provision governing actionability.
          Without an express provision, actionability is left to judicial interpretation.
   c. **Liability based on fault** — negligence.   **[571]**
      A statute imposing liability based on fault may only require exercise of reasonable care in the circumstances.
      (1) Same as duty of care in common law negligence action.
      (2) **Example:** Safety, Health & Welfare at Work Act 1989.
      (3) **Note:** Statutes may impose strict liability (no fault required). *See* Chapter 6.
      (4) Breach of the statutory duty is often referred to as negligence *per se*.

B. Determining legislative intent

Factors for determining whether the statute sets a standard of care:

1. Court must determine what type of *harm* the statute was
   designed to protect.   **[572]**
   a. **Classic example**: *Gorris v Scott* [1874] LR 9 Exch. 25.
      Plaintiff sued when his animals were washed overboard
      while being transported on the defendant's ship. In his
      negligence action the plaintiff tried to use as the standard
      of care a provision of a Contagious Disease Act that
      required animals on ships to be kept in pens. The court
      refused to use the provision in the Act instead of the rea-
      sonable person standard, because the Act's purpose was to
      prevent the transmission of disease and not to prevent their
      death from drowning.
   b. **Statutory interpretation techniques** used by the courts:
      (1) Examine the preamble of Act,   **[573]**
      (2) Examine other sections to determine if an intention to
           create civil liability for breach may be inferred,
      (3) Look to previous statutory enactment's on the subject,
           and/or
      (4) Look to the previous status of the common law.
2. **Plaintiff within protected class**
   Plaintiff must be within the class: **[574]**
   a. Protected by the statute — rather than a member of the
       public at large, and
   b. Within the class of persons the statute is trying to protect.
   c. **Example:** The Control of Bulls for Breeding Act 1985
       provides that all non-pure-bred bulls must be registered.
       Failure to register such bulls could result in a fine, castra-
       tion or slaughter of the bull. A plaintiff suffering person-
       al injury by an unregistered bull could not use the Act as
       imposing an actionable standard of care. The injured per-
       son is not within the class of persons the statute is trying
       to protect, i.e. breeders.
3. **Availability and suitability of other remedies**   **[575]**
   a. **The inadequacy of criminal penalties** has been used as
       grounds for allowing tort actions. (*Obiter* by Hanlon, J.
       in *Parsons v Kavanagh* [1990] ILRM 50.)
   b. **Adequacy of alternative remedies** may provide grounds
       for rejecting the claim. *ILSI v Carroll* [1995] 3 IR 145.
                                                            [576]

C. *Breach of actionable duty*

Breach of statute: The defendant *must* be in breach of the statute.
[577]

D. *Causation: The defendant's breach must be the cause of the harm or loss. See Causation in Chapter 3 [458] et seq.*

E. *Statutory defences*

1. The statute may provide *special* defences: **[578]**
   a. For duties imposed by statute, or
   b. May restrict the application of general defences.
      (1) **Examples:**
         (a) **Contributory negligence.** Courts are reluctant to allow contributory negligence for breaches of statutory duties, especially under occupational and safety statutes. **[579]**
         (b) **Voluntary assumption of the risk.** Courts are also reluctant to allow this defence under occupational and safety statutes.
      (2) **Rationale:** these types of defences would reduce the effect of the statutes.
2. **Contributory negligence** is generally *not* the same for a breach of a statutory duty as it has in a common law negligence action. *Stewart v Killeen Paper Mills Ltd* [159] IR 436 (SC). **[580]**
   a. **Rationale:** the policy of statutory protection is to protect workers from their own carelessness.
   b. Plaintiff's required care is less under statutory duties.
      (1) Plaintiff carelessness, inattention or forgetfulness does not rise to contributory negligence.
      (2) Plaintiff's negligence or carelessness in a positive manner does rise to contributory negligence. *Kennedy v East Cork Foods Ltd* [1973] IR 244 (SC). **[581]**

F. *Remedies*

1. General rule:
   a. **Proof of damage** is required in an action for *damages*. **[582]**
   b. **Proof of risk of harm or damage** is required in action for *injunctive relief*. **[583]**

2. **Damage threatened or suffered** must be of the type the statute was designed to prevent. *Gorris v Scott* [1874] LR 9 Exch. 125.

[584]

II. Occupiers' Liability Act 1995

A. General principles

1. **Replaced the common law rules** that concerned the occupiers' duty owed to entrants based on the condition of his land or premises. **[585]**
   a. **Occupancy Duty**. The Act only applies to harm caused by the dangerous condition of premises.
   b. Act *does not* affect other duties owed for harm occurring on the premises, i.e. activity duties. **[586]**
      (1) **Example:** Tilly was visiting her friend Betty. Betty was frying chips. Betty negligently poured water into the hot oil causing it to splatter and burn Tilly. The Act does not apply and it does not affect the common law negligence duty owed to Tilly.
      (2) **Example:** Trespassing Theresa was injured when the occupier negligently discharged his shotgun while trying to clean it. The Act does not apply and it does not affect the common law negligence duty owed by the occupier to Theresa.
2. **Note:**
   a. There may be more than one occupier. **[587]**
   b. An occupier is *not* necessarily the owner.
3. **Premises** includes land, water, fixed or moveable structures and means of transport. **[588]**
   a. A caravan could be a movable structure.
   b. A means of transport could be a train.
4. **Entrants**. Under the Act entrants are broken down into three primary groups: **[589]**
   a. **Visitors**
   b. **Recreational users**
   c. **Trespassers.**
5. **Negligence of independent contractors,** *see* **s. 7.**
   a. **General rule:** An occupier is not liable to any entrant for injury or damage caused to the entrant or his property because of a danger on the premises caused by the negligence of an independent contractor hired by the occupier. **[590]**

Note: Menial Tasks — An occupier cannot avoid liability by assigning all tasks to an independent contractor, especially those things that an occupier is competent to do.
Crowe v Merrion Shopping Centre Ltd [1995] 15 ILT (CC).
[591]

    b. **Exception**: Unless the occupier knows or should know that the work was not properly done. **[592]**

    c. **Reasonable care** requires that the occupier should verify that the independent contractor was competent to do the work. **[593]**

6. **Act not applicable, s. 8(b).** The Act does not lower or affect the duties owed by three classes of persons: **[594]**

    a. Commercial carriers (operators of trains, planes, ships etc.),

    b. Commercial bailees,

    c. Employers with regard to the duties owed to their employees.

B. Duty owed to a visitor

1. **A visitor** (*see* s. 1(1)) is a lawful entrant who enters: **[595]**

    a. As of right,

    b. Under a contractual provision,

    c. By invitation of, with the permission of, the occupier,

    d. As a member of the occupier's family,

    e. At the express invitation of a member of the occupier's family, or

    f. For social purposes connected with the occupier or one of his family members.

2. **Duty owed to visitor**. The act imposes a common law duty in negligence.

    a. **General rule: S. 3(2)** requires that an occupier must take *reasonable care* in the circumstances to ensure that a visitor does not suffer any injury or damage because of any danger or unsafe condition on the premises. **[596]**

    Note: Duty of care owed to an entrant is affected by:

    (1) Contributory negligence, and

    (2) Expected supervision. *See* [604].

    b. **Exception: (S. 5(2)(a)) restricted or excluded**. The duties imposed by the Act on an occupier for visitors may be restricted or excluded by: **[597]**

        (1) **Express agreement**, or **Strangers to agreement (S. 6).** Any restriction or exclusion under an express agreement is not binding on strangers to the agreement. **[598]**

(2) **Notice** given by the occupier.

(a) **Reasonable in all the circumstances, s. 5(2)(b)(ii).** Any modification must be reasonable in all circumstances. **[599]**

(b) **Lowest duty, s. 5(3).** Any restriction or exclusion cannot allow the occupier to intentionally or recklessly cause injury or damage to a visitor.

c. **Notices:** To restrict or exclude liability a notice must be:

(1) **Reasonable**, and **[600]**

(2) Must be reasonably *brought to the attention* of the visitor. **Presumed**: A notice will be presumed reasonable if the occupier prominently displayed it at the normal place of entry. **[601]**

(3) **Adequacy of the warning, s. 5.** This must enable a visitor to avoid injury and damage. **[602]**
O'Donoghue v Green [1967] IR 40. Person injured while on the premises to use the toilet facilities.

d. **Exception: expansion of duties, s. 5 (1).** The duties imposed by the Act on an occupier to an entrant may be extended by: **[603]**

(1) Express agreement, or

(2) Notice given by the occupier.

3. **Reasonable care, s. 3.** Factors for determining what is reasonable under the circumstances include: **[604]**

a. (1) The level of care the visitor can be expected to take for his/her own safety, and

(2) **Example:** *Roles v Nathan* [1963] 2 All ER 908. An expert warned of a particular risk on the premises. It was held to be a sufficient warning to the plaintiff (an entrant) to avoid the risk of harm. The court found the defendant not liable for injury resulting from the plaintiff's failure to heed the warning.

b. The level of supervision and control a visitor can exercise over another visitor.

(1) **Examples:** supervised school groups, parent and child.

C. Duty owed to a recreational user

1. A **recreational user** is: **[605]**

a. A person who is present on the occupier's premises to engage in recreational activity with or without the occupier's consent.

b. A recreational user is *not* a:

    (1) Member of occupier's family,

    (2) Entrant at the express invitation of the occupier or a member of his family.
      Not a social visitor to the premises.

    (3) Entrant whose recreational activity is in connection with the occupier or a member of his family, or

    (4) Person who paid an admission fee to enter the premises.
      Note: A recreational user may be charged a reasonable amount for parking his car.

  c. **Distinction** between social guest and recreational user.**[606]**
    Social guest: is a person whose presence is desired by the occupier or his/her family.

2. **Recreational activities, s. 1(1)** include open-air activities such as: **[607]**

  a. Sport,

  b. Nature studies (such as exploring caves), or

  c. Visiting sites and buildings of importance:

    (1) Historically,

    (2) Architecturally,

    (3) Traditionally,

    (4) Artistically,

    (5) Archaeologically, or

    (6) Scientifically.

3. **General rule:** The Act imposes a duty on an occupier *not to intentionally injure* or *damage* their property, or to *act with reckless disregard* for the recreational user's *person* or *property*. **[608]**

  a. **Note: No common law duty** in negligence is imposed. **[609]**

    (1) **No liability is imposed** on an occupier due to the dangerous state of his/her land or premises.

    (2) For criticism *see* [616].

  b. **Duty owed** to a recreational user cannot be reduced by agreement or notice, but the duty can be increased. **[610]**

  c. **Reckless disregard**
    See [620–7] for the determining factors.

4. **Special duty imposed, s. 4(4).**

  a. **Structures** provided for recreational users must be maintained in a safe condition. **Example:** playground equipment. **[611]**

  b. **Exception:** The special duty does not include entry structures such as gates or stiles.

D. Duty owed to a trespasser

1. **A trespasser is**: [612]
   a. Any person entering who is not a visitor or recreational user, or
   b. Any person entering without legal authority and for reasons other than recreational activities.
   c. Not a criminal entrant. [613]
      (1) Person who enters to commit an offence, or
      (2) Person who while on the premises commits an offence.
2. **General rule**: The Act imposes duty on the occupier *not to intentionally injure* or damage a trespasser's *property*, or to *act with reckless disregard* for a *trespasser's person or property*. [614]
   a. No common law duty in negligence is imposed. [615]
      (1) **No liability imposed** on an occupier due to dangerous state of his/her land or premises. [616]
         (a) Legal commentators are critical of this provision especially with regard to children.
         (b) McMahon refers to the 'adventurous urban child'.
      (2) This overturns *McNamara v Electricity Board* [1975] 1 (SC). An eleven-year-old climbed over a fence around an electric station and while attempting to slide down a drainpipe came into contact with a high-tension cable. **Held:** An occupier owes a duty to take reasonable care to foreseeable trespassers.
   b. Duties imposed by the Act on an occupier *may not* be restricted or excluded. [617]
      Duties imposed by the Act on an occupier *may* be increased or extended by:
      (1) Express agreement, or
      (2) Notice given by the occupier.
   c. **Note**: **Criminal entrants**, **s. 4(3)(a)**, are not owed the non-reckless duty. [618]
      (1) McMahon: 'Occupiers are now free to act reckless' toward criminal entrants. However,
      (2) (a) Immunity toward criminal entrants is not absolute.
         (b) S. 4(3) — in the interests of justice — an occupier may owe a duty not to act reckless.
      (3) (a) **Note**: The occupier is always under a duty not to intentionally injure the entrant or his property. [619]
         (b) However, an occupier is entitled to use reasonable force for self-defence and the defence of his/her property. *See* [105] *et seq.*

3. **Factors** for determining intentional or reckless disregard: *S. 4(2)* — *objective test.*

   a. Whether the occupier *knew*, or had *reasonable reason to know* that a *danger existed* on the premises. **[620]**

   b. Whether the occupier *knew*, or had *reasonable reason to know* that the *trespasser* or his *property* was, or was likely to be, on the premises. **[621]**

   c. Whether the occupier *knew*, or *had reasonable reason for believing*, that the trespasser or his property was *near* or likely to go near the area of the *danger*. **[622]**

   d. Whether the *danger* was such that the occupier should provide protection. **[623]**

   e. The *burden* of eliminating the danger or providing protection. **[624]**

   f. The *character* of the premises. **[624]**

   Example: traditional hill walking path or mass path.

   g. *(i)* The *conduct* of the person entering and the level of care that could reasonably be expected of persons entering, regarding their own safety. **[625]**

   (ii) Distinguishes between innocent (children) and bad trespassers (burglar).

   h. The nature of any *warnings* given by any person regarding the danger. **[626]**

   i. The expected level of *supervision* by persons entering in the company of others. **[627]**

   Examples: Parents with children, teachers with pupils.

E. Damages — S. 1

1. **Injury** includes: **[628]**

   a. Death of entrant, or

   b. Physical personal injuries, and/or

   c. Mental injuries.

2. **Damage** includes: **[629]**

   a. Loss of property — and includes all property in the possession or control of the entrant while on the premises.

   b. Injury to an animal.

   c. The Act is silent on pure economic loss. **[630]**

   Quill argues that since definition of damage is not exhaustive in the Act economic loss could arise under it.

F. Common law principles apply to: **[631]**

1. Causation, *see* [458] *et seq.*
2. Remoteness, *see* [487].
3. **Defences,** *see* [537].
    a. **S. 8(a)** preserves the common law rules regarding the defence
       of persons or property. *See* [105] *et seq.*   **[632]**
       Common law defence of persons or property still apply
       notwithstanding language in the Act regarding occupiers' duty
       not to intentionally harm trespassers or recreational users.
    b. Contributory negligence — *see* [537] *et seq.*

III. Revision questions

(1) Georgia was invited to her friend Penny's house to go swimming.
    Is Georgia a recreational user under the Occupiers' Liability Act
    1995?

(2) Tina was injured when a table in the dining car of the Waterford
    to Dublin train collapsed onto her legs. Can Tina bring an action
    under the Occupiers' Liability Act 1995?

(3) The Having Fun Amusement Company opened a haunted castle
    in Cork City. Due to the nature of the activities — i.e. scaring
    patrons — the company erected a large notice inside the first
    haunted room. When the room is entered by the patrons it is very
    dimly lit and then goes completely dark.
    (a) If Sally takes her two daughters to the fun house what type of
        entrants are they?
    (b) What duty of care is owed to them?
    (c) If the notice restricts or excludes liability for all injuries on
        the property is the notice valid?

(4) Hillary the hillwalker attempted to enter the land of Farmer Fred
    by climbing on his field gate. While the gate looked sound it was
    in fact rusting from the inside out. When Hillary stepped onto
    one of the bars it broke and she fell to the ground breaking her
    neck.
    (a) What type of entrant was Hillary to Farmer Fred's land?
    (b) Can Farmer Fred be liable for entrants he did not know were
        present on his land under the Occupiers' Liability Act 1995?
    (c) Is Farmer Fred liable under the Act for Hillary's injuries?

(5) Tom is being bullied by other students at his school. One day
    while walking home from school he notices that Elmer Fudd's
    window is open. He climbs through the open window and begins

to search the house. Tom knows that Elmer Fudd is an avid rabbit hunter. Eventually, Tom locates Elmer's gun safe and continues searching until he finds the key to the safe hidden in another room. Tom steals one of Elmer's shotguns and shells for the gun. Tom hides the gun in the garden and retrieves it after dark. Once he has it at home he saws off the barrel so it can easily be hidden under his coat. The following day at school Tom shoots Richard one of the students who has made Tom's life a living hell. Richard is severely injured.

Assume that Ireland has enacted a statute that makes it a criminal offence to fail to keep guns locked in an approved gun safe when not in use. The statute is silent as to whether a person can bring a cause of action against any person violating the statute. The legislative intent of the statute is to keep legally held guns from falling into the hands of criminals to be used in robberies and other violent crimes.

(a) What factors will a court weigh to determine whether the statute sets a standard of care?

(b) Is Richard within the group intended to be protected by the statute?

(c) Has Elmer Fudd breached the statute?

(d) Can Richard maintain a cause of action against Elmer Fudd pursuant to this statute?

SECTION 3: STRICT LIABILITY

5

STRICT LIABILITY

Chapter synopsis

I. Common law strict liability
    Fire
    Animals
    Vicarious liability
    Rule in *Rylands v Fletcher*
II. Statutory-based strict liability
    Liability for Defective Products Act 1991
    Common law liability for defective products

I. Common law strict liability

A. Historical background of strict liability

1. **Definition**: Strict liability is liability imposed without intent or
   fault by the defendant.   **[633]**
2. Early law of torts was *not* concerned with moral responsibility.
   a. **Example:** affirmative duties.
   b. It was argued that early torts provided a remedy that would be
      accepted instead of private vengeance. (Holmes). *See* [285].
3. Originally, strict liability was imposed in the sense that any
   person who injured another, even if by pure accident or self-
   defence, was responsible for damages.
   a. Until the end of the nineteenth century tort liability slowly
      began to lean toward recognition of *fault* or moral responsi-
      bility as its primary concern:
      (1) Due to growing moral consciousness in the community.
      (2) Led to legal liability based on achieving conduct expected
          of a good member of the community — i.e. negligence.
   b. **Near death of strict liability**   **[634]**
      (1) Eventually, arguments emerged that there should never be
          liability without fault.

(2) McMahon refers to this period in tort history as the 'no liability without fault' era.

c. Twentieth century: Since the beginning it has been generally accepted that in some cases a defendant may be liable although he has:

(1) No moral wrongdoing, nor

(2) Departed from a reasonable standard of care. **[635]**

B. *Reasons for imposing strict liability*

1. **Social justice**: Who best can bear the loss? **[636]**

a. Often referred to as *loss shifting* by creating liability where there was no fault.

b. **Deep pockets**: The person or entity with the *deepest pockets* (resources) is made responsible for the loss.

   Example: Workers' compensation statutes.

2. **Social policy**: What is best for the public at large? **[637]**

a. Strict liability imposed on the keepers of animals, and

b. Abnormally dangerous activities or conditions.

Fire

A. Historical background

B. Present fire liability — the Accidental Fires Act 1943

C. Survival of common law strict liability

A. *Historical background*

1. **Early common law** imposed strict liability on landowners for fire. **[638]**

a. Allegation was for *negligently* keeping fire, but commentators think that this was not the negligence of today. (Wigmore)

b. Defences included:

(1) Act of God,

(2) Act of stranger.

c. Strict liability rule was considered unduly harsh.

2. **Early fire statutes** **[639]**

a. England passed statutes in the early eighteenth century.

(1) The Prevention of Fires (Metropolis) Act (1707) 6 Anne.6. c. 31, made permanent by (1774) 10 Anne. 1. c. 14.

No action allowed for a fire accidentally occurring in a person's *building or estate*.

   (2) An Act for Preventing Mischief That May Happen by
       Fire (1715) 2 Geo.1. c. 5.
       No action allowed against a person 'in whose house,
       chamber or out-house' a fire was accidentally caused.
   b. English courts held:
       (1) Landholder not liable:
           (a) Unless the fire started or spread through landholder's
               negligence, *Vaughan v Menlove* [137] or
           (b) Fire was intentionally started. *Filliter v Phippard*
               [1847] ER 490.
       (2) **Note**: Strict liability is *still applied* to *arson* or intentional
           fires.

3. **Industrialisation**   **[640]**
   a. **Caused a reversion to common law strict liability** for fires
      started because of *abnormally dangerous activities*. *Musgrove v
      Pandelis* [1919] 2 KB 43.
      Musgrove facts: A fire accidentally started in the carburettor of
      the defendant's automobile. The defendant's employee negli-
      gently failed to turn off the petrol tap and the fire spread. The
      defendant was held liable for the spreading of the fire, but not
      for the original fire.
   b. Led to the Railway Fires Act 1905 & 1923.
      Provided statutory compensation for damages to land caused
      by sparks from railway engines.

4. **Irish approach**   **[641]**
   a. *Richardson v Athlone Woollen Mills* [1942] IR 581. A fire acci-
      dentally started in a factory. The court held that it was not
      protected by the 1715 statute and the owners were liable
      for damages to adjoining premises. The reasoning was that
      factories were not covered by the Act.
   b. In response to this case the Accidental Fire Act 1943 was
      enacted.

B. *Present fire liability — the Accidental Fires Act 1943*   **[642]**

   1. **No legal action** can be initiated by any person who has suffered
      damage because of a fire accidentally occurring on or in the
      buildings or lands of another person.
      a. Definitions
         (1) Building: is any structure made of any material.
         (2) Appears to extend to any occupier.

(3) Accidental: means without negligence. *Rutledge v Land* [1930] IR 537.

b. **Purpose**: The Act grants *immunity* for non-negligent fires. A similar statute in Northern Ireland (Accidental Fires Act 1944) suggests that accidental includes all *non-intentional* fires.

2. **Occupiers**

a. May be vicariously liable for the negligent act of anyone but a stranger. *Balfour v Barty-King* [1957] 1 QB 496. **[643]**

(1) A stranger is not a:
   (a) Member of the occupier's family,
   (b) Guest of the occupier,
   (c) Employee acting within course of employment, or
   (d) Licensee of the occupier.

(2) Negligent act may include: **[644]**
   (a) Creation of the fire, or
   (b) Failure to control a fire caused by:
      i   The defendant or the defendant's employee,
      ii The act of stranger such as a trespasser,
      iii Natural sources such as lightening, or
      iv Fires of unknown origin.
   (c) *McKenzie v O'Neil & Rose Ltd* (1977) unrep. (HC). The defendant's employee burned papers on the defendant's land. The day was windy. Although the employee thought that the fire was out it spread to another's land. Liability was imposed for negligent failure to control the fire.

c. **Immunity** under the Act includes: **[645]**

(1) Injuries to land,
(2) Injuries to chattels, and
(3) Personal injuries.

d. **Onus** **[646]**

The burden of proof is on the plaintiff to show that fire was caused by non-accident. *Woods v O'Connor* [1958] IR Jur Rep 71.

C. Survival of common law strict liability

Intentional fires

a. **Accidental Fires Act 1943** provides *no immunity* for intentional fires such as arson. **[647]**

b. The person setting the fire will be strictly liable.

Animals

A. Historical background
B. Present strict liability — animals
C. Cattle trespass

A. Historical background

1. Earliest common law held the owner of the chattel strictly liable for any harm caused by the chattel.   **[648]**
    a. Owner was held strictly liable for the damage an animal, slave or other chattel had inflicted on others.
    b. Owner could escape liability by surrendering the chattel to:
        (1) The injured party, or
        (2) The king. This was referred to as *noxal surrender.*
2. Today, ancient notions of strict liability have survived because of modern social policy.   **[649]**
    a. **Rationale**: Certain animals create an obvious danger to others even if they are carefully kept.
        (1) Strict liability for dangerous animals is of ancient origin.
        (2) First modern case dealing with dangerous animals was *May v Bundett* [1846] 115 ER 1213.
    b. Those who keep animals are required to protect the community from damage caused by the animals.

B. Present strict liability — animals

1. **General rule:** Liability for injuries caused by animals can be: **[650]**
    a. Strict, and/or
    b. Based on negligence. *See* Chapter 3 for negligence principles.
2. The law has divided animals into classes.   **[651]**
    a. *Ferae naturae* or wild animals.
        Examples: elephants, bears, seals, alligators, tigers.
    b. *Mansuetae naturae* or domestic animals.
        Examples: dogs, cats, bees, horses, cattle, pheasants.
    c. **Distinction** between domestic and wild animals is: **[652]**
        (1) Based on the traits of the species *rather* than an individual animal, and
        (2) Determined by the likelihood of finding such an animal in jurisdiction.
            Example: An elephant is a common domesticated animal in Asia, but it is not native to Ireland. Hence, the

elephant is considered wild even if the particular animal is domesticated.

3. Liability

a. **Domestic**: Under common law the keepers of domestic or tame animals with vicious, fierce or 'mischievous propensity' to do the damage suffered, were held strictly liable for the damage suffered.

(1) Liability based on *possession or control* rather than ownership. *Breen v Slotkin* [1948] 4 DLR 46. **[653]**

(2) **Onus**: The plaintiff has the burden of establishing the defendant's knowledge of dangerous nature of the animal.

(3) *Scienter* **doctrine**: Once the defendant had knowledge of the dangerous nature of an animal in his possession, strict liability would attach. **[654]**

Scienter: is knowledge of the dangerous propensity.

(4) **Knowledge**:

(a) *Must* be proved for domestic animals. **[655]**

(b) May be imputed to the owner.

Example: *Bennet v Walsh* [1936] 70 ILTR 252. The defendant's nine-year-old daughter knew of the animal's mischievous propensity. The defendant was held to have imputed knowledge.

(c) Knowledge *must* be of the *damage suffered*.

Examples:

i *Quinn v Quinn* 39 ILTR. The defendant's sow had previously killed a fowl and then killed the plaintiff's cow. Defendant was held to have knowledge of dangerous propensity of the sow.

ii *Glansville v Sutton & Co. Ltd* [1928] 1 KB 571. The defendant's horse with a bad habit of biting other horses was not proof that horse had a vicious tendency to bite humans.

(d) Awareness does not require injury: Animals can display dangerous or mischievous propensity without inflicting injury. **[656]**

Duggan v Armstrong [1992] 2 IR 161 (SC). A dog showed aggressive behaviour toward children although he did not bite. Owner held to have knowledge of propensity.

(e) **Mere friskiness** is not dangerous or mischievous propensity. **[657]**

Example: Excited dogs may jump on people and bark. Horses may run about wildly kicking up their heels.

b. **Wild**: Under common law the keeper of a wild animal keeps the animal at his peril. **[658]**

  (1) The keeper of a wild animal is *strictly liable* for all damages caused by such an animal.

Liability is based on *possession or control* rather than ownership.

  (2) **Doctrine of *scienter*** **[659]**

    (a) **Knowledge is presumed** of the dangerous nature of a wild animal.

    (b) **Presumption cannot be rebutted**. *Behrens v Bertram Mills Circus Ltd* [1957] 1 All ER 583.

c. **Dogs** — statutory liability **[660]**

  (1) **Control of Dogs Acts 1986 & 1992** impose strict liability on dog owners for:

    (a) Damage caused by the dog attacking a person, or

    (b) Damage done to livestock by the dog.

  (2) Old common law rule of *one free bite*, abolished.

    (a) **One free bite**: This was because the owner needed knowledge of the dog's dangerous propensity for liability to attach, it was said that the dog was allowed one free bite.

    (b) **Note**: Today the owner *does not* need knowledge of the dog's dangerous propensity for liability to attach.

  (3) **Owner** — includes occupiers of land where dog: **[661]**

    (a) Is kept, or

    (b) Allowed to stay.

Requires knowledge and consent. *Leahy v Leader and Cork Diocesan Trustees* (1999) (HC). The plaintiff was bitten on the defendant's church property. The dog belonged to another and the parish priest had no knowledge that the dog was present. No liability.

    (c) **Exception** — if that person can prove he is not the owner of the dog.

  (4) **Statutory exceptions to strict liability** **[662]**

    (a) If a dog injures a trespasser, strict liability will not apply. The trespasser must prove negligence to bring action.

    (b) If a dog injures trespassing livestock strict liability will not apply, unless the defendant caused the dog to attack the livestock.

C. *Cattle trespass*

1. **Definition**: The person keeping livestock that strays onto the land or chattels of another is held strictly liable for the trespass itself and any resulting harm. **[663]**
2. **Does not apply** if cattle are being lawfully driven on the road and break into property adjoining the road. **[664]**
3. Cattle trespass *applies* to all farm animals.
   Exception: cats, dogs and wild animals.
4. **Resulting harm** includes:
   a. Damage to land,
   b. Damage to chattels e.g. crops and other animals, and
   c. Personal injuries. *Wormald v Cole* [1954] 1 All ER 683.
5. Under common law, livestock *straying* onto the public road did not commit cattle trespass. **[665]**
   Animals Act 1985, s. 2: any person placing animals on land is required to take reasonable care to avoid damage being caused by the animals straying onto a public road. **[666]**
6. **Defences to cattle trespass**
   a. **Act of God** **[667]**
      Definition: An act of God is a result of natural forces.
      Example: In tornado country it is common for livestock to be picked up in a tornado and put down several miles away unharmed.
   b. **Contributory negligence** **[668]**
      Example: The plaintiff left the defendant's gate open and the defendant's horses trampled the plaintiff's garden.
   c. **Act of stranger** **[669]**
      Moloney v Stephens [1945] IR Jur Rep 37. A third person left the defendant's gates open so that his cattle strayed onto the plaintiff's land. Act of stranger was a valid defence.

Vicarious liability

A. General background
B. The doctrine of *respondeat superior*
C. Duty to control others

A. *General background*

1. **Definition**: Where one person is held liable for the acts of another person.

2. The modern form of vicarious liability dates from the end of the seventeenth century. Arises in: **[670]**
   a. **Formal legal relationships** such as:
      (1) Employer/employee, *see* [380] *et seq.*
      (2) Principal/agent,
      (3) Firm/partner: This was imposed by Liability of Partners under the Partnership Act 1961.
   b. **Informal relationships** where one person has *control* over another.
      (1) Driver/passenger — *Curly v Mannion, see* [677].
      (2) Social host/guest — *Moynihan v Moynihan, see* [683].
      (3) Owner of vehicle/driver, **s. 118, Road Traffic Act.**

B. *The doctrine of respondeat superior — see [365] et seq.*
   1. **Definition**: An employer is vicariously liable for any tortious acts committed by his employees within the scope of the employment. **[671]**
   2. **General rule**: An employer may be liable for the tortious acts committed by employees within the scope of employment. *See* [365] for crucial requirements.
      a. An employee may be: **[672]**
         (1) An ordinary worker,
         (2) A casual or part-time worker, or
         (3) An unpaid volunteer.
      b. **Factors for determining** if employment relationship exists: **[673]**
         (1) **Dominant factor** — *right to control* the worker.
         (2) Method of payment (salary or fee).
         (3) Right to hire and fire worker.
         (4) Degree of skill of worker.
         (5) Whether the worker provides his own employment.
         (6) Contract for services, or of services?
         (7) Worker integrated into the business?
      c. **Medical staff**: Those people in the full-time service of hospitals are employees for vicarious liability purposes.
   3. **Independent contractor**
      a. **General rule**: There is no vicarious liability to employers for the tortious acts of independent contractors. **[674]**
      Legal commentators generally agree that:
         (1) There is no precise rule for determining difference between an employee and an independent contractor.

(2) Some courts have gone to extraordinary lengths to find that contractors are employees.

b. **Exception**: An employer may be vicariously liable for torts committed by independent contractors if the employer's degree of control was *comparable* to that of an employee. **[675]**

(1) *Phelan v Coillte Teo* [1993] 1 IR 18. The plaintiff was injured due to negligence of an independent contractor (a welder/fitter) with whom the plaintiff was working.

(2) Test of control is not settled.

(3) English approach — regarding issue of control:
   (a) Was the wrongful act authorised by the employer, or
   (b) Was the act authorised by the employer, but the method of performance was not authorised?

C. Duty to control others — see [358] et seq.

1. **Parent/child relationship**
   a. **General rule**: Parents are not vicariously liable for the torts committed by their child. *See* [370]. **[676]**

2. **Owners of vehicles**
   a. **General rule**: A driver has a duty to control his/her passengers so that third parties using the public road are not injured. **[677]** *Curly v Manion* [1965] IR 543 (SC). The driver of a car was held vicariously liable for the negligent acts of her passenger. The passenger (a child) negligently opened the car door causing injury to the plaintiff (a cyclist).

   b. **Road Traffic Act 1961, s. 118** imposes liability on the owner of a vehicle for the conduct of any person using the vehicle with the owner's consent. **[678]**

   (1) **Consent to use required**: To hold the owner vicariously liable the plaintiff must show that the driver had the owner's consent to use the vehicle, *and*

   (2) **Conduct within scope of consent**: The conduct causing the injury was within the scope of the consent.
   Example: *Guerin v Guerin & McGrath* [1992] 2 IR 287 (HC). The owner of a car left the country. He gave the keys to his father, but before leaving he asked a neighbour to drive his family. However, the father asked another person to drive the family and the plaintiff was injured. **Held:** The consent granted by the owner extended to any person driving on behalf of his family and was not confined to the neighbour.

     (3) **Fraud:** Consent obtained by fraud bars vicarious liability. *Kelly v Lombard Motor Co. Ltd* [1974] IR 142.   **[679]**

     (4) **Onus:** is on the owner to show that conduct is outside the scope of the consent. *Buckley v Musgrave Brook Bond Ltd* [1969] IR 440.   **[680]**

  3. **Partners**

    a. **Common law**: Persons who engaged in a partnership or joint venture were vicariously liable for the conduct of the other members within the scope of the enterprise.   **[681]**

    Rationale: Persons engaged in a partnership or joint venture had an equal right to control the operation of the enterprise.

    b. **Partnership Act 1890**

    Each partner is vicariously liable for the tortious acts of the other partners committed in the course of the partnership's business.   **[682]**

     (a) Extends to all activities that the partner has authority to do.

     (b) This may include fraud. *Allied Pharmaceutical Distributors Ltd and All-Phar Services Ltd v Walsh* (1990) unrep (HC).

  4. **Gratuitous services**

    Hostess/social guest   **[683]**

    Moynihan v Moynihan [1975] IR 192. A two-year-old was burned by a pot of tea that the child pulled off of her granny's table. The tea was left on the table by her aunt who went to answer the phone. The mother and granny were in the kitchen doing the dishes. **Held:** The gran was vicariously liable for the negligence of her daughter the mother. As the hostess, the grandmother was in control of her daughter, the serving of the tea, and/or if the tea was to be served.

Rule in Rylands v Fletcher

A. Historical background

  1. **Landmark case — *Rylands*.** Facts: The defendant, a mill owner, hired an independent contractor to make a reservoir on his land to supply water to a mill. During construction of the reservoir the independent contractor found a shaft of an old coalmine on the site. The contractor could have blocked the mineshaft, but he did not. He was not aware that it joined shafts of mines on neighbouring land. When the reservoir was filled with water it

flooded the shaft thus flooding the plaintiff's mine — (1868) LR 3 HL 330.

2. The *Rylands Rule* was developed because under existing law the plaintiff was without a cause of action.   **[684]**
   a. **Negligence**: The defendant was not negligent because he did not know about the shafts.
   b. **Vicarious liability**: The defendant could not be vicariously liable because the contractor was an independent contractor.
   c. **Trespass**: The plaintiff could not bring an action in trespass because the damages he suffered were not direct and immediate.
   d. **Nuisance**: The plaintiff could not bring an action for nuisance because it did not apply to a single event.
3. **The rule**: An occupier who brings anything likely to do damage onto his land and keeps it on his land: he/she will be held strictly liable for the damage caused if it escapes.   **[685]**
4. **Irish approach**: There are very few Irish cases.

B. *Requirements*

1. **Accumulation**
   a. The thing must be brought onto the land by the defendant.
                                                              [686]
      (1) Does not include things naturally occurring on, or already on, the land.
      (2) *Healy v Bray Urban District Council* [1963–4] IR Jur Rep 9. Stones forming part of a hillside injured the plaintiff. The stones had not been brought to the land by the defendant.
   b. Accumulation must be for the benefit of the defendant.
   c. Early cases required that the parties be owners or occupiers of land. Requirement has been eased.   **[687]**
      (1) In *Crown River Cruises Ltd v Kimbolton Fireworks Ltd* [1996] 2 Lloyd's Rep 533, it was held that a barge moored to a riverbank could qualify as land. (Defendant not held liable under rule in *Rylands*.)
      (2) Liability can be incurred for bringing a dangerous thing onto the highway. *Rigby v Chief Constable of Northampton* [1985] 2 All ER 985 (QB). While attempting to capture a man, police fired tear gas into a shop where he was hiding. The tear gas set the shop on fire. **Held:** The rule would apply to a thing escaping from the highway.

2. **Non-natural use of land**: The principle is applied *only* to the non-natural use of the land.   **[688]**
   a. Non-natural use of land is a vague concept.
      (1) Without a meaningful test — *Burnie Port Authority v General Jones Pty Ltd* (1994) 68 ALJR 331 (HC) (Australian).
      (2) Natural does not mean primitive. *Read v Lyons* [1947] AC 156 (HL).
   b. English decisions have placed an emphasis on the use being:
      (1) Abnormal,
      (2) Inappropriate,
      (3) Extraordinary, or
      (4) Exceptional etc.
   c. **Special use**: This required that the use must bring with it an increased danger to others, not merely ordinary use or use of land for the benefit of the community. *Rickards v Lothian. See* [697].   **[689]**
3. **Dangerous or hazardous thing**
   a. **Anything likely to do mischief if it escapes.**   **[690]**
      (1) **Examples:** fireworks, water, poisonous gases and chemicals.
      (2) **Not relevant:** that the thing could be safe if not allowed to escape.
         (a) Dangerous chemical substances: *Hanrahan v Merck Sharp & Dohme. See* [830]. Decided on non-*Rylands* grounds.
         (b) However, *see obiter* Goff, J. in *Cambridge Water* — the storage of chemicals was a classic case of non-natural use. (Liability denied, *see* [694].)
   b. **Standard of foreseeability**: The defendant will not be liable for damages caused by something that could not be foreseen as causing damage if it escaped.   **[691]**
   c. **Strict liability**: The fact that the possibility of escape is not foreseeable is not a defence.
4. **An escape**
   a. Required from the defendant's occupation or control.
      Read v Lyons [1947] AC 156. The plaintiff, an inspector, while inspecting the defendant's munitions factory was injured when a shell exploded. The defendant had not been negligent, so the plaintiff sued under *Rylands*. The court held that the dangerous thing was required to escape.

b. **Escape defined**: When something goes outside a place where the defendant has occupation or control. The plaintiff was injured on the defendant's premises, liability denied. **[692]**

5. **Damage and causation**

a. Occupier of neighbouring land can recover for: **[693]**
   (1) Damage to:
      (a) Chattels, and
      (b) Land.
   (2) Economic loss suffered because of damage to land.
   (3) Personal injuries.

b. Person with no right of occupation of land — such as a guest.
   (1) Quill argues that a person with no right of occupation:
      (a) Should have the right to recover under *Rylands*. Otherwise, two persons with similar damage in the same incident would be treated differently.
      (b) Should be treated the same as in nuisance. Once the damage falls within the risk generated by the activity, the injured party should be allowed to recover independently of any interest in the property on which the injuries occurred.

c. **Foreseeability requirement**: The damage suffered must be foreseeable. Camb*ridge Water Co. v Eastern Counties Leather* [1994] 2 AC 264 (HL). **[694]**
   (1) If damage is foreseeable: The manner in which the damage occurs need not be foreseeable.
      (a) Having escaped, was the damage the type/kind that was a reasonable consequence of the escape?
      (b) Was the damage the type that was foreseeable at the time of the escape?
   (2) *Cambridge Water*: Notwithstanding the fact that the storage of chemicals is a classic case of non-natural use (*obiter* Goff, J.), it was held that it was not foreseeable that a solvent used in industry that seeped into the ground would be found in a borehole over a mile away. Liability under *Rylands* denied. **[695]**
   Per Lord Goff: The historical basis of *Rylands* was the tort of nuisance with a particular application to isolated escapes.
   (3) Applied in: *Superquinn Ltd v Bray UDC* (1998)(HC). *See* [699].

d. **Causation:** *see* [458] *et seq.* regarding causation.

(1) Plaintiff must prove: **[696]**
    (a) That the escape of the dangerous accumulation caused the loss, and
    (b) The loss was not too remote a consequence of the accumulation and escape.

C. Defences

1. Act of stranger

  a. **General rule**: Where a stranger causes the release of the dangerous accumulation the defendant will not be liable in the absence of negligence. **[697]**
    (1) **Example:** *Rickards v Lothian* [1913] AC 263 (HL): An unknown person blocked a sink and left a tap turned on in the defendant's premises thereby causing damage in the plaintiff's premises on a lower floor.
    (2) **Stranger**: A stranger is defined as any person without authority to interfere with the dangerous accumulation.

2. Act of God

  a. **General Rule**: Absent negligence — a defendant will not be liable if a natural force caused the escape. **[698]**
    Greenock Corporation v Caledonian Railway Co. [1917] AC 556 (HL). The corporation built a concrete paddling pool for children and changed the flow of a stream. After an exceptionally heavy rain the stream flooded and water poured down a public street into the plaintiff's premises. **Held:** The rainfall was not an act of God that the defendants could not have predicted.
  b. **Exception**: There is no liability if the escape is caused by a natural force, in circumstances which the defendant could not have been expected to foresee or guard against. **[699]**
    (1) *Nichols v Marsland* [1874–80] All ER Rep 40. The defendant dammed a natural stream on his land in order to create three artificial lakes. The lakes were well built and precautions against flooding were adequate. However, an exceptionally heavy rain caused the banks of the lakes to burst. The flooding water swept away four bridges on the plaintiff's land. **Held:** No liability because the storm could not have been reasonably predicted. Witnesses had described it as the heaviest rain in living memory.
    (2) *Superquinn Ltd v Bray Urban District Council* (1998) unrep. (HC). The defence was successful for flooding caused by Hurricane Charlie.

3. **Consent**
   a. **Complete defence**: If the plaintiff consented to the risk associated with the dangerous accumulation. **[700]**
   b. **Partial defence**: If the plaintiff consented to the accumulation, the defendant would remain responsible for any negligence. **[701]**
      (1) *Victor Weston (Eire) Ltd v Kenny* [1954] IR 191 (HC). The flat occupied by the plaintiff was flooded by water from the defendant landlord's flat. The water was part of the ordinary supply to the building. **Held:** no liability. The plaintiff implicitly consented to the accumulation of the water for supply to the building as a whole — there was no negligence committed by the defendant.
      (2) In other jurisdictions this defence is called *common benefit*. The presence of the thing brings a benefit to the plaintiff.
4. **Contributory negligence:** If the plaintiff causes the dangerous thing to escape she may be held contributorily negligent. *See* [537] *et seq.* **[702]**

D. *Other approaches*

1. **Australian approach**: The rule has been subsumed within the general law of negligence. *Burnie Port Authority v General Jones Pty* (1994) 68 ALJR 331 (HC). **[703]**
2. **American approach**
   a. **General rule: S. 519 2nd Restatement** — A person who maintains an abnormally dangerous condition or activity on his land or engages in an activity that presents an unavoidable risk of harm to others, may be liable for the harm caused even though reasonable care has been exercised.
      (1) Ultra-hazardous activities: This term was used in the 1st Restatement.
         (a) **Examples:** Blasting, manufacturing explosives, etc.
         (b) **Examples:** of merely dangerous activities, e.g. use of vehicles, fire, boilers etc.
      (2) Abnormally dangerous activities: used in the 2nd Restatement. Terminology changed to give more weight to the context in which the activity was performed.
   b. **Factors for determining** if an activity is abnormally dangerous.
      (1) Does the activity involve a high degree of risk?
      (2) What is the gravity of the risk?

(3) Can the risk be eliminated by the exercise of reasonable care?

(4) Is the activity a matter of common usage?

(5) Is the activity appropriate to where it is being conducted?

(6) The value of the activity to the community.

II. Statutory-based strict liability

A. Statutes may impose:

1. **Strict liability**: Liability is imposed where the defendant may not be at fault.

2. **Exercise of reasonable care**: The defendant's exercise of reasonable care will *not* relieve him of liability.   **[704]**

B. Common features of strict liability statutes:

1. Statute phrased in the *imperative* form.
   Containing language such as 'shall' 'must' instead of 'may' or 'should'.

2. Statute does *not* provide: restrictions, defences or conditions for meeting the duty imposed.
   Example: The Liability for Defective Products Act 1991.

3. May provide limitations on amounts recoverable under the statute and types of damages covered.
   Example: Warsaw Convention — International Aeroplane Crashes: This is designed to meet the problems of inter-national legal conflicts and it provides the victims of any international air mishap with a strict liability recovery of a limited amount of damages. There is no recovery for emotional distress without some physical injury.

Liability for Defective Products Act 1991 (LFDPA 1991)

A. General background

1. **Focus**: The law of products' liability focuses on the liability of a manufacturer or other supplier of a product for harm to the person or property of the plaintiff, caused by a defect in the product.   **[705]**

   a. Harm to the person can be physical or psychological.

   b. **Strict liability, s. 2** imposes strict liability on a producer for damage caused wholly or partly by a defect in his product.
   Rationale: (for strict liability) is imposed on the party best able to stop similar future harm.

2. **Sales problems** are *not* covered under products' liability. **[706]**

a. A sales problem may occur:
   (1) **Performance**: Where a product simply does not perform as well as expected, causing a purely economic loss to the buyer.
   (2) **Damage**: Where the product is damaged and it is worth less than the price paid for the product.
b. Sales problems may be covered under: [707]
   (1) Contract law, or
   (2) The Sale of Goods Act 1893 and the Sales of Goods and Supply of Services Act 1980. (SGSSA 1980)
c. The Act differs from the SGSSA 1980. [708]
   (1) Act is based on safety.
   (2) SGSSA 1980 places two implied conditions in every contract for sale:
       (a) That the product or goods are of merchantable quality, and
       (b) That they are reasonably fit for the purpose for which they are intended.
   (3) **Note**: The sale of goods legislation provides remedies not available in the Act for flaws in products that have *not* caused any personal injuries or damage to other property.

3. **EEC Directive 85/374/EEC of 30 July 1985.** [709]
   a. **LFDPA 1991** gives effect to the directive.
   b. **Note: Supplements existing law, s. 10** provides that the Act *supplements*, rather than replaces, the existing remedies in tort and contract. *See* [739] *et seq.* for common law products liability.
   c. **Not retrospective — Art. 17:** The Act is *not* retrospective in its operation.
      (1) It does not apply to products put into circulation *before* the date the Act went into force.
      (2) The Act went into force on 16 December 1991.
   d. **Failed to comply**: Member states were to give effect to the directive within three years.
      (1) Ireland did not comply.
      (2) **Grey area:** There is the question of the *direct effects* of the directive during the period after 30 July 1988 and before implementation on 16 December 1991.

4. *Prima facie* **case** under the Act: In order to succeed an injured party is required to prove: [710]
   a. A covered *injury*, and

b. **Causation**: that the injury was *caused* by a defect in the product that was produced or manufactured by the defendant.

B. *Definitions: The Act provides definitions of the requisite elements.*
1. **S. 2, a producer is**: [711]
   a. The manufacturer or producer of a finished product,
   b. Producer of a component,
   c. Manufacture or producer of any raw material,
   d. Person who holds himself out as being a producer, which may be done by:
      (1) Applying a trade mark, or
      (2) Own brand on the product.
   e. Importer of products from outside the European Union (EU),
   f. The person who carried out the processing in the case of products of soil, stock farming, fisheries and game which have undergone initial processing.
      Initial processing: This is any processing of an industrial nature of these products that could cause a defect.
   g. **Extended definition: S. 2(3) — suppliers (retailers)** [712]
      (1) **The supplier** may be liable to the plaintiff if the producer cannot be identified by taking reasonable steps.
      (2) **Reasonable steps:** If the plaintiff requests, the supplier must identify any person who is the producer of the product within a reasonable time.
   h. **A producer is not a repairer** (common law still applies, *see* [739]). [713]
2. **Product**: S. 1 includes all *movables*, except primary agricultural produce.
   a. **Directive 99/34/EC:** Effective 4 December 2000, primary agricultural produce is no longer exempt. [714]
   b. **Includes incorporated movables** whether as a component part, raw material or otherwise into:
      (1) Another product, or
      (2) An immovable.
      Example: A house (immovable) collapses because of faulty bricks (movables). The producer of the bricks is liable.
   c. **Includes electricity** [715]
      (1) Where damage is caused as a result of a *failure* in the process of generation,
      Examples: Damage resulting from a surge in electricity,

or conversely damages resulting from inadequate voltage being produced.

(2) Does *not* cover defects that are due to external agents intervening after the electricity has been put into the network.

Example: Damage resulting to a television from a surge in electricity caused by lightening.

(3) Does *not* cover *damage from failure* to supply.

Example: Would not cover food in a freezer that thaws and is ruined because of a power failure lasting several days.

3. **Defective product**: **S. 5** is one that fails to provide the safety that a reasonable person is entitled to expect, taking all circumstances into account. **[716]**

   a. **Circumstances** include:

   (1) Presentation of the product. **[717]**
   Presentation includes: advertising, labelling and instructions for use.

   (2) The use to which it could *reasonably* be expected that the product would be put.

   (a) The more unusual or extreme the use the less likely it could be said to be reasonably expected.

   (b) **Example:** The producers of a haemorrhoid cream would not reasonably expect that the product would be used to reduce *bags* under the eyes.

   (3) The time when the product was put into circulation.

   b. **Exception**: A product is not considered under the Act to be defective because a better product is later put into circulation.

4. **Damage**: **S. 1** means death or personal injury, or loss of, damage to, or destruction of, any item of property other than the defective product itself.

   a. **Personal injury** **[718]**

   (1) Includes mental impairment, but

   (2) There is some doubt as to whether pain and suffering is included. (McMahon)

   b. **Requirements for damaged property** **[719]**

   (1) **Type**: The property must be of a type *ordinarily* intended for private use or consumption, and

   (2) **Private use**: The property must have been used by the injured person mainly for his own *private* use or consumption.

(3) **Damage to defective product itself** is not covered.[720]
Example: An electric kettle is defective and catches fire.
Under the Act no damage occurs unless it causes injuries
to a person or damage to other property.

C. Liability

1. **The producer: S. 2** is liable for damage caused *wholly or partly*
by a defect in his product.   [721]
2. **A retailer may be liable**: **S. 2(3)** if: [722]
   a. He does not, or
   b. Cannot identify someone above him in the chain of distribu-
      tion, (i.e. manufacturer, producer, importer etc.). *See* [711].
      Within a reasonable time of being requested to do so.
3. **Joint and several**: **S. 8** is where two or more persons are liable
   under the Act for the same damage,   [723]
   a. They are held liable jointly and severally liable as *concurrent
      wrongdoers*. *See* [464] *et seq.*
   b. Persons may be concurrent wrongdoers where:
      (1) One has *vicarious liability* for another,
      (2) There is a *breach* of a joint duty,
      (3) Where there is a *conspiracy* or a concerted action to a
          common end.
   c. **Concurrent wrongdoers** are each liable for the whole of the
      damages.   [724]
      Important to an injured person — if one or more of the
      responsible parties is unable to pay their share of the damages.
4. **Reduction of liability — s. 9**   [725]
   a. The liability of a producer *cannot be reduced* when damage is
      caused both by a defect in his produce and by an act or omis-
      sion of a third party.
   b. The doctrine of contributory negligence applies. *See* [580].
5. **Prohibition on exclusion from liability — s. 10**   [726]
   A producer is *prohibited* from limiting or excluding his liability:
   (1) Contractually,
   (2) By notice, or
   (3) By any other provision.

D. Damages

1. The **onus (S. 4)** is on the injured person to prove: [728]
   a. **Damages,**

b. The *defect*; and

c. The *causal relationship* between the defect and damage.

2. **Limitation of damages — s. 3**   [729]

   a. **No award** if property damage is *less* than £350.

   b. For damage to property greater than £350 — *only* the amount in excess of £350 shall be awarded.

E. Defences

1. **S. 6**: A producer shall not be liable if he proves: [730]

   a. **Circulation**: That he did not put the product into circulation. **Put into circulation** means when:

      (a) It is *delivered* to another in the course of business, or

      (b) When it is *incorporated* into another immovable product.

   b. **No defect at circulation**: This is where when having regard to the circumstances, it is *probable* that the defect did not exist at the time: [731]

      (1) When the product was put into circulation, or

      (2) That the defect came into being afterwards.

      Difficulty: This is determining when precisely a defect came into being.

   c. **Private non-commercial transactions**: The product was neither:

      (1) Manufactured by him for sale or any form of distribution for an *economic purpose*, nor   [732]

      (2) Manufactured or distributed by him in the course of his business.

   d. **Compliance with law**: The defect is *due* to compliance by the product with any requirement imposed by, or under, any enactment or any requirement of the law of the EU.   [733] In other words, any producer who abides by the law and, in doing so, causes a defect in his product, the producer will have a good defence to the strict liability in observing the law.

   e. **State of the art**: The *state* of scientific and technical knowledge at the time when the product was *put into circulation* did not enable the existence of the defect to be discovered. [734]

      (1) Also known as the *development risks* defence.

      (2) To avail, a producer will have to show that *no* producer of a similar product *could have* been expected to have discovered the defect which caused the injury.

      (3) The Act does not specify whether EU or international *state of the art* standards should apply.

(4) This defence was optional in the Directive.

    (a) Complete exclusion: Luxembourg and Finland.

    (b) Partial exclusion: Spain excluded it for medicines and human foods, but included it for everything else.

(5) **Scope of the defence** was considered in *E.C. Commission v UK* [1997] 3 CMLR 923. Commission alleged that the UK had failed to properly implement the Directive. Although the wording of the defence written into UK legislation was different from the wording of the EU Directive, the Court of Justice concluded that there was no substantial difference in the effect. Important factor: English courts had not interpreted the language of the UK legislation.

(6) **Defence is controversial.** Commentators see it as undermining the strict liability intended to be imposed by the Act.

(7) **American approach**: In the US, strict liability for defective products developed within the common law.

    (a) **Statutory intervention for vaccines.** In 1986, the US Congress enacted legislation (42 USC, ss 300aa–10 *et seq.*) to insulate the producers of vaccines from liability, with a modified no-fault compensation scheme for injuries resulting from certain childhood vaccines.

    (b) **Rationale:** Vaccines are important, but there is a great liability risk for any company producing them.

  f. **Component and raw material producers** will have a defence if the defect is attributable *entirely*: [735]

    (1) To the *design* of the product in which the component has been fitted or the raw material has been incorporated:

    (2) To the *instructions given* by the manufacturer of the product.

    (3) This defence protects subcontractors where:

        (a) Their products are clearly not responsible for the defect, or

        (b) They produced specifically to order and the defect is the result of the design of the product or as a result of the instructions given by the manufacturer.

2. **Contributory negligence — s. 9**

  a. Will apply where *any* damage is caused: [736]

    (1) *Partly* by a defect in the product, and

(2) *Partly* by the fault of the injured person or any person for whom the injured person is responsible.

b. Proportion: The plaintiff will have his/her damages reduced in proportion to her fault.

F. *Limitations of actions — s. 7*

1. All actions under the Act must be brought within *three years*:[737]
   a. *After* the date on which the cause of action accrued, or
   b. The date on which the *plaintiff became aware, or should reasonably have become aware*, of the damage, the defect and the identity of the producer.
2. **Action barred**: A right of action shall be *barred* ten years from the date on which the producer put into circulation the actual product which caused the damage, regardless of whether or not the right of action accrued during the ten years.   **[738]**
   Exception: If the injured person has instituted proceedings against the producer within the ten years the action is not barred.

Common law liability for defective products

Note: Because the Liability for Defective Product Act 1991 supplements rather than replaces the common law, the common law is outlined below.

Remember: The common law principles are based on *negligence*, i.e. fault-based liability rather than strict liability (under the Act).[739]

A. *Historical background*

1. **Privity of contract**: The manufacturer or supplier of a product could only be held liable for injuries sustained through the use of the product with which he was in privity of contract.   **[740]**
   a. Restrictive — allowing only parties to a contract to sue upon it.
   b. In other words, if the plaintiff was *not* a purchaser of the defective product there was usually *no privity of contract* and therefore no ability to sue the manufacturer.
   Example: *Winterbottom v Wright* (1842) 152 ER 402. The plaintiff, a coach driver, was seriously injured when his coach broke down due to a latent defect. The plaintiff's employer had a contract with the Postmaster General to deliver mail. The Postmaster General had a contract with defendant to keep the coach in good repair. The plaintiff could not recover because he had no privity of contract with the defendant.

2. **Inroads on the privity of contract requirement**
    a. **False representation of safety** [741]
    If the defendant knew that a product was dangerous, yet he made false representations as to its safety, a basis of recovery was recognised. *Langridge v Levy* (1837) 150 ER 863.
    b. **Failure to give warning**
    Liability also recognised in cases where there was failure to give a warning when there was an awareness of a defect. *Quinn v Tedcastles & Co.* (1898) 32 ILTR 137. [742]
    c. **Inherently dangerous things**
    Liability was recognised in *O'Gorman v O'Gorman* [1903] 2 IR 573.
3. **Abolition of privity requirement** [743]
    Despite early inroads on the privity requirement, the abolition of the requirement came about in the US in the landmark case of *MacPherson v Buick Motor Co.* (1916) 217 NYS 382.

B. *Modern common law products' liability* — before *LFDPA 1991*.

1. **Manufacturers' liability for simple negligence**
    a. **Duty of care owed to *all* foreseeable users** [744]
    MacPherson: Cardozo J. reasoned that if the reasonable person could foresee that the chattel would create a risk of harm to human life or limb if not carefully made or supplied, the manufacturer or supplier of such chattel is under a duty of care in the manufacture or supply thereof.
    (a) Cardozo J. — other important opinion, *see* [316].
    b. **Duty of care owed to the ultimate consumer** [745]
    (1) *Donoghue v Stevenson* [1932] AC 562. Lord Atkin, in addressing the case of a plaintiff who allegedly found a decomposed snail in her ginger beer that had been purchased for her by a friend, stated that the manufacturer of products which sell in such a way as he intends them to reach the ultimate consumer with no reasonable possibility of exam, with the knowledge that the absence of reasonable care in the preparation will result in an injury to the consumer's health or property; owes a duty to the consumer to take reasonable care. *See* [275] and [315].
    (2) Principle accepted in Ireland — in *Kirby v Burke* [1944] IR 207 (HC).
2. **Expansion of liability to include:**
    a. **Repairers**

(1) **Duty of care owed to *all* persons** who may be *exposed* to danger by the repaired article: **[746]**
   (a) If it was foreseeable that it would be used without inspection.
   (b) **Example:** *Power v Bedford Motor Co.* [1959] IR 391 (SC). Liability was imposed on the defendant garage for the negligent repair of a car. The repair left the steering mechanism in a dangerous state. **Held:** The duty extended to all persons exposed to the danger — other drivers, passengers, property owners adjoining the road etc.

(2) **Duty of care to inspect for pre-existing faults** **[747]** *Andrew v Hopkins* [1957] 1 QB 229. A garage selling a used car had a duty to inspect the car for defects or to warn the buyer that the car had *not* been inspected.

b. **Installers and assemblers**
   (1) **Duty of care owed** to all persons injured by the defective work. **[748]**
   (2) *Brown v Cotterill* (1934) 51 TLR 21 (KBD). Liability was imposed on a monument mason when a tombstone that he had erected fell on a little girl who was placing flowers on her grandmother's grave. The court held that the mason could not shift responsibility away from himself onto the person who had contracted with him for the erection of the tombstone.

c. **Suppliers** of chattels for reward:
   (1) **Duty of care owed** to all persons likely to use or be injured by the chattel. **[749]**
   (2) *Keegan v Owens* [1953] IR 267 (SC) held that there was evidence capable of supporting a verdict for the plaintiff against the supplier of swingboats, hired out to a carnival committee, for injuries sustained by a worker (a volunteer) who assisted the committee by operating the swingboats.

3. **Expansion dealing with dangerous substances** **[750]**
   a. A person in control of a dangerous substance — whether as supplier, manufacturer or vendor — has a duty to take reasonable care that any person acquiring it from him does not suffer injury or loss. *Bolands v Trouw Ireland Ltd* (1978) unrep. (HC).
   b. **Duty to warn**: *Bolands*: The vendor of an ingredient in a poultry food mixture did not owe a duty to explain to the

purchaser who compounded the food mixture, the manner in which the ingredient could be used safely with other ingredients. **[751]**

- (a) The purchaser (as a compounder) had, or should have had, *special knowledge* of the product and its correct usage.
- (b) Finley P. did not find the product to be *particularly dangerous*.

4. **Expansion dealing with non-dangerous substances**   **[752]**
   a. **Neighbour principle** A manufacturer of a product which is *not* dangerous may be liable for what he knew or should have known when he released the product on the market. *Donoghue v* Stephenson, *see* [745] above.
   b. *Kearney v Paul & Vincent Ltd* (1985) unrep. (HC). The plaintiff claimed that his calves died as a result of the defendant's product. **Held:** No liability — the plaintiff failed to produce scientific evidence that the deaths were due to the product.

5. **Duty to warn**
   a. **New products**
      (1) **Risk of injury due to use**: Manufacturers placing new products on the market have a duty to inform of dangers which are known, or should be known, if the product is used in a certain manner.   **[753]**
      (2) *O'Byrne v Gloucester* (1988) unrep. (SC). Makers of a brushed cotton skirt were held liable in negligence for failure to attach a warning that the skirt was highly flammable. The teenage plaintiff suffered severe burns after the hem touched a butane heater.
   b. **Continuing nature of duty**   **[754]**
      (1) Manufacturers discovering a defect after their product has been put into circulation must issue a warning concerning the dangers. *Hobbs (Farms) v Baxenden Chemical Co.* [1992] 1 LR 54.
      (2) **Recall of product** may be the proper course of action if the risk is serious enough.
         (a) **Example:** Adulterated baby foods.
         (b) American approach: Duty to recall a product arises:
            i   Where the product developed hazards only after use, or
            ii Hazards which become apparent in similar products. *Comstock v General Motors Corp.* 99 NE2d 627 (Mich. 1959).

III. Revision questions

(1) Cowboy Conor started a tourist dude ranch near Ennis. After building a replica Wild West town, Conor imported rattlesnakes to keep in a glass enclosure in the gift shop. One of the snakes escaped and bit Rose in the bunkhouse. Can Rose bring an action based on the rule in *Rylands* against Conor?

(2) Farmer Fred has a bull named Jean Luke. Jean Luke is a huge inquisitive animal who enjoys exploring. Hillary the hillwalker lost her way and opened the gate to enter Jean Luke's field — the bull rushed out past her.

    (a) If the bull injures Hillary will Farmer Fred be held strictly liable?

    (b) If Jean Luke injures Michael the Milkman will Farmer Fred have a valid defence?

(3) The day after Irene's big party she was not feeling well. While ironing her blouse for work she had to rush to the loo. Unfortunately, the blouse caught fire. Upon returning to the kitchen Irene grabbed a glass and threw the contents on the fire. The glass contained vodka and it caused the fire to spread rapidly. If the neighbours' chattels are destroyed by the fire will Irene be held strictly liable?

(4) Cyril the sheepdog saw ten heifers enter his master's field. Knowing the heifers did not belong to his master, Cyril chased the heifers over the ditch into the road. One of the heifers was injured going over the ditch. Under the Control of Dogs Act 1986 & 1992 is Cyril's master strictly liable for the injured heifer?

(5) Bobby, the bouncer at the Dew Drop Inn disco, was irritated by an obnoxious patron named Patrick. Bobby broke Patrick's arm while throwing Patrick out of the disco. Is Bobby's employer strictly liable for Patrick's injuries?

(6) The Zipper Circus visited Cork. Someone let Larry the lion out of his cage. As Larry lazily wandered the streets of Cork everyone ran away from him. Cowboy Conor saw the lion and tried to capture him by enticing him into a horse-box. When Larry would not climb into the horse-box Conor hit the lion with a long whip to drive him into the horse-box. Larry knocked Conor to the ground and continued his walkabout until he was tired — then he returned to his cage.

    (a) Will Larry's owner be able to escape some liability by alleging that Conor was contributorily negligent?

(b) Assume that Aine climbed onto a chair to look out of her kitchen window to watch Larry as he strolled by. While leaning forward to get a better view Aine fell off the chair and broke her leg. Will Larry's owner be held strictly liable for the injuries suffered by Aine?

(7) Johnny asked his neighbour Michael if he objected to him building a large goldfish pond in his back garden. Johnny intended to put several fountains in the pond and wanted to make certain that the sound of running water would not disturb Michael. Michael's house is located very close to the proposed site of the pond and slightly downhill. Michael assured Johnny that the sound of the water would not disturb him, but he stressed to Johnny that the pool must be well made and maintained because he did not want several hundred gallons of water and fish to flow into his kitchen. If the pond water escapes and floods Michael's kitchen will Johnny escape all liability because Michael consented to the accumulation?

(8) Maurice the mechanic fixed the brakes on Stephanie's car. Later the same day the brakes failed and Stephanie crashed into Walter. Both Stephanie and Walter were injured in the crash.

(a) Can Stephanie sue Maurice under the Liability for Defective Products Act 1991?

(b) Can Walter sue Maurice under the Liability for Defective Products Act 1991?

(c) Did Maurice owe a common law duty of care to Stephanie?

(d) Did Maurice owe a common law duty of care to Walter?

(9) Jane bought a Curl Up and Dye branded hairdryer at Shultze's Department Store for £25. The next morning she washed her hair. When Jane turned on the dryer it worked fine for a few minutes then burst into flames setting her hair on fire. Jane quickly threw down the dryer and smothered the flames in her hair with a towel. The dryer landed on the floor and ruined her new carpeting. While recovering from her burns Jane has found out that a North Korean manufacturer makes the Curl Up and Dye branded hairdryer.

(a) Pursuant to the Liability for Defective Products Act 1991, can Jane bring a cause of action against the North Korean manufacturer?

(b) Pursuant to the Liability for Defective Products Act 1991, can Jane bring a cause of action against Schultze's Department Store even though she knows the name of the manufacturer?

(c) Pursuant to the liability for Defective Products Act 1991, will Jane have her damages reduced due to contributory negligence?

(d) Pursuant to the Liability for Defective Products Act 1991, will Jane recover for the cost of the hairdryer?

(e) Pursuant to the Liability for Defective Products Act 1991, will Jane recover for the cost of her carpeting?

(f) Pursuant to the Liability for Defective Products Act 1991, will Jane recover for her personal injuries if her medical bills are less than £350?

(10) Iggy the inventor designed a rat trap in 1990 for his mother. His mother liked the trap so much that Iggy decided to manufacture his rat trap. Iggy sold thousands of traps from 1990–99 when he retired. In 2001, Ziggy the Dublin Rat Catcher was injured by one of Iggy's 1990 rat traps.

(a) Can Ziggy bring a cause of action under the Liability for Defective Products Act 1991 against Iggy?

(b) Assume that Ziggy was injured when he attempted to use the rat trap as a paper weight on his desk. Is the rat trap defective?

SECTION 4: MISCELLANEOUS

6

NUISANCE

Chapter synopsis

I.   General principles
II. Public nuisance
III. Private nuisance
IV. Causation
V.   Defences
VI. Remedies

I. General principles

A. Nuisance

1. **Definition**: Nuisance is an act or omission that amounts to an unreasonable interference with, disturbance of, or annoyance to another person in the exercise of his rights.   **[755]**
   a. Historically, nuisance dates back to the Middle Ages. It was connected to land.
   b. Today it is important as a tool of environmentalists. Generally, no connection to land is required.
2. Nuisance is generally regarded as a continuing wrong and is divided into two categories: **[756]**
   a. **Private nuisance**
      Definition: If the rights relate to the ownership or occupation of land, easement, profit or other right enjoyed in connection with land, then the acts or omissions amount to a private nuisance. *Connolly v South of Ireland Asphalt Co.* [1977] IR 99 (SC).
   b. **Public nuisance**
      Definition: If the rights interfered with belong to the person (as a member of the public) the act or omission is a public nuisance. *Connolly v South of Ireland Asphalt Co.*

B. *Compare with trespass*

1. **Similarities** [757]
   a. Many acts may be both a trespass and a nuisance, for example:
      (1) Both protect possession rather than ownership.
      (2) Both protect against physical damage to land.
   b. A direct interference may be a trespass as well as a nuisance.
      Example: Excavations on the defendant's land near the plaintiff's home may cause vibrations which crack the foundation of plaintiff's home which is a nuisance. At the same time, the excavating may cause stones to land in the plaintiff's garden — this is a trespass.
2. **Differences**
   a. **Nuisance** [758]
      (1) Is usually said to be more concerned with the interference with the *use* or *enjoyment* of land.
      (2) **Note:** Nuisance is not generally actionable *per se* — proof of damage is required. *See* [810] for exceptions.
   b. **Trespass** [759]
      (1) Is more concerned with physical invasion of land.
      (2) Trespass is actionable *per se* — *no* proof of damage required.

C. *Compare with negligence*

1. **Negligence** [760]
   a. In negligence, the conduct of the defendant is of central consideration.
   b. **Objective analysis** is made of the defendant's actions.
2. **Nuisance** [761]
   a. Involves a balancing process between the competing interests of the plaintiff and the defendant.
   b. **Analysis** is of an objectively reasonable plaintiff at the time of the invasion or interference.

D. *Required elements for nuisance* [762]

1. Act by the defendant
2. Invasion or interference
3. Intent, negligence, or strict liability
4. Unreasonable and substantial harm
5. Causation.

II. Public nuisance

A. *Definition: If the rights interfered with belong to the person (as a member of the public) the act or omission is a public nuisance. Connolly v South of Ireland Asphalt Co. [1977] IR 99 (SC).* **[763]**

B. *The essence of a public nuisance is injury to the reasonable comfort and convenience of the public.* **[764]**

C. *Standing to sue*

1. **General rule:** only the Attorney General can bring a civil action for a public nuisance. **[765]**
   This requirement avoids a multiplicity of actions against the defendant arising from the same event.

2. **Special damage requirement** a private individual may maintain an action only if a special, particular or peculiar damage is suffered by him/her and his/her damage must be more serious than the damage suffered by the general public. **[766]**

   a. **Special, particular or peculiar damage** may consist of injury to the plaintiff's pecuniary interests where his/her person, or property is damaged. Alternatively, it may include the deprivation of the opportunity to earn a living. **[767]**
   Note: a personal injury *is* a particular or special damage.

   b. **No interest in land necessary**: A person suffering a particular or special damage as a result of a public nuisance is not required to have an interest in land to bring an action. **[768]**

      (1) *Boyd v Great Northern Railway.* [1895] 2 IR 555. The plaintiff was a doctor who was delayed for twenty minutes at a level crossing due to the fault of the defendant's agents. The Court found that the plaintiff had a huge practice and his time was of pecuniary value. He was found to have suffered an appreciable damage peculiar to himself beyond that suffered by other members of the public ordinarily using the road. Accordingly, the plaintiff was awarded ten shillings.

      (2) *Smith v Wilson* [1902] 2 IR 45. The plaintiff, an elderly man, walked to town on a public road until the defendant obstructed the road by removing a bridge and erecting a fence. As a result of the obstruction the plaintiff had to take a much longer route and sometimes had to hire a car to drive him. Plaintiff was awarded damages for his peculiar damage.

(3) **Breach of planning law** — Local Government (Planning and Development) Act 1976, s. 27. **[769]**
Any person can go to the High Court (if an activity constitutes a breach of the planning law) and seek an injunction.

D. *Onus of proof*

Once a public nuisance is proved by the plaintiff and the defendant is shown to have caused it, the onus is shifted onto the defendant to defend his actions. *See* Defences below [831] *et seq.* **[780]**

E. *Public nuisance on the highway*

1. **Note:** Public nuisance can arise in any number of contexts. Public nuisance on the highway is the most common — but it is not the only public nuisance.
2. **Obstructions**
   a. Generally any obstruction on the public highway is a public nuisance. *Cunningham v McGrath Bros.* [1964] IR 209 (SC). **[781]**
   b. **Exception**: Not every obstruction creates a cause of action for a person injured or inconvenienced. *McKenna v Stephens & Alexander E. Hull & Co.* [1923] 2 IR 112 (SC).
      (1) **Temporary blocking**: This generally refers to streets or footpaths because the unloading of goods does not create a nuisance. **[782]**
      (2) **Building or renovation:** Generally, the blocking or closure of footpaths in front of buildings being built or renovated (in order to protect the public from falling building materials) does not create a nuisance.
   c. **Temporary obstructions that may constitute nuisance** **[783]**
      (1) Allowing picketers or queues to form across footpaths or streets so as to cause an obstruction. *Boyd v GN Ry Co.* [1895] 2 IR 555.
      (2) Allowing animals to obstruct the highway. *Gillick v O'Reilly* [1984] ILRM 402 (HC).
      Note: Lawfully driving animals on a roadway is not an obstruction. *See* generally cattle trespass [633] *et seq.*
      (3) Allowing a ladder to remain on a public footpath for an unreasonable period of time.
      (4) Allowing railway gates to remain closed for longer than is

reasonable and necessary. *EI Co. Ltd v Kennedy* [1968] IR 69 (SC).

d. **Permanent obstructions which may constitute nuisance** [784]
  (1) Digging a trench in the highway. *Wall v Morrissey* [1969] IR 10 (SC).
  (2) Building a structure that obstructs a road. *AG v Mayo Co. Council* [1902] 1 IR 13.

3. **Dangers on a Highway**: A nuisance may consist of anything that makes the use of the highway unsafe or dangerous to the public whether temporary or more permanent in nature. [785]
  a. **Temporary dangers** rendering roadway hazardous. [786]
    (1) Placing dangerous material on or about a roadway.
      Example: Diverting water onto the roadway in freezing weather.
    (2) Inappropriate use of road [787]
      Example: Holding unauthorised motor rallies on unsuitable roads.
  b. **Permanent dangers** rendering roadway hazardous. [788]
    (1) Damaging the road surface.
      Example: Digging up the road.
    (2) Excavating near a road or footpath causing the surface of the road or footpath to collapse. *Baker v Alliance & Dublin Consumers' Gas Co.* [1946] IR Jur 48 (CC).

4. **Special consideration for misfeasance/nonfeasance** [789]
  a. **Common law**: A road authority may be liable in misfeasance but not nonfeasance.
    (1) **Nonfeasance:** There is no legal duty to act.
      In other words the road authorities are under no legal duty to maintain or repair roads, however negligent that failure may be.
    (2) **Misfeasance**: If a road authority decides to perform maintenance or repairs on roads, it has a *legal duty* not to negligently maintain or repair the roads.
  b. County councils are not liable in public nuisance for permitting extensive development without the necessary road infrastructure. *Convery v Dublin Co. Council* [1996] 3 IR 153 (SC). [790]

III. Private nuisance

A. Definition: If the rights relate to the ownership or occupation of land, easement, profit, right(s) enjoyed in connection with land, then the acts or omissions amount to a private nuisance. Connolly v South of Ireland Asphalt Co. [1977] IR 99 (SC). **[791]**

B. *Act or omission by defendant generally required*

1. **Proper defendant:** Who is liable in nuisance?
   a. **Creator** **[792]**
      (1) **Person creating** the nuisance is liable for it. This is true even if he is not in occupation of the land.
      (2) **Continuing liability**
      Example: A builder constructs a building that constitutes a nuisance. The builder will be liable and will continue to be liable even where he has no power to abate it. *Thompson v Gibson* (1841) 151 ER 845.
   b. **Occupier**
      (1) **Personal creation**: An occupier will be liable if s/he personally creates a nuisance. **[793]**
      (2) **Authorised creation**: An occupier may be liable where he *authorises* its commission or where his servants (and in some circumstances) his invitees or licensees create the nuisance. *Daly v McMullan* [798]. **[794]**
      Tetley v Chitty [1986] 1 All ER 663. The defendant council allowed a club to use its land. The neighbours complained regarding the noise and dust generated by the go-karts. **Held:** Permitting the use of the land by the club amounted to authorisation of the nuisance.
      (3) **Adopts of fails to reduce**: An occupier may be liable when he begins occupation and adopts or fails to take reasonable steps to reduce the interference created by the nuisance of another, such as the previous occupier. *Penruddock's Case* (1597) 5 Co Rep 1006. **[795]**
         (a) **Expansion**: If the nuisance is created by a stranger, trespasser or from natural causes the occupier will be liable if he fails to take reasonable steps to stop it within a reasonable time. *Sedleigh-Denfield v O'Callaghan* [1940] AC 880.
         (b) *Vitalograph Ltd* v Ennis UDC & Clare Co. Council (1997)(HC). An injunction was issued restraining the defendants from allowing a group of travellers, who were creating a nuisance, from remaining on the defendant's land near the plaintiff's business. **Held:**

The County Council adopted the nuisance by failing to take steps within a reasonable time to stop it.

(c) *Lind v Tipperary Council* (1998)(HC). An injunction was granted against the local authority for intensifying a nuisance that already existed by providing an inadequately supervised halting site.

c. **Landlord**

   (1) **General rule:** A landlord will not be liable for a nuisance on the demised premises unless he is an occupier. **[796]**

   (2) **Exception**: Where the landlord has authorised the creation or continuation of the nuisance.

Goldfarb v Williams & Co. [1945] IR 433 (HC). Liability was imposed on the defendant lessors because they let premises to a social club. The social club operated dances and other activities causing a noise nuisance to neighbours in the building. During lease negotiations dancing was specifically mentioned as an activity the club was going to engage in. **Held**: The lessors were responsible as having authorised the nuisance. Landlords are presumed to know the characteristics of their buildings, such as for soundproofing. **Rationale**: The nuisance was inevitable if the premises were used as intended.

2. **Act or ommission**

a. *See* [431] regarding act(s) and omissions.

b. **Traditional rule**: A person is under no duty to avoid harm to neighbours from natural conditions. **[797]**

   (1) Exception: Failure to repair or maintain property to prevent or minimise risk. Persons in control of property will be liable in nuisance if they do not reasonably prevent or minimise the risk of foreseeable damage where they know, or should know, that something on the land has or will encroach on neighbouring land. **[798]**

     (a) *Leakey v National Trust* [1980] QB 485. The defendant occupied land that was a large naturally occurring mound known as the 'Burrow Mump' located at the rear of the plaintiff's home. The topsoil began to slide onto the plaintiff's property due to the weather, causing damage and creating a significant risk of further damage.

     (b) *Leakey* approach followed in *Daly v McMullan* [1997] 2 ILRM 232 (CC). See [793].

(2) **Exception**: *Trees adjoining roadways or neighbouring land.* A landowner with trees adjoining the roadway or his neighbour's land must take reasonable care to guard against damage from his tree falling. **[799]**

    (a) Reasonable care does *not* mandate that an expert must inspect the trees for the occupier. *Gillen v Fair* (1956) 90 ILTR (HC).

        Lynch v Hetherton [1991] 2 IR 405 (CCA). The plaintiff's car was damaged in a crash with a tree that fell from the defendant's land onto the road. **Held**: The landowner must exercise reasonable care.

    (b) **Note**: What is reasonable is subject to change.

        Lynch v Dawson [1946] IR 504 (HC). Liability was imposed on the defendant landowner for allowing a tree branch to project onto the highway. The top of a turf lorry hit the branch causing an injury to the plaintiff. **Rationale**: Changing times require changes in the level of vigilance required.

3. Classification of liability

a. General rule: **[800]**

    (1) Defendant's liability for nuisance may arise because the defendant's action or omission is *intentional, negligent* or because it is imposed by *strict liability*.

    (2) **Classification** is important to determine what defences are available to the defendant.

b. **Intentional**

    (1) Liability imposed where the defendant has wilfully failed or refused to abate the nuisance. **[801]**

        Example: Hosting weekly wild parties knowing that the noise disturbs the other occupants in the apartment building.

    (2) Reasonable care is not a defence.

c. **Negligent** **[802]**

    (1) **Liability imposed** where the defendant has *failed* to exercise due care to abate a condition under his control.

        Example: Allowing manure to become heaped on the defendant's land near the plaintiff's home, thus exposing plaintiff to a constant stench of rotting manure.

    (2) **Fault based nuisance** tends to involve omissions (failure to act).

d. **Strict liability**

(1) **Liability imposed** where the law (statutory or common
law based) imposes liability without either intent or fault
on the defendant's part.   **[803]**
Example: Vicarious liability.
(2) Liability for third parties tends to be strict or fault based.

C. Interference with plaintiff's interests

1. Standing to sue

a. **Traditional rule**: Any person with a proprietary interest in
the affected land had the right to bring an action in nuisance.
                                                            [804]
b. **Expansion**: This was to include the rights of occupiers with
no proprietary interest such as mere occupation of a home.
(1) Family members of an owner or occupier. *Hanrahan v
Merck, Sharp & Dohme* [1988] ILRM 629. *See* [830].
(2) Personal harassment, not connected with land.
Khorasandjian v Bush [1993] 3 All ER 669 (CA).
(a) *Khorasandjian* facts: A teenager broke up with her
21-year-old boyfriend. He took the break up badly
and for months was violent and threatening toward
the girl. He followed her and made repeated menac-
ing phone calls to her home where she lived with her
parents. After he threatened to kill her he was jailed,
but continued to harass her. She successfully sued
him for private nuisance despite the fact that she had
no traditional proprietary interest in the family
home.
(b) *Khorasandjian* may no longer be relevant since the
enactment of the Protection From Harassment Act
1997 in England.

c. **Retreat to traditional rule?**   **[805]**

(1) English approach: *Hunter v Canary Wharf* [1997] AC 655
(HL). Hundreds of residents sued for the interference
caused to their television reception due to the construction
of the huge Canary Wharf tower in East London. **Held**:
The House of Lords rejected the claim relying on old cases
where it was held that the obstruction of a person's view
was no grounds for a nuisance action. Further, only plaintiffs with a right in land can sue in private nuisance. This
limits actions to those who own land, rent land or have
exclusive possession of it. **Rationale**: There needs to be a

clear distinction between nuisance and negligence. Nuisance is limited to protecting a person's right to the use and enjoyment of land, whereas negligence is limited to protecting a person's bodily security.

(2) Irish approach: This is not settled, but the High Court does not appear willing to follow *Hunter*.

    (a) *Royal Dublin Society v Yates* (1997)(HC). Shanley J. observed that the Supreme Court in *Hanrahan* was more flexible regarding the standing to sue than the House of Lords in *Hunter*.

    (b) *Molumby v Kearns* (1999)(HC). A legal interest over and above being in occupation of land is not necessary.

2. **Interference** may consist of:

  a. **Physical injury to the land.** [806]

    (1) **Examples:** Blasting, vibrations, dust, sewage and smoke.

    (2) *Halpin v Tara Mines Ltd* [1976–7] ILRM 28. It was held that cracks in a building due to vibrations was actionable. The plaintiff failed as he did not prove the required causal link between the damage he suffered and the activities of the defendant.

  b. **Substantial interference with the use and enjoyment of land**

    (1) **Definition**: Personal inconvenience or interference with one's enjoyment, quiet, freedom or anything that injuriously affects the senses or the nerves. *St. Helens Smelting Co. v Tippin* (1865) 11 HLC 642. [807]

    (2) **Examples:** Noise, loud music, strong odours.

    (3) **Note**: The term land refers to more than the real estate — it also refers to buildings, minerals, fixtures and the airspace above the land. *See* [117] *et seq.*

  c. **An interference with servitudes** [808]

  Example: Air, or right to sunlight, blocked by a neighbour's new twenty-foot garden wall.

  d. **Personal injury** [809]

    (1) Is material damage sufficient to allow a claim in private nuisance. *Hanrahan v Merck, Sharp & Dohme. See* [830].

    (2) English approach: Nuisance only applies to property damage and negligence is the tort for personal injuries caused by a neighbour's activities. *Cunard v Antifyre Ltd* [1933] 1 KB 551.

D. Harm must be unreasonable and substantial

1. a. Nuisance is not actionable *per se* — the plaintiff must prove actual damage.
   b. **Exception**: There are three exceptions where the plaintiff is not required to prove actual damage: **[810]**
      (1) The court may infer damage, if to require the plaintiff to prove damage would be superfluous. *Fay v Pentice* (1845) ICB 828.
      (2) No damages required where the plaintiff is seeking damages for interference with an easement or profit *à prendre*.
      (3) An injunction may be granted where harm is reasonably feared to be imminent.
2. In deciding whether an interference is unreasonable, the court will take into account all the circumstances including: **[811]**
   a. The locality of the area, and
   b. The duration and cause of the nuisance.
3. **Two strand competing interest test** is used by the courts to *weigh* the competing interests of the parties, as follows: **[812]**
   a. **Utility of the defendant's conduct**, and
   b. **Gravity of the harm** resulting or likely to result from it to plaintiff's interests.
4. **Substantial**
   a. **General rule**: The interference to the plaintiff's interest must be something that a reasonable person would take offence at, rather than a mere annoyance.   **[813]**
   b. **Sensitivity of the plaintiff**
      (1) **Reasonable person:** The interference must be something at which a reasonable person would take offence, rather than a mere annoyance.   **[814]**
      (2) **Standard nuisance:** This is based on reasonable give-and-take between neighbours and the standard of tolerance is that of the normal neighbour.
         Unduly sensitive plaintiffs will not be able to compel their neighbour into accommodating their own unusual needs.   **[815]**
      (3) **Usual characteristics:** Some characteristics of a plaintiff will not be deemed unusual.
         Example: *O'Kane v Campbell* (1985)(HC). The defendant was enjoined from 24-hour trading. Elderly people may sleep more lightly than young people, but they are not abnormal because of that and are entitled to their night's sleep.

(4) **Sensitivity may be taken into account** if the sensitivity was caused by the defendant's earlier nuisance. *Mullin v Hynes* (1972) unrep. (SC).

c. **Gravity of harm resulting or likely to result from defendant's conduct**

   (1) **General rule**: An injury must be of a substantial character, *not* fleeting or unlikely to recur. *See* Duration [811].

   [816]

   Allowances must be made for the incidents of neighbourly relations.

   (2) **Exception — material injuries:** If an injury is of a material nature, the courts will *not* have regard to competing considerations, such as public benefit or the character of the neighbourhood. **[817]**

     (a) **Material** means not trivial, fanciful or just exaggerated inconvenience.

     (b) **Interference** generally must cause damage that is a *discomfort or inconvenience* — *no* requirement of actual injury to land.

     (c) **Personal injuries** are always material. *Hanrahan v Merck Sharp & Dohme* [1988] ILRM 629.

     (d) **Damage to chattels** may be material. **[818]**

       i *Halsey v Esso Petroleum Co. Ltd* [1961] 2 All ER 145. Damage to laundry on a line was held to be material harm.

       ii *Hanrahan* [830] — damage to farm animals.

       iii *St. Helens Smelting Co. v Tippin* (1865) 11 ER 1483. The owners of a copper smelting works were held liable in nuisance for damage done to trees and shrubs from fumes.

5. **Unreasonable utility of the defendant's conduct**

  a. **General rule**: Where an intentional or negligent nuisance is alleged by the plaintiff, the defendant's conduct must be unreasonable for liability to attach. **[819]**

  Example: *Baxter v London Borough of Camden* [1999] 1 All ER 237 (CA). The defendant council converted a house into flats. The plaintiff lived in one of the flats. She sued the council, claiming that the building was poorly soundproofed and she suffered from the everyday noise generated by the other occupants of the flats. **Held:** The ordinary use of residential premises could not amount to a nuisance because there was nothing unusual about the way the building had been converted and the noise was normal for the residential use of the building.

b. **Utility of the defendant's conduct.** *See* [434] generally.

(1) **General rule:** Allowances may be made for the social and economic contexts in which the interference takes place.

[820]

(2) **Exception — public convenience or benefit**
A court is not entitled to take the public convenience into consideration when dealing with the rights of private parties, or to deprive the plaintiff of his legal rights because of public convenience. *Bellew* v *Cement Ltd* [1948] IR 61 (SC). [821]

(a) *Bellew.* The only cement factory in Ireland was forced to close for causing a nuisance, even though cement was desperately needed for new building projects.

(b) **Exception? — public interest**
Clifford v Drug Treatment Centre Board (1997)(HC). The High Court declined to enjoin the defendant drug treatment centre for the nuisance created by its patients because it would be against the public interest in not having the addicts treated. The Court did enjoin further expansion of the centre.

(3) **No allowances for malice** [822]

(a) **General rule:** The court will take into account the defendant's, intention of causing annoyance to his neighbour or use of his property in an unneighbourly fashion.

    i **Classic example:** *Christie v Davey* [1893] 1 CH 316. The defendant, upset by the noise from music lessons given late at night by the plaintiff, wrote a letter asking the plaintiff to stop. When this letter was ignored the defendant resorted to making noise by performing a *mock concert* to annoy the plaintiff. **Held:** The defendant committed a nuisance.

    ii *Hollywood Silver Fox Farm Ltd v Emmett* [1936] 2 KB 468. The defendant's farm bordered the plaintiff's fox farm. The defendant, knowing that noise near the breeding pens would put the vixens off mating, began shooting on his own property near the mating pens. The noise caused the vixens to stop mating and some killed and devoured their young. Liability was imposed against the defendant.

  (b) **Note**: Malice is not relevant if the plaintiff does not have a protectable interest. *Bradford v Pickles* [1895] AC 587.

c. **Suitability of locale**
  (1) What may be acceptable in one part of a city may be unacceptable in another.   **[823]**
    (a) Courts often give more weight to the demands of a neighbourhood with a fixed character over the demands of a neighbourhood in change.
    (b) This is referred to as 'judicial zoning' in the United States.
  (2) Difficulties may arise in mixed-use areas.   **[824]**
    O'Kane v Campbell [1985] IR 115 (HC). The defendant, a shop owner on the corner of the intersection of a wide busy street and an old established residential street, began trading twenty-four hours a day. The increase in his operating hours caused the neighbours to be disturbed at night by the defendant's customers. The court enjoined the defendant from opening his business between midnight and six a.m.

d. **Duration of nuisance**
  (1) **General rule**: The longer an interference continues the more likely it is to be considered unreasonable.   **[825]**
    However, there is no requirement that a nuisance must last a long time. *Crown River Cruises v Kimbolton Fireworks Ltd* [1996] 2 LR 533. It was held that a twenty-minute fireworks display could amount to a nuisance.
  (2) **Single act**: While nuisance is generally regarded as a continuing wrong, an action will lie where damage results from a single act such as the escape of gas.   **[826]**

e. **Utility may also be relevant** to determining the proper remedy.
  (1) **Recreation and innocent amusement:** *New Imperial & Windsor Hotel Co. v Johnson* [1912] 1 IR 327. The plaintiff hotel sought an injunction against the defendant who operated a tea room and restaurant across the street. The defendant held dances and other entertainment at night disturbing the guests sleeping in the plaintiff's hotel. The court held that one of the necessary incidents of the social life of the industrial city is a certain amount of recreation

and innocent amusement. A limited injunction was granted ordering the defendant to keep his windows shut after midnight and to prevent patrons from making undue noise as they entered or left.

(2) **Sunday recreation:** *Dewar v City & Suburban Racecourse Co.* [1899] 1 IR 345. The defendants organised race meetings on Sundays to take place in a residential area. The area residents complained that it interfered with the ordinary comfort and enjoyment of the property users and with religious services in an adjacent church. The Court granted an injunction prohibiting the Sunday races.

(3) **24-hour trading:** *O'Kane. See* [824].

IV. Causation

A. Intentional nuisance

1. **Causation** is basically the same as for other intentional torts such as battery. **[827]**

2. **General rule:** The intentional wrongdoer is liable for the direct and indirect consequences of his acts, whether or not the harm is foreseeable. *See* Causation [31]. **[828]**

   a. **Harm:** The injury or damage to the plaintiff's interest must be caused by the defendant's act or omission, or brought about by some force that the act or omission set in motion.

   b. Intention to cause harm disposes of any questions of remoteness or foreseeabliity of harm caused.

   c. **Defendant's conduct:** Causation is satisfied if the defendant's conduct directly or indirectly results in the injury.
   Example: The defendant drives piles into his land. The resulting noise may be a nuisance to the plaintiff and it is a direct result of the act. If the vibrations disturb the plaintiff this too is a direct result. However, if the vibrations cause structural damage to plaintiff's home, this is an indirect result of defendant's act.

B. Negligent nuisance and nuisance predicated upon principles of strict liability

1. **Require** that the defendant's act be the *cause* of plaintiff's injuries for liability to be imposed. **[829]**

   a. The courts use a *two strand test*.

      (1) **Actual cause:** Whether the defendant's conduct was the actual cause or the cause in fact of the plaintiff's injuries.

Example: *But for* the defendant burning tyres on his land, the plaintiff (a weaver) would not have been forced to rewash all his linen due to the smoke and soot drifting into his shop from the fire.

(2) **Proximate cause:** Whether the defendant's conduct was the proximate or legal cause of plaintiff's injuries.

Proximate cause deals with the defendant's liability for unforeseeable or unusual occurrences or consequences of defendant's act. *See* [487] remoteness.

2. **Onus on the plaintiff to prove causation** **[830]**

Hanrahan v Merck, Sharpe & Dohme [1989] ILRM 629 (SC). The plaintiff argued that to prove causation was harsh and amounted to a failure of the State to fulfil the constitutional mandate under Article 40.3 to vindicate the personal rights of the citizen. The plaintiff had alleged emissions from the defendant's neighbouring chemical factory was causing a variety of illnesses suffered by the plaintiff, as well as death of plants and animals on the plaintiff's farm. The plaintiff argued that the defendant had the capacity to prove or disprove causation better than the plaintiff. The Supreme Court rejected the plaintiff's argument to place the onus of proving causation on the defendant.

V. Defences

A. Contributory negligence

1. **General rule:** Any negligent act on the part of the plaintiff will afford the defendant a defence in an action for nuisance, based on the defendant's negligence for failure to exercise due care to abate a condition under his control. **[831]**

Civil Liability Act 1961 — apportionment principles apply.

2. No defence available for contributory negligence based upon plaintiff 'coming to the nuisance'. **[832]**

Example: The plaintiff bought property knowing that it was subjected to a nuisance from the neighbouring property. The defendant does not have a valid defence merely because the plaintiff bought the property knowing of the nuisance.

B. Assumption of the risk

1. **Consent**

   a. **General rule:** If the plaintiff consented to the act giving rise to nuisance, *knowing* that it would create a nuisance, the

defendant may have a good defence to the nuisance.   **[833]**
   b. **'Coming to the nuisance'**: The fact that an activity creating a nuisance existed before the plaintiff came within its scope is ordinarily not a defence.   **[834]**
2. **Civil Liability Act 1961, s. 34(1)(b)**
Apportionment principles apply.

C. *Inevitable accident: Injury could not be avoided by taking ordinary and reasonable precautions.*   **[835]**
   1. Available where liability in nuisance *depends* on negligence.
   2. **Onus** of proof is on the defendant.

D. *Prescription: A defendant may acquire a right to commit a private nuisance by prescription.*   **[836]**
   1. Prescription applies where it can be shown that the nuisance has been actionable for at least twenty years and that the plaintiff was aware of this fact during the relevant time.
   2. **Note**: The fact that the nuisance has existed for twenty years is not enough.
      a. It must have been a nuisance to the plaintiff or his predecessors on the land.
         (1) The defendant throughout the period had to act openly with the knowledge of the plaintiff or his predecessors.
         (2) It is not enough that it may have been a nuisance to other neighbours.
      b. Period runs from the date the nuisance began.
   3. **Classic example: *Sturges v Bridgman*** (1879) 11 Ch D 852. The plaintiff, a doctor, built a consulting room at the end of his garden. Nearby, the defendant had used heavy machinery for over twenty years. The noise from the machinery constituted a nuisance to the room, but prescription did not apply because no nuisance existed until the room was built.
   4. Prescription *does not* apply to all types of nuisance.   **[837]**
      a. Prescription is *not* a defence to public nuisance.
      b. Prescription has been successfully applied to:
         (1) Discharging water from eaves onto neighbours land, and *Harvey v Walters* (1873) LR 8 CP 162.
         (2) Sending smoke through flues in a party wall. *A.G. v Copeland* [1902] 1 KB 690.

E. Legislative authority **[838]**

1. **General rule**: Legislation may, either in express terms or by implication, authorise the commission of what would be a nuisance in common law.

 Example: Legislation creating a transit authority to develop and run commuter trains through the city cannot be sued in nuisance for the normal noise generated by the commuter trains.

2. **Exception:** The person or authority so acting under legislation and creating a nuisance cannot be negligent in the exercise of the statutory duty or power. **[839]**

 a. **Classic example:** *Smith v Wexford Co. Council* [1953] 87 ILTR 98. The defendants, who had a statutory duty to keep rivers clean, deposited large amounts of soil and vegetable matter on the plaintiff's land. Some of his cattle ate the roots (which were poisonous) and died. It was held that the defendant could not have reasonably foreseen the poisonous nature of the roots. Statutory authority was a good defence.

 b. *Superquinn v Bray UDC* (1998)(HC). The defendant local authority had a statutory duty to drain the area. The court held that the defendant was not negligent in the exercise of that duty. Liability denied.

3. Defence limited: The statutory authorisation to commit a nuisance extends only to its delegated function. **[840]**

 Example: *Kelly v Dublin Co. Council* (1986)(HC). The defendant had statutory authority to maintain and construct roads. In furtherance, the defendant built a depot for vehicles and materials. This depot was a nuisance to the plaintiff because it caused noise, dust and fumes close to his home. **Held:** The defendant exceeded the function of the authority granted.

4. **Planning**

 a. Is treated similarly to statutory authority. **[841]**

 The grant of planning permission does not make the planning authority responsible for authorising the creation of a nuisance. *Convery v Dublin County Council* [1996] 3 IR 156.

 b. Planning permission can only be taken as authorising a nuisance if the effect alters the character of the locale, so now after the change the nuisance is reasonable. **[842]**

 (1) *Wheeler v JJ Saunders* [1995] 3 WLR 466. The defendant was granted planning permission to build two piggeries close to the plaintiff. The strong pig smells affected the plaintiff. **Held**: The planning permission did not alter the character of the locale.

(2) *Hunter v Canary Wharf* — *obiter.* The fact that a building is part of an enterprise area does not mean that the legislators intended such developments to have blanket immunity for nuisance. For case facts see [803].

F. Act of stranger

1. **General rule**: If a person acting independently (over whom the defendant had no control) causes the nuisance, the defendant will not usually be liable.   **[843]**
   Example: A trespasser at night dumps several loads of slurry on the defendant's land next to the plaintiff's water well. The well becomes polluted from the slurry.
2. **Exception**: If the defendant's land is a well-known illegal dumping site, it could be said that the pollution of the well was a foreseeable consequence of the defendant's failure to secure his land against the act of the stranger.
3. Exception, if the defendant fails to remedy the situation within a reasonable time. *See* [795].

G. Act of God

Definition: Is an event which 'no human foresight can provide against, and of which human prudence is not bound to recognise the possibility.' *Tennent v Earl of Glasgow* (1864) 2 M (HL) 22.   **[844]**
a. **Examples:** Extraordinary and unprecedented floods, storms and other weather conditions.
b. **Note:** This defence has seldom been used successfully.

H. Non-valid defences

1. **Exercise of reasonable care and skill**: Generally it is not a defence in nuisance to allege that the defendant used due care and skill in seeking to avoid committing a nuisance.   **[845]**
   Exception: Where the defendant pleads statutory authority he must exercise reasonable care and skill.
2. **Public convenience or benefit**: Traditionally the defendant that created a nuisance to benefit the public did not have a valid defence. *See* [821–2].

VI. Remedies

A. *Damages: Compensatory damages may be awarded for interference with plaintiff's interests.*   **[846]**

B. *Injunctions: These are equitable remedies and therefore it is discretionary on the court as to whether or not to grant.* **[847]**

1. ***Quia timet* injunction**: If nuisance is of a recurring nature, an injunction against future nuisance may be sought.
   May be granted where damage is imminent but has not yet occurred.
2. **Prohibitory or mandatory injunctions** may be sought to stop current nuisances.

C. *Self-help*

1. **Abatement of the nuisance** is an ancient principle. **[848]**
   a. This remedy is *not* favoured by the law and is usually not advisable. *Sedleigh-Denfield v O'Callaghan* [1940] AC 880.
   b. **Confined**: Today, abatement of the nuisance is generally confined to:
   (1) **Simple cases** such as an overhanging branch or an encroaching root would not justify legal proceedings, and
   (2) **Urgent cases** requiring an immediate remedy.
   Burton v Winters [1993] 3 All ER 847.
2. **Traditional common law rule**: The plaintiff may take action to terminate or stop the nuisance. **[849]**
   Examples:
   (1) Cut off the overhanging branches of a neighbour's tree. *Lemmon v Webb* 1895 AC 1.
   (2) Sever roots from neighbour's tree entering the plaintiff's land. *Butler v Standard Telephone* [1940] 1 KB 399.
3. **Exception**: The plaintiff can only enter land of another to abate the nuisance:
   a. In cases of an emergency.
   Emergency: This is where the nuisance risks immediate harm to persons or property. *See Lemmon v Webb* above.
   b. **After notice**
   The plaintiff may enter the land of another to abate a nuisance if the plaintiff has given notice of his intention to abate and the notice has been ignored. *See Lemmon v Webb* above.
   c. A proper abatement will give the plaintiff a valid defence to any action of trespass brought by the defendant for the entering of his land.
4. **Retaliation by abatement** **[850]**

    a. **Unnecessary damage**: Any damage done while abating a nuisance is an actionable wrong against the plaintiff. *Roberts v Rose* (1865) 4 (HC) 103.

    b. **Malicious retaliation** to the nuisance can itself be a nuisance making the initial victim the wrongdoer. *See Christie* [822]. **But** there is no nuisance if the malicious behaviour does not infringe on any legally protected right. *Bradford Corporation v Pickles* [1895] All ER Rep 984.

5. **Alternative remedy:** If the plaintiff chooses to abate the nuisance he cannot seek damages for the injury suffered. *Baten's Case* (1610) 9 Co.Rep 53b.

VII. Revision questions

(1) Glow In The Dark Chemical Company manufactures various weedkillers. Recently, it has been discovered that a leak in the plant has allowed various chemicals to enter the local river killing all the fish.

   (a) Assume that Erica the environmentalist sues Glow In The Dark on behalf of humanity for the pollution. Will Erica be able to maintain a nuisance action against Glow In The Dark?

   (b) Felix, a fisherman who earns his living by fishing in the affected river, sues Glow In The Dark in nuisance. Will Felix be able to maintain his action against Glow In The Dark?

   (c) Farmer Fred uses the river water for his cattle. He pumps the water to his land. The chemicals in the water poisoned several of Fred's cattle. Will Fred be able to maintain a cause of action in nuisance against Glow In the Dark?

(2) Kevin is a secondary school student who dreams of becoming a great chemist. Recently he found a *recipe* for making stink bombs on the Internet. While his parents were at work Kevin carefully constructed a stink bomb in a jam jar using common household products in his kitchen. When he went to take it outside to test he tripped in the hall of the apartment complex dropping the stink bomb in the hall next to Clean Jean's front door. Clean Jean's apartment soon smelled like rotten eggs. The stench only lasted for ten minutes but it turned the walls, furniture and floors a dirty brown.

   (a) Can Kevin's single act be a nuisance?

   (b) Assume that there was no permanent damage to Clean Jean's apartment or furnishings, is the ten minutes of unpleasant odours enough to amount to a nuisance?

(c) Can Kevin's parents be held responsible for any torts committed by Kevin?

(d) Assume that Clean Jean is fastidious about her appearance and keeping her apartment clean. Does this make Clean Jean an unduly sensitive plaintiff?

(3) In 1980, Tony began repairing lawn mowers, chain saws and bicycles in his garage. In 1998, James moved next door to Tony and found the noise generated by Tony's repair business a disturbance to the use and enjoyment of his home.

(a) Will the defence of prescription apply?

(b) Does Tony have a valid defence that his business existed long before James bought his home?

(c) Assume that James was fully aware of Tony's business and the noise it generated before James bought his house. Will Tony be able to plead contributory negligence?

(d) Would it make any difference that in 1980 James obtained planning permission to convert his garage into a repair shop?

7

DEFAMATION

Chapter synopsis

I.   Historical background
II. Present status of defamation
     Libel
     Slander
     Slander *per se*
III. Defences
IV. Remedies
V.   Proposals for change

I. Historical background

A. Development of defamation

All commentators agree that the tort developed in a haphazard fashion. **[851]**

(1) 'It contains anomalies and absurdities for which no legal writer ever has had a kind word.... (Prosser)

(2) 'The law went wrong from the beginning in making the damage and not the insult the cause of action.' (Pollock)

(3) It was '...marred in the making.' (Winfield)

B. Slander originally applied to spoken words. **[852]**

1. **Seigneurial courts:** Originally, defamatory utterances were dealt with in the local courts of the feudal lord.

2. **Ecclesiastical courts**: These courts dealt with slander when the local seigniorial courts went into decline.
   Sin: Ecclesiastical courts generally regarded slander as a sin and punished it with penance.

3. **Common law courts**: As ecclesiastical courts lost power in the sixteenth century, slander began to appear in common law courts.
   a. **Conflicts** developed between the Church and the common law courts over jurisdiction of the slander cases.
   b. The common law courts held that:

(a) **Temporal damage or secular damage** was to be heard by common law courts, and

(b) **Spiritual damage** was to be heard by the church courts.

C. Libel   [853]

1. **Star chamber court**: At the start of the fourteenth century this court began to punish *political* libel.
   a. **Star chamber court** was an administrative court which was *outside* the common law system.
      (1) It was a tool of the monarchy used to persecute perceived enemies of the throne.
         Actions were arbitrary and without a jury.
      (2) It was abolished in the eighteenth century.
   b. **Political libel** — seditious publications.
      These types of publications had become widespread with the printing press.
   c. **Expansion of role**: Later, the role of the star chamber court extended to non-political libel.
      (1) **Damages** were awarded to the person defamed.
      (2) Damages provided a legal substitute for duelling that had become illegal.
2. **Common law courts** gained jurisdiction over libel.   [854]
   a. Remember: The common law courts already had slander.
      Continued to recognise differences between:
      (1) Criminal libel,
      (2) Tortious libel, and
      (3) Slander.
   b. Present distinctions between libel and slander survives.

D. Synopsis of common law defamation   [855]

1. **Strict liability**
   No fault necessary: The plaintiff could recover without proving any fault on the part of the defendant.
2. **Falsity of statement** was presumed.
3. **Damages** were presumed.
4. Plaintiff had to *prove* that the defamatory statement:
   a. Was *made* by the defendant,
   b. Was *about* the plaintiff, and
   c. Was *published* to a third party.

II. Present status of defamation

A. Definition: Defamation is the wrongful publication of a false statement about a person:

1. Which tends to lower that person in the eyes of right-thinking members of society, or
2. Tends to hold that person up to hatred, ridicule or contempt, or
3. Causes that person to be shunned or avoided by right-thinking members of society. *Berry v Irish Times* [1973] IR 368.   **[856]**

Defamation requirements are:
1. Defamatory communication,
2. Published to third person,
3. Causation,
4. Damages.   **[857]**

B. General principles

1. **Defamation Act 1961**: This generally *supplements* common law defamation.
    a. Controversial retention: Irish law retains the common law presumption of falsity.   **[858]**
    b. A statement is presumed false and the defendant bears the onus of proving that his statement is true.
2. Defamation deals with *competing interests*:   **[859]**
    a. **Right of free speech,** and
    b. **Right of the person to preserve his *good name* or reputation**.
        (1) All legal commentators question whether the balance between the two competing interests is presently proper.
        (2) 'Whatever is added to the field of libel is taken from the field of public debate.' *New York Times Co. v Sullivan,* 376 US 254(1964)(SC).
        (3) The criticism of the public conduct of a government official has caused dilemmas in many jurisdictions.
            (a) US approach: *New York Times v Sullivan*
                No libel without *actual malice* or *reckless disregard* for the truth.
            (b) English approach: *Reynolds v The Sunday Times* [1999] 4 All ER 609 (HL).
                Rejected the recognition of a political information category of information that would always be entitled to qualified privilege regardless of the circumstances.

(c) *Lange v Atkinson & Australian Consolidated Press* [1998] 3 NZLR 424 (CA).
No libel unless the statements were motivated by ill will or in order to take improper advantage.

3. Defamation is still divided into two primary torts: libel and slander. **[860]**

C. Standing to sue

1. **Person defamed**: Only a living person is able to bring and maintain an action. **[861]**

2. **Legal persons** such as a company or incorporated body may bring defamation actions. **[862]**
   a. *Upjohn v BBC & Others* (1994) unrep.: The plaintiff, as the manufacturer of Halcion, was accused that it had concealed the dangerous side effects of the drug for over twenty years.
   b. McLibel case: *McDonalds Corp. v Steel* [1995] 3 All ER 615. The defendants unsuccessfully argued that there is a public interest in free speech concerning the activities of huge multinational corporations such as McDonalds — rendering such businesses unable to sue for libel.

3. a. **Local authorities** in Ireland may bring an action for defamation. **[863]**
   b. But not in England.
      (1) *Derbyshire Co. Council v Times Newspapers Ltd* [1993] AC 534 (HL). A local authority was denied the right to bring an action for defamation. **Reasoning:** It would inhibit freedom of speech and be contrary to Art. 10 of the European Convention on Human Rights.
      (2) Individual members may bring an action if they are identifiable as individuals.

4. **Trade unions:** **[864]**
   a. Can sue in defamation. *ATGWU v Cork Examiner* (1987).
   b. But a trade union cannot be sued in tort. (S. 4 Trade Dispute Act 1906 & Industrial Relations Act 1990.)

D. False statement

1. **Required**: Defamation *requires* a *false* statement that is *not* an expression of opinion. **[865]**

2. **Statement: This includes any manner of communicating, such as:**

a. Oral,

b. Written, or

c. **Defamation Act 1961, s. 14(2):** By visual images, gestures and other methods of signifying meaning.   **[866]**

   (1) **Examples:** Photos, drawings, cartoons, films, music, satire.

   (2) By Act(s) such as by challenging persons suspected of shoplifting. *McEntee v Quinnsworth* (1993) (SC).

3. **False fact(s)** about the plaintiff: **[867]**

a. Could include inaccurate information or errors, for example:

   (1) Transcription errors — *Clarke v Independent Newspapers* (1991).

   (2) Printing wrong photo of man — *O'Kelly v Evening Press* (1992).

b. **Must** be defamatory in nature causing others to avoid the person.

   (1) **Objective standard:** Would the statement cause a reasonable person to form a negative or adverse view of the plaintiff's reputation?   **[868]**

     (a) **Speaker's intent** is not relevant regarding the issue of whether his statement is defamatory.

     (b) **Example:** *McDonagh v News Groups* [893].

   (2) **Mere abuse** such as foul language, common name-calling is not defamatory.   **[869]**

     (a) **Rationale:** It has no effect on reputation because people generally recognise it for what it is.

     (b) **Example:** Calling a person a 'Dutch Bastard' is not defamatory. *Harberagen v Koppens* [1974] 2 NXLR 597.

     (c) **Example:** Calling a woman a 'bitch' at a public meeting though abusive was not defamatory. *Ward v Zelikovsky* 643 A.2d 972 (NJ 1994).

c. **Allegations of crime** are not required.   **[870]**

   (1) Alleging that the plaintiff is a criminal is clearly defamatory.

   (2) However, there is no requirement that the allegation must concern a crime to be defamatory.

     (a) *Reynolds v Malocco* (1998) (HC). The defendant described the plaintiff as a 'gay bachelor'. The plaintiff is not a homosexual and (while the court noted that homosexuality is no longer a crime) this means that the statement could be defamatory.

(b) **Example:** Reference to Kelly J. in *Reynolds*. Adultery is no longer a crime, but an allegation of adultery could be defamatory. To lie is not a crime, but calling someone a liar is defamatory.

E. *Publication*

1. **Definition**: A publication is a communication made to a third party. [871]
2. **General rule**: The defamatory statement must be published to a person other than the plaintiff. [872]
   Rationale: Falsely accusing the plaintiff of being a thief will not injure the plaintiff's reputation or good name unless the statement is made to someone other than the plaintiff.
3. **Acts of publication**
   a. **Making a statement** [873]
      (1) Speaking in a loud voice and allowing others to overhear. *White v JF Stone* [1939] 2 KB 827.
      (2) Allowing an unauthorised defamatory statement to remain on the premises. *Byrne v Deane* [1937] 1 KB 818.
   b. **Distribution of a statement**
      (1) **General rule**: The person making an alleged defamatory statement will only be liable if he could have *reasonably foreseen* the particular publication. [874]
      (2) **Foreseeable publications**: These are circumstances where it would be likely to be seen by a third party. [875]
         (a) Placing a defamatory statement in a letter and addressing the letter to the wrong person. *Hebdith v MacIlwaire* [1894] 2 QB 54.
         (b) A clerk opened a letter for the employer. *Pullman v Walter Hill & Co. Ltd* [1891] 1 QB 524.
         (c) Addressing a letter to 'Mr Paul' when it is known, or should be known, that two Mr Pauls live at the address. *Paul v Holt* (1935) 69 ILTR 157.
         (d) Making a defamatory statement on the envelope and sending it through the mail. *Hinderer v Cole* (1977) unrep. *See* [883].
   c. **Dissemination of a statement**
      (1) **General rule**: A person who did not author the alleged defamatory statement may be held liable in defamation for *disseminating* the statement. [876]
      (2) Everyone in the publication *process* is technically liable:

(a) **Example:** Reporters, sub-editors, editor, newspaper owner, printer and distributor.

(b) *Berry v Irish Times* [1973] IR 368. The defendant printed a photo of a placard containing a false statement about the plaintiff.

(3) **Exception**: **innocent dissemination**. No liability if:

(a) The defendant did not know about the defamatory nature of the publication.   **[877]**

(b) There was nothing in the publication or circumstances that gave the defendant grounds to *suspect* the defamatory nature of the publication.

(c) The defendant was not negligent in *failing* to discover the defamatory nature of the publication. *Fitzgibbon v Eason & Son* (1910) 45 ILTR 91.

(4) **Onus** is on the defendant to prove the exception. *Ross v Eason & Son and The Winning Post* (1911) 45 ILTR 91.
          [879]

(5) Exception successfully applied to:

(a) Retailers, and

(b) Libraries.

(6) Exception does not apply to:

(a) Media organisations, and

(b) Printers.

d. **Repeating a statement to a third party**

(1) **Repetition**: Every act of repeating the statement is a new publication.   **[880]**

Repetition by another person: The original person making the statement is not liable for the statement later repeated by someone else. *Ward v Weeks* (1830) 7 Bing 211.

(2) Making a statement *likely* to be repeated: The original person making the statement may be liable for the statement later repeated.   **[881]**

Slipper v BBC [1991] 1 All ER 165. The defendant was held liable for the original statement made in a television broadcast. Later, he was also held liable for the newspaper articles reporting on the statement.

4. *Not* **acts of publication**

a. Making a statement to a person about themselves.   **[882]**

(1) In person — as long as no-one else can hear the statement.

(2) Via telephone — as long as it is a private call.

(3) Letter — as long as it is done in a private letter.

b. **Accidental publications**: Where the defendant was not negligent regarding the communication of a false statement to a third person, he is not liable. *Paul v Holt* (1935) 69 ILTR157 (NICA). **[883]**

c. If the *plaintiff* shows the defamatory statement to someone else.

(1) Plaintiff has published the statement, not the defendant.

(2) *Hinderer v Cole* (1977) unrep.: The plaintiff was sent a letter by his brother-in-law. In the letter, the defendant assassinated the character of the plaintiff. The plaintiff showed the letter to other people, so the plaintiff published the contents — not the defendant. The plaintiff did obtain nominal damages of £75 because the defendant had addressed the letter in a defamatory manner that was, or could have been, seen by others.

d. **Spouses** **[884]**

(1) A statement made by a person to his spouse is *not* a publication. *Wennhak v Morgan* (1888) 20 QBD 635.

(2) However, a statement made by the defendant to the plaintiff's spouse is a publication. *Wenman v Ash* (1853) 148 ER 1432.

F. *Referring to the plaintiff*

1. **General rule**: The plaintiff must be able to show that the defamatory statement refers to the plaintiff. **[885]**

2. **Identification can be inferred**

a. **Name not required**: The plaintiff is not required to show that his name was used. **[886]**

(1) The plaintiff must show that anyone who knows him/her knew that the statement refers to him/her. **[887]**

(a) **Example:** *Knupffer v London Express Newspaper Ltd* [1944] AC 116. The statement would lead a reasonable person acquainted with the plaintiff to believe that he was the person referred to in the published statement.

(b) **Fictitous person:** Even if the article claims to use a fictitious name this will not stop a real person from succeeding in showing that the article referred to him and was false. *Murphy v Times Newspapers Ltd* (SC) 280/98

(17 Jan 2000) citing *E. Hulton & Co v Jones* [1910] AC 20.

    (c) **Multiple actions**: If the article claims to use a fictitious name, more than one real person may succeed in showing that the article referred to him and was false. *Murphy v Times Newspapers Ltd.*

  (1) That plaintiff belonged to a limited class of persons. **[888]**

    (a) **Example:** The defendant alleged that a female member of the County Council was working as a prostitute. The plaintiff is one of the two female members of the County Council.

    (b) **Example:** *Doyle v The Economist Newspaper* [1981] NI 171 (HC). The defendant stated that a recent Catholic appointee was considered a *token* by his peers.

  b. **Extrinsic facts** can be admitted to establish the link between the plaintiff and the published statement. **[889]**

    (1) Evidence of the reactions of third parties.

    (2) **Example:** *Fulham v Associated Newspapers Ltd* [1955–6] IR Jur Rep 45. Evidence of jeering crowds greeting the plaintiff after the publication of the statement was admitted.

3. **Unintentional reference to the plaintiff**

  a. **Common law**: Identification of the plaintiff, whether intentionally or negligently published, was actionable. **[890]**

  b. **Defamation Act 1961, s. 21.**

  A *defence* is available for unintentional identification.

  Reasonable Care & Offer of Amends. *See* Defences [907] *et seq.*

G. Innuendo

1. If a statement has two meanings — one innocent and one defamatory: **[891]**

2. **Onus**: The plaintiff must prove that the statement has a secondary meaning that makes it defamatory.

  a. **Proof of second defamatory meaning:**

    (1) From words themselves, or **[892]**

    (2) Extrinsic information.

    (3) **Example:** *The Irish People's Assurance Society v The City of Dublin Assurance Co. Ltd* [1929] IR 25 (SC). The defendant took figures out of context from the plaintiff's balance sheet concerning amounts the plaintiff owed to the bank. The plaintiff successfully claimed that the defendant's statement was intended to represent that the plaintiff was in financial difficulties.

H. Right-thinking members of society [893]

b. Frequently, it is not easy to determine the right-thinking members of society.

Example: *Byrne v Deane* [1937] 1 KB 818. A golf club was raided by the police. The police removed an illegal gambling machine and a poem appeared on the club notice board with a line, '...he who gave the game away may he byrne in hell...'. The plaintiff sued the club alleging that the line accused him of being the police informer. It was held that the statement might lower the plaintiff in the eyes of the club members, but not in the eyes of right-thinking members of society. Right-thinking members would be against crime.

c. Appears to require the application of community norms. *Quigley v Creation Ltd* [1971] IR 269 (SC).

Example: *McDonagh v News Group Newspapers Ltd* (1998) (HC). The plaintiff, a barrister, was appointed by the Irish Government to represent it at an inquest. The defendant published an article entitled 'Leftie Spies Pack Gov Inquest'. The jury found that it falsely meant that the plaintiff was a terrorist sympathiser and lacking in integrity.

I. Injury

Statement must ruin reputation: A statement will not be defamatory if it does not injure the plaintiff's reputation or *good name*.

[894]

a. A statement merely causing anger or upset is not enough.

Example: *Berkoff v Burchill* [1996] 4 All ER 1008. The plaintiff was called ugly by the defendant — a journalist. The defendant argued that the statement was not defamatory. The court generally agreed, but because the plaintiff was an actor the words were likely to lower him in the eyes of the public or make him the object of ridicule.

b. The plaintiff must have a reputation or name to ruin. [895]

(1) At common law a plaintiff whose reputation is so bad that a false statement could not hurt it could not recover more than nominal damages.

Example: A convicted multi-murderer's libel action was dismissed when he attempted to sue over the false statement that he had also raped his victims. *Jackson v Longcope* 476 NE2d 617 (Mass. 1985).

(2) No Irish case. *See* [941].

J. Malice

1. **Definition**: Malice is a defamatory statement published with spite, ill will or recklessness.   **[896]**
2. Destroys the defences of:
   a. Justification,
   b. Fair comment.
   c. *Halpin v Oxford Brookes University* [1995] QBENF 94/0863 (CA). The plaintiff was the subject of several memos. He alleged that the writer had acted out of malice. **Held:** Malice was proved if it was shown that the writer knew that what he was publishing was not true or he was reckless as to its accuracy — or in the case of qualified privilege where he said it out of spite, rather than in order to perform the alleged duty to inform others.

K. Limitations

Statute of Limitations 1957, s. 11.

Six years: A plaintiff has up to six years after the publication to bring an action for defamation.   **[897]**

Libel

A. Definition: Libel is a defamatory statement that is in some permanent form.   **[898]**

1. **Examples:**
   (a) A defamatory statement contained in a letter.
   (b) A defamatory statement contained in a book.
   (c) A defamatory statement contained in a newspaper article.
2. **Expanded: Defamation Act 1961, s. 15.**
   Libel includes defamatory statements contained in radio or television broadcasts.   **[899]**

B. General rule: libel is:

1. Actionable *per se.*
2. A crime as well as a tort.
3. Forever a libel.
   a. Once a libel is made it remains forever a libel.
   b. **Example:** *Forrester v Tyrrell* (1983) 9 TLR 257. A defamatory script was read to an audience and held to remain a libel.

C. Forum

1. Due to the increase in international communications, more foreign communications are heard in Ireland than ever before.**[900]** **Examples:** The Internet, satellite television and radio.
2. EU Communications: **Brussels Convention, s. 5(3).**
   a. Forum proper — either:
      (1) Where the tort was committed.
          Note: The plaintiff is entitled to all damages suffered within that jurisdiction.
      (2) Where the defendant is domiciled.
          Note: The plaintiff is entitled to all damages suffered within the signatory states of the Convention.
   b. A tort is committed:
      (1) Either where the damage occurred, or
      (2) Where the event causing the damage occurred.
   c. **Example:** *Ewins v Carlton UK Television Ltd* [1997] ILRM 223 (HC). The plaintiff sued under libel for two documentaries concerning the IRA that were made by the British defendant and published in Britain and Ireland. **Held:** The plaintiff could choose whether to sue in Britain or Ireland for defamation.

Slander

A. *Definition: Slander is a defamatory statement that is transitory in nature.* **[901]**

B. *General rule:*
   1. Not a crime — slander is only a tort, not a crime.
   2. Not actionable *per se* — damages must be proved.
   Example of damages:
   (1) Loss of material benefit of friends.
   (2) Loss of a contractual or other tangible business advantage.

Slander per se

A. *Definition: In slander per se the law finds that certain transitory statements are defamatory without proof of damages.* **[902]**

B. *Four categories were developed in the common law:*
   1. **Imprisonable offence:** Where there is an imputation that the plaintiff has committed an imprisonable offence. **[903]**

a. **Specific criminal offence required** — not a vague reference to wrongdoing.

b. **Example:** Imputation that the plaintiff stole. *Corcoran v W. & R. Jacob Ltd* [1945] IR 446.

2. a. **Socially undesirable disease**: Where there is an imputation that the plaintiff is suffering from a socially undesirable disease. **[904]**

b. **Examples:**

(1) Venereal diseases,

(2) AIDS.

3. **Unchaste females**: Where there is an imputation that a female has committed adultery or otherwise behaved in an unchaste fashion. **[905]**

a. Adopted by **Defamation Act 1961, s. 16.**

b. **Allegations of lesbianism**: included in the term *unchaste*. *Kerr v Kennedy* [1942] 1 All ER 412.

c. Legal Commentators agree that this provision would not survive a constitutional challenge — unequal protection.

4. **Unfit in job**: Where there is an imputation that the plaintiff is not fit in his trade, profession or calling. **[906]**

a. **Common law requirement**: The statement must disparage the plaintiff in the way in which he exercises his profession or job.

Hopwood v Muirson [1945] 1 KB 313. Allegations that a headmaster had committed adultery was not actionable *per se*. It could have been if the adultery had been alleged with a student or teacher at his school.

b. **Defamation Act 1961, s. 19.**

Slander may be about anything regarding the plaintiff's character so long as his *commercial reputation* is affected.

III. Defences

A. *Five common law defences to defamation — these have been expanded by the Defamation Act 1961 and are:* **[907]**

1. Consent,

2. Justification,

3. Fair comment,

4. Absolute privilege,

5. Qualified privilege.

B. Consent

General rule: A person who consents to the actual publication of a defamatory statement about himself cannot later bring an action for defamation. **[908]**

a. Consent must be to the actual publication itself.

Green v Blake [1948] IR 242. The plaintiff, a racehorse owner, sued the defendant Racing Calendar for printing the decision of a complaint made against the plaintiff. The plaintiff argued that the entry of his horse in a race did not amount to consent to the publication of the decision of a complaint about the race. It was held that the publication was defamatory. The mere submission to a set of rules was not sufficient consent for the publication of the decision of the racing board.

b. **Civil Liability Act 1961, s. 34(1)(d).**

As interpreted by *O'Hanlon v ESB* [1969] IR 75. The plaintiff cannot complain if he consented under contract to the publication or he agreed to waive his legal rights.

C. Justification

1. **Traditional common law rule:** Truth is an absolute defence to defamation. **[909]**

2. **General rule**: If the statement is *true in substance* justification is a valid defence. **[910]**

   a. **Justification does not require:**
      (1) That every detail of the statement is true.
      (2) That the defendant acted with malice.
      (3) That the defendant believed the statement to be false at the time of he made the statement.

   b. **Justification requires** that the statement is true in *substance*.
   [911]

   Example: *Alexander v N.E. Railway Company* (1865) 122 ER 1221. While on the defendants train the plaintiff failed to pay his fare and was convicted. The defendant published a poster stating that the sentence given to the plaintiff for his failure to pay his fare was a fine or three weeks' imprisonment. The alternative to the fine was two weeks' imprisonment. **Held:** The inaccuracy was minor. The statement was true in substance and the defence of justification prevailed.

3. **Partial or literal truth (half-truths):** If the defendant fails to prove the truth of significant parts of his allegations or statement he will be liable. **[912]**

a. **Example:** *Irish People's Assurance Society v City of Dublin Assurance* [1929] IR 25. Figures taken out of context from the plaintiff's balance sheet were true figures, but taken out of context they gave the impression that the plaintiff was in poor financial condition. Defence of justification denied.

b. *Lewis v Daily Telegraph* [1964] AC 234. Stating that the fraud squad was investigating the plaintiff was held not to infer guilt.

4. **Expansion: Defamation Act 1961, s. 22.**

a. **Multiple allegations**: The *falsity* of *some* allegations will be *excused* if the *effect* on the reputation caused by the publication is merited. **[913]**

b. **False minor allegations** may be excused if the more serious allegation is proved to be true, and
   (1) The main allegation does not materially injure the plaintiff's reputation, and
   (2) The minor false allegations are not a bar to the defence.

5. **Onus** of proving justification rests on the defendant. **[914]**

a. Justification is seldom used.

b. If the defence of justification fails:
   The court may award exemplary damages.
   Because each repetition of the statement throughout the trial is a new publication of the defamatory statement.

D. Fair comment

1. **General rule**: A statement of opinion, made in good faith, on a matter of public interest is protected by the defence of fair comment. **[915]**

2. **Onus** is on the defendant to prove:

a. That the statement of opinion was fair.
   (1) Only applies to opinions or comments. It does not apply to statements of fact.
   (2) **Fair** **[916]**
      (a) Meaning honest or capable of being honestly held by a rational person in light of the facts which are either true or privileged. *Stopes v Suterland* [1925] AC 47.
      (b) Generally does not mean reasonable.

b. That the statement was made in *good faith*, and **[917]**
   Not motivated by malice.

c. That the statement of opinion concerned a matter of public interest or concern. **[918]**

(1) Public matters relating to the government, the administration of the State, any body that occupies a position of
prominence in the State or in State affairs.
Examples: The conduct of politicians, judges or the
treatment of victims of violent crimes.

(2) Such examples as literary and artistic matters submitted
to the public for approval. **[919]**

   (a) **Examples:** Book, art and restaurant reviews.

   (b) **Note:** To avail of the defence the review should not
exceed the public aspect of the work.

d. Under the common law the defendant was required to prove
that all of the facts upon which the opinion or comment was
based upon were true. **[920]**

(1) **Defamation Act 1961, s. 23**. The defence will not fail
simply because the facts upon which the opinion is based
are not true — but the opinion or comment *must* be fair.

(2) *Foley v Independent Newspapers* [1994] 2 ILRM 61. The
defence of fair comment failed because the defendant
failed to report in its commentary criticising the fees paid
to the plaintiff that the fees had been negotiated in
advance.

2. **Difficult** to determine what is a fact and what is an opinion.
[921]

Lingens v Austria [1986] 8 EHRR. The European Court of Human
Rights held that the difference between fact and opinion is:

(a) Facts are susceptible to scientific proof.

(b) Opinions are not susceptible to scientific proof.

E. *Absolute privilege*

1. Is generally granted in the limited circumstances where complete
freedom of expression is of paramount importance.

2. **Constitution provisions** **[922]**

a. **Art. 13.8.1 — Presidential privilege**
The President has absolute privilege for the exercise of any
official functions or powers.

b. **Art. 15.13 — Parliamentary privilege** **[923]**

(1) (a) Members of the Oireachtas: No defamatory action
can be brought for any utterances in either house.

   (b) **No extension to tribunals.** *AG v Hamilton II* [1993]
3 IR 227 (SC). During the Beef Tribunal an argument
was made that parliamentary privilege should extend to

statements made to the Tribunal because it was an agent of the Oireachtas. The argument was rejected.
(2) **Art. 15.12.** Privilege extends to official reports and publications of either house.
  c. **Expansion: Committees of the Houses of the Oireachtas (Privilege & Procedure) Act 1976, s. 2.**   [924]
  Privilege extends:
  (1) To statements made before committees of the Oireachtas by members of either house.
  (2) To utterances of members, advisors, officials and agents of the committees.
  (3) To documents and reports of the committees.
3. **Common law provides**:
  a. **Judicial privilege**: No defamatory action can be brought for any statements made in the course of judicial proceedings by: **[925]**
    (1) **Judges**
      (a) **Exception:** A judge of an inferior court may lose the privilege if she acted outside her jurisdiction. *Desmond & MCD Management Services v Riordan* (1999) unrep. (HC). Relying upon *Sirros v Moore and Ors* [1975] QB 118 — holding that a superior court always has power to determine the limits of its own jurisdiction. A wrong conclusion as to jurisdiction is merely an abuse of its jurisdiction and not an act outside it.
      (b) **Extended** to coroners acting under the Coroners Act 1962. Absolute privilege — unless he acts without jurisdiction and is aware of it. *Desmond.*
    (2) Counsel, or
    (3) Witnesses.
      (a) **Privilege absolute:** *Looney v Bank of Ireland & Morly* [1996] 1 IR 157 (HC). The plaintiff claimed he had been libelled in an affidavit made by Morly — an employee of the defendant bank. **Held:** Witness privilege is absolute.
      Relied upon *Kennedy v Hilliard* (1859) 10 IR.CLR 195 — discussing wide-ranging immunities for material statements made by witnesses and parties.
      (b) **Privilege not absolute:** *In re Haughey* [1971] IR 217 (SC). Ignored *Kennedy* and found that that immunity for witnesses does not exist to benefit the witness, but

for the administration of justice. Immunity would apply only to material statements.

b. **Trial statements**: No defamatory action can be brought for statements made in connection with a trial. **Examples:[926]**

  (1) **Court pleadings** and documents prepared for trial.

  (2) **Reports of court proceedings.**

  Exception: A spectator's accusation that the witness testifying was committing perjury was not protected when reported by the defendant. *Lynam v Gowing* (1882) 6 LR IR 259.

  (3) **Expanded: Defamation Act 1961, s. 18(1).** Reports of court proceedings that are a fair and accurate report published in a newspaper or broadcast in Ireland or Northern Ireland are absolutely privileged.

  (a) Statutory provisions apply only to media in Ireland and Northern Ireland.

  (b) Blasphemous or obscene matters are not covered.

c. **Inter-spousal communications**: Absolute privilege applies to communications between spouses.   **[927]**

F. Qualified privilege

1. Under the Common law, qualified privileges exist to encourage a person to speak.   **[928]**

  a. Unlike an absolute privilege, qualified privileges can be lost through malice or abuse.

  b. **The communication:**   **[929]**

  (1) **Must not** be wider than is necessary.

  (2) **Must not** be motivated by malice.

  c. **An honest but mistaken belief** by the speaker: **[930]**

  (1) That the person receiving the statement had an interest in receiving the statement — is *not* privileged.

  (2) *Hynes-O'Sullivan v O'Driscoll* [1988] IR 436. A fee dispute between the plaintiff psychiatrist and the defendant solicitor over the plaintiff's fee resulted in the plaintiff making a complaint to the Law Society about the defendant's conduct. The defendant then made complaints to the Medical Council and the Irish Medical Association about the plaintiff. The plaintiff was not a member of the Irish Medical Association and had no interest in the statement made by the defendant. Statement held not privileged.

2. **Duty to report**: The defence applies to statements made under some duty to make a communication to a person who has some corresponding interest in receiving it. The duty may be: **[931]**
   a. **Legal**
      (1) *Kirkwood Hacket & Tierney* [1952] IR 185 (SC). While it is defamatory to accuse a student of receiving money by false pretences, the President of UCD had a legal duty to investigate the matter. **Held:** The alleged statement made in front of the College Secretary was privileged in the absence of malice.
      (2) *Hartley v Welltrade* [1978] ILRM 38 (HC). Accusing police of assault and brutality is defamatory, but in making it in a complaint to the police about to investigate it, was privileged.
   b. **Social**
   c. **Moral: Protections for Persons Reporting Child Abuse Act 1998**. Provides statutory protection to certain specified categories of people who report child abuse in good faith.
3. **Protection of interests**: A defendant is conditionally privileged to defame another if there is:
   a. **Protectable personal interests**. The defendant must have a reasonable belief that some important personal interest is threatened.   **[932]**
      (1) **To a person**
      Example: Calling the police to report a domestic disturbance in a neighbouring flat.
      (2) **To property**   **[933]**
         (a) Investigation of wrongfully obtained money was privileged. *Kirkwood Hacket v Tierney. See* [931].
         (b) Statement made to suspected shoplifter is conditionally privileged. *Coleman v Keans Ltd* [1946] IR Jur Rep 5.
         (c) Complaint to police regarding possible blackmail is privileged. *Hartery v Welltrade. See* [931].
         (d) Accusation of theft made against an employee by the employer was conditionally privileged. *Hyland v Cleary Ltd* (1964) unrep. (SC).
   b. **Protection of public interests**: A defendant is conditionally privileged to defame another if the defendant reasonably believes that his statement is necessary to protect a legitimate public interest.   **[934]**

(1) The person receiving the statement must have the power to protect the interest.

Example: While walking past the bank Marge saw three armed gunmen. She ran to the police station and reported that her neighbour Bart was holding up the bank.

(2) **Note:** The media cannot claim the privilege of protecting the public interest for having published an article defaming a politician. *Reynolds v The Sunday Times* [1999] 4 All ER 609 (HL). **[935]**

Reynolds v The Sunday Times. The House of Lords rejected that the common law should develop political information as a category of information that will always be entitled to qualified privilege regardless of the circumstances. *Offending statement:* The plaintiff, Albert Reynolds, while Taoiseach, misled the Oireachtas. **Held:** The plaintiff was defamed. Nominal damages were awarded.

4. **Qualified privilege may be lost** through:
   a. **Bad faith** **[936]**
      (1) The failure to give the plaintiff's explanation in an article was unfair and not entitled to privilege. *Reynolds. See* [934].
   b. **Malice** **[937]**
      (1) **Onus** is on the plaintiff to establish the defendant's malice. Whether the plaintiff has shown malice to destroy the defence of qualified immunity is a matter for the jury. *Hynes-O'Sullivan v O'Driscoll* [1988] IR 436 (SC).
      (2) Proof may be intrinsic or extrinsic.
         (a) **Intrinsic proof** — such as the tone of the communication.
         (b) **Extrinsic proof** — evidence of the circumstances under which the statement was made.

G. Offer of amends

Defamation Act 1961, s. 21. **[938]**

Defence under certain conditions where the publisher was not aware of the possibility that the plaintiff would be defamed — because there was no knowledge either of identification or circumstance by which an innuendo would arise.

(1) **S. 21(5) — Innocent publication:** The publisher's innocence is dependent on having exercised reasonable care.

(2) **S. 21(3):** An offer to publish a correction and a suitable apology in a manner reasonably suited to *reaching recipients of the original publication* may be a defence, if:

(a) Accepted by the plaintiff — bars further action.

(b) Rejected by the plaintiff — *s. 21(1)* is allowed as a defence
if the offer was made as soon as possible after the defendant
became aware of the potential defamation.

H. Not valid defences

1. **Apology**
   Defamation Act, s. 17   **[939]**
   (1) An offer by the defendant of an apology made before an action
   is commenced or as soon after as possible, is not a defence.
     (a) **Example:** *McDaid v The Examiner* (1999) unrep. (HC).
         The defendant printed a false article on the front page
         regarding the plaintiff. The next day the defendant
         printed a full apology admitting the inaccuracy of the
         front-page article. The plaintiff testified that because of
         the article he was jostled on a public street and threat-
         ened. The plaintiff was awarded damages.
     (b) The apology must be genuine and to the plaintiff's sat-
         isfaction. *Campbell-Sharp v Magill* (1985) unrep. (HC).
   (2) However, if the action has commenced, the offer of an
       apology can be used as evidence in mitigation of damages.

2. **Use of quotation marks**
   a. Will not provide protection or a defence.   **[940]**
   b. They may actually cause more problems.
     (1) The quote may be inaccurate and lead to a defamatory
         meaning and a suit from the speaker.
     (2) The words quoted may defame another person who could
         sue the speaker and the media.

3. **Inserting phrases of doubt**
   Use of such phrases as 'it is rumoured' or 'it is alleged' is not a
   valid defence.   **[941]**

4. **Evidence of the bad reputation of the plaintiff**
   a. No Irish case
      Law Review Commission, 38–91. Recommends that evidence
      of bad reputation of the plaintiff be allowed for mitigation of
      damages purposes.
   b. English approach: Defamation Act 1996, s. 13.
      Not as a defence — but to mitigate damages.
      Rationale: Basis of tort of defamation is the protection of
      reputation. If the plaintiff does not have a good reputation, if
      defamed, how much has he been damaged?

IV. Remedies

A. Damages

1. Are generally the *standard remedy* in defamation.   **[942]**
2. Compensatory: The plaintiff is being compensated for the damage to his reputation.
3. **Emotional distress**
   Damages may be awarded for anxiety, distress and injury to feelings arising from the publication. *Barrett v Independent Newspapers Ltd* [1986] IR 13.

B. Injunctive relief   **[943]**

1. An injunction may be granted to prevent either the publication or further publication of defamatory material.
2. Interlocutory injunction: To stop the publication of a libel pending the hearing of the action should only be exercised in the clearest case where the court would find that the matter complained of was libellous.
3. **Example:** *Sinclair v St. John Gogarty* [1937] IR 377. An injunction was granted to prevent the publication of a novel which contained clear defamatory material.

V. Proposals for change

A. The Law Reform Commission (LRC) has recommended: **[944]**

1. **The abolition** of the *distinction* between libel and slander.
   With the introduction of a single tort of defamation.
2. a. That *printers* and distributors be granted *immunity* where they are not the original publishers.
   b. **LRC 38–91, s. 12.32**: The defamed person would retain an entitlement to compel the disclosure of information concerning the publisher and to prevent further publishing.
3. The abolition of the common law *presumption of falsity*.
   a. **Currently**, the defendant bears the onus of proving that his statement is true.
   b. In all other areas of tort, the plaintiff has the onus of proof.

B. United Nations (March 2000)   **[945]**

Abid Hussain, a special UN representative, has recommended that:
a. Sanctions for libel should be reduced. High awards have a *chilling effect* on free speech.

b. Onus of proof should be on the plaintiff to prove the falsity of the statement, rather than on the defendant to prove the truth of the statement.

c. Establishment of an independent press ombudsman.

d. **Amendment of Broadcasting Act, s. 31.**
Currently allows a minister to ban representative(s) of proscribed organisations from being heard on the airwaves.

VI. Revision questions

(1) Mary is a lecturer in a prestigious university. Mary has information that marks are being altered and inflated to make it appear that the students at the university are doing better than they really are: so she writes a report concerning the altering of student marks and sends the report to the university's Academic Council. The council is responsible for maintaining standards at the university. When the council refuses or fails to take action, one member of the council sends the report to a newspaper in Boston where the contents appear on the front page of the newspaper and on the newspaper's website.

   (a) Can a university bring an action in defamation?

   (b) Mary, in her report to the Academic Council did not accuse any person of a crime. Is accusation of a crime necessary for a defamation action?

   (c) Assume that the report is false. Will Mary be liable in defamation for sending the report to the Academic Council?

   (d) Assume that the report is false. Will Mary be liable in defamation for the report appearing on the front page of the newspaper or on the newspaper's website?

   (e) If the university suffers damage because students refuse to attend or withdraw from courses, will the university be able to bring an action in Ireland against the newspaper pursuant to s. 5(3) of the Brussels Convention.

   (f) Assume that the report is false, but the university does not appear to lose any students or grants etc. If the university discovers the person that sent the report to the newspaper, can the university maintain a defamation action against the person?

(2) Hamish is a food critic. Last week, incognito, he visited the hottest new restaurant in town. The following Sunday in his column he likened the asparagus soup to snot and the steak to shoe leather. Within days of his column appearing in the Sunday paper no-one is eating in the restaurant.

(a) Does Hamish have a valid defence to defamation?

(b) Assume that Hamish also reported that he found the toilet in a filthy condition. Has Hamish exceeded the public aspect of the work?

(c) Assume that Hamish referred in his article to the person that served him as being 'fat'. Can the server sue Hamish for defamation?

(d) Assume that Hamish was once in love with the owner of the restaurant, but the owner rejected Hamish. Could this fact be important?

(3) Ricky is a reporter for the Daily News. Ricky received a tip from a teller at the local bank that the assistant manager was about to be fired for embezzling. Ricky went to see the assistant manager and told him that he wanted to discuss a delicate matter. Once inside the assistant manager's office Ricky told him that the news on the street was that he was an embezzler. The assistant manager strongly denied the allegation. Unknown to both men Lilly, a trained lip reader, was outside the door waiting to speak to the assistant manager. She knew the content of the conversation because she could see the men through the window in the door, but she could not hear the conversation.

(a) Assume that Ricky accused the wrong assistant manager of embezzlement. Can the man falsely accused bring an action against Ricky for defamation?

(b) Assume that the wrongly accused assistant manager told his secretary of the allegations. Has a publication to a third person taken place?

(4) Andrew is the founder of the Anti-Gambling League. Recently, Ricky the reporter heard that Andrew was the winner of the first £1 billion lottery payout. When Ricky telephoned Andrew to inquire if the rumour was correct, the conversation was overheard by Andrew's secretary Susan. Susan immediately told Andrew's wife Winnie about the conversation. Winnie exclaims, 'Why that sanctimonious bastard. I hope he does not lose his job as president of the Anti-Gambling League if word gets out. All my friends belong to the League.'

(a) Assume that the statement is false. Is the false statement that Andrew won the lottery defamatory in nature?

(b) Assume that the statement is false. Has Susan committed slander?

  (c) Assume that the statement is false. Has Winnie committed slander with her outburst to Susan?

  (d) If Winnie confronts Andrew and accuses him of being a hypocrite and a liar, has Winnie committed slander?

(5) During a recess of a high profile murder case the judge tells another person via the telephone that the defendant's barrister is 'walking malpractice'.

  (a) Can the judge rely on judicial privilege?

  (b) What type of defamation, if any, has the judge committed?

  (c) Assume that the defendant's barrister begins defamation proceedings against the judge, but the barrister suffers a heart attack and dies two days before his case is to be heard. Will his estate be able to maintain the cause of action?

  (d) Assume that the judge was speaking to his wife via the telephone. Has he committed defamation?

8

ECONOMIC RELATIONS

Chapter synopsis

I.   Injurious falsehood
II. Passing off
III. Deceit
IV. Interference with contractual relations

I. Injurious falsehood

A. Historical background [946]

1. The earliest cases arose around the beginning of the seventeenth century. (Action on the case.)
   Cases involved oral statement by the defendant that cast aspersions upon the plaintiff's ownership of land that results in his inability to lease or sell the land. *Earl of Northumberland v Byrt* (1606) 79 ER 143.
2. The tort became known as 'Slander of title'.
   'Because of the unfortunate association with slander, a supposed analogy to defamation has hung over the tort like a fog and has had great influence upon its development.' (Keeton)
3. In the nineteenth century the tort was enlarged slowly to include:
   a. Written aspersions — *Malachy v Soper* (1836) 132 ER 453.
   b. Title to property other than land — *Malachy v Soper* (1836).
   c. Disparagement of the quality of the property — *Western Counties Manure Co. v Lawes Chem. Manure Co.* (1874) LR 9 Ex. 218.
   d. Aspersions cast on business itself. *Bromage v Prosser* (1825) 107 ER 1051. (This dealt with bank closure.)
4. The tort, at various times, was called various things, such as:
   a. Disparagement of property.
   b. Slander of goods.
   c. Commercial disparagement.

       d. Trade libel.

       e. Finally, Salmond coined the term *Injurious Falsehood* that immediately became popular.

   5. Principle has been applied to:

       a. Interference with an expectancy of a marriage. *Shepherd v Wakeman* (1662) 82 ER 982.

       b. Defamatory words concerning the plaintiff's employees. *Riding v Smith* (1876) 154 ER 38.

B. *Present injurious falsehood*

   1. Required elements: **[947]**

       a. False Statement by the defendant,

       b. Publication,

       c. Resulting pecuniary (economic) damage to the plaintiff,

       d. Intent,

       e. Causation.

   2. a. Modern rules stem from *Ratcliffe v Evans* [1892] 2 QB 524.

       b. **Definition**: Action for written or oral falsehoods maliciously published that produce or are likely to produce pecuniary damage(s).   **[948]**

         (1) Falsehoods are not required be actionable *per se*.

         (2) Falsehoods are not required to be defamatory.

         (3) Falsehoods must be calculated to produce or likely to produce a pecuniary damage.

   2. **Publication** — *see* Defamation, Chapter 7.

   3. **Falsehood**   **[949]**

       a. Must be distinguished from sales talk or 'puffing'.

         (1) Mere sales talk could include statements such as 'best buy'.

           (a) *DeBeers Abrasive Products Ltd v International GE Co. of New York* [1975] All ER 599. The parties were competitors. The defendant produced a pamphlet for potential customers claiming scientific tests proved the superiority of their product to the plaintiff's product. **Held:** The claim of scientific evidence was sufficiently specific and serious to maintain an action.

           (b) **Test** used in *DeBeers* — *Reasonable Consumer*.
Would a reasonable person believe that the claim was serious?

         (2) American approach — Falsehood

A defendant cannot falsely claim that the plaintiff's goods are *seconds*, prison made or contain impurities. *National Refining Co. v Benzo Gas Fuel Co.*, 20 F.2d 763 (US 8th Cir 1927).

4. **Intent**
   a. **False statement** alone is not enough to establish tort. **[950]**
   b. Defendant must *know* that the statement is false.
      (1) **Careless or negligent** false statement is not enough.
      (2) *Irish Toys & Utilities v The Irish Times Ltd* [1937] IR 298, citing *Balden v Shorter* [1933] All ER 249. *Irish Toys* failed on the facts.
   c. **Malicious**: Defendant must have intended to produce harm or intentionally acted without 'just occasion or excuse'. *Ratcliffe v Evans* [1892] 2 QB 524.
   d. **Recklessness:** Gross negligence may be enough for liability. *Malone v McQuaid & Registrar of Titles* (1998)(HC).

5. **Damages**
   a. Generally, the tort is designed to protect against interference with economic interests. **[951]**
      (1) **Common law** required the plaintiff to prove *special damages*.
      (2) **Causation**: If it could not be proved that loss flowed from the act the plaintiff could not recover.
   b. **Defamation Act 1961, s. 20.**
      (1) Special damages no longer required.
      (2) Present requirements:
         (a) The representation is calculated to cause pecuniary damage to the plaintiff, and
         (b) The representation is contained in a permanent form, or
         (c) The representation relates to 'any office, profession, calling trade or business' or the plaintiff's.

6. **Defences**
   a. **Consent** — *see* [908]. **[952]**
   b. **Truth**: The falsity of disparagement is an essential element of the tort. **[953]**
   c. (1) **Defamation** defences: The same defences are recognised. *See* Defamation Defences, Chapter 7. [907] et seq **[954]**
      (2) Action for defamation and injurious falsehood was defeated by the qualified privilege defence. *Murphy v Dow Jones Publishing* Co. (1995) unrep. (HC).

d. Other approaches: US — Protection of private interests **[955]**
  (a) A conditional privilege to defame or disparage to protect one's own interest or the interests of others.
  (b) Competitors may make general claims. **Examples:**
    (1) Best product in the world.
    (2) Tests have shown X to be superior to all other cleaning products.
  (c) Cannot make specific false claims about the plaintiff's property or business. *National Refining Co. v Benzo,* 20 F.2d 763 (8th Cir. 1927).
  (d) Non-competitor: A defendant is usually protected if he honestly believes the truth of his statement and was speaking in any of the situations recognised in the US in which defamation would provide a privilege. **Examples:**
    (1) Response to inquiry, and
    (2) Protection of others — 2nd Restatement, s. 646A: Reports by consumer research groups on new products or doctors evaluating new medicines are privileged if reports are made in good faith.

II. Passing off

A. Historical background [956]

1. Developed as a subset of Injurious Falsehood.
   Ancient origins go back to deceit, but the requirement of fraudulent intent was abandoned.
2. Generally applied when a person was misled as to:
   a. Origin of goods, or
   b. Origin of services.
   Resulting in damage to the plaintiff's business
3. Originally involved, for profit, the misappropriation of:
   a. Trade names, and
   b. Trade marks.
     (1) The defendant makes a profit on the success of another business by deceiving consumers.
     (2) The result is that the defendant wrongfully takes a portion of the successful business's place in the market.

B. Present requirements — passing off [957]

1. Misrepresentation by the defendant,
2. Made in the course of trading,

3. Made to customers,
4. Calculated to injure,
5. Damage or the likelihood of damage to the plaintiff.

C. *Misrepresentation*

1. **Definition**: Some aspects of the plaintiff's business is used to confuse the public into thinking that the defendant's goods or services are the plaintiff's goods or services.   **[958]**
   a. **Commercial**: The misrepresentative must take place in a commercial context.
   b. **Generally**: Courts are reluctant to find misrepresentation absent compelling evidence due to serious consequences of intervention.
   c. The plaintiff must have a commercial reputation associated with the marketing of its product, services, etc.
2. **Appropriated business aspects**
   a. **Names** of business, product or service.   **[959]**
      (1) **Registered names**: Registration of a trade name provides extensive protection of it to the registered owner.
      (2) **Unregistered names** may develop a specific association, which may easily allow for the confusion of the public by misrepresentation.   **[960]**
         (a) **Example:** *Muckross Park Hotel v Randles* (doing business as Muckross Court Hotel) [1995] 1 IR 130. The defendant's hotel was outside the area known as Muckross.
         (b) **Example:** *J. Bollinger v Costa Brava Wine Co. Ltd* II [1961] 1 All ER 561. The use of the word 'champagne' in relation to sparkling Spanish wine was held to constitute a misrepresentation regarding the place of origin of the Spanish wine.
   b. **Packaging**
      (1) **Distinctive**: Some packaging is so unique that if a defendant copies it consumers may be confused and purchase the defendant's product when they intended to buy the plaintiff's.   **[961]**
      (2) **Example:** *Coca-Cola v AG Barr & Co.* [1961] RPC. The plaintiff's distinctive bottle shape was held entitled to protection under passing off.
   c. **Design: Distinctive**: Like packaging, some designs are so unique and distinctive that if the defendant copies it, consumers may become confused and purchase the defendant's

product when they intended to buy the plaintiff's. **[962]**

(a) *Adidas Sportschahfabriken Adi Dassler KA v Charles O'Neill & Co. Ltd* [1983] ILRM 112. The Supreme Court held that the use of three stripes on sportswear was the adoption of a fashion trend rather than a misrepresentation.

(b) *Gabbicci v Dunnes Stores* (1991) unrep. (HC). An interlocutory injunction was granted for the sale of sweaters that were identical to the plaintiff's design.

d. **Advertising**

(1) **Association**: Businesses spend huge sums of money developing unusual and unique advertising to sell their goods and services. **[963]**

(a) **Examples:** The Budweiser Lizards, Hibernian Insurance's 'Jack and Jill'.

(b) **Capable of misrepresentation**: If it provides the required association with the plaintiff's goods or services and copying of it would lead to consumer confusion.

   i *Cadbury Schweppes v Pub Squash Co.* [1981] 1 All ER 213.

   ii **Not unique**: *Ragget v Findlater* (1872) LR 17 Eq. 29. A brewer who customarily placed the phase 'nourishing stout' on his label had not created something uniquely associated with his product.

(2) **Source** of advertising **[964]**

Associated Newspapers plc v Insert Media Ltd [1991] 3 All ER 525. The defendant produced an advertising flyer and inserted it into the plaintiff's newspapers without the plaintiff's consent. It was held that the insertion was a misrepresentation, i.e. the public would be deceived into thinking that the advertisement came from the plaintiff.

3. **Commercial context** **[965]**

a. Misrepresentation *must* take place in a commercial context.

(1) **Trade association** not actively engaged in trade, but representing members who were tradesman, was allowed to bring an action against the defendant for falsely claiming to be a member of the association. *An Board Trachtala v Waterfood Foods plc* (1992) unrep. (HC).

(2) **Charities** allowed to bring an action. *British Diabetic Association v Diabetic Society Ltd* [1995] 4 All ER 812.

(3) **Political parties** are not allowed to bring an action.

4. **Onus** is on the plaintiff [966]

   a. To establish that the business aspect appropriated is publicly associated with the plaintiff.

   b. **Confusion**: The business aspect appropriated has or is likely to deceive the public.

      (1) The plaintiff is *not* required to prove actual deception of the public, just the likelihood of deception. *An Post v Irish Permanent plc* [1995] I IR 140.

      (2) **Must be widespread**: The confusion must be widespread with a general tendency to occur.
      Private Research v Brosman [1996] ILRM 27. It was held that there was not sufficient proof of a misrepresentation where the plaintiff only showed a similarity between the businesses, with a few customers mistakenly contacting the defendant instead of the plaintiff.

   c. The plaintiff must prove that the misrepresentation has had an adverse impact on the plaintiff's business — or it is likely that it will have an adverse impact. [967]

5. **Remedies**

   a. **Injunctions**

   b. **Damages** [968]

      (1) Actual damages must be shown.

         (a) An adverse impact has occurred to the plaintiff's business.

         (b) Or that actual damage is imminent to the plaintiff's business.

      (2) Commercial impact is required. [969]
      Day v Brownrigg (1878) 10 Ch D 294. Copying the name of another person's house was held not actionable because it did not have a commercial impact.

      (3) Measure of damages
      Falcon Travel Ltd v Owners Abroad Group plc t/a Falcon Leisure Group [1991] 1 IR 175. The plaintiff was operating in Ireland and the defendant was operating in England under a similar name. When the defendant opened offices in Ireland the plaintiff was able to show that the goodwill and reputation of its business was getting mixed with the defendant's. It was held that proof of adverse

consequences was not necessary. The court found that the defendant had been acting in good faith and refused to issue an injunction. The measure of damages was based on the cost of advertising the differences between the two businesses.

D. Further expansion?

1. **Appropriation of the plaintiff's name or likeness**   [970]
   a. Many celebrities make income from endorsing various goods and services.
   b. American approach: It is a tort for a defendant for a commercial purpose to use the plaintiff's name or likeness without authorisation.
      (1) (a) **Celebrity**: The use of the name or likeness of a celebrity has a commercial value.
          (b) Using a celebrity's name or likeness is an invasion of the celebrity's right to sell endorsements for goods or services.
          Haelan Labs v Topps Chewing Gum Inc., 202 F.2d 806 (2d Cir.), cert. denied, 346 US 816 (1953).
      (2) (a) **Non-celebrity**. The unauthorised use of a non-celebrity's name is an invasion of privacy.
          (b) The non-celebrity would have a right to damages for interference with his/her right to peace. *Fairfield v American Photocopy,* 138 Cal.App.2d 82 (1955).

III. Deceit

A. General principles

1. **Definition**: A person is misled and suffers damage (usually economic) by the fraud of another.   [971]
2. **Present requirements:**
   a. Misrepresentation by the defendant,
   b. Scienter,
   c. Intent to induce the plaintiff's reliance,
   d. Actual reliance,
   e. Resulting damage.

B. False representation

1. The defendant must make a representation of fact that is not true.   [972]

a. False representation may be an inference *implicit* in a statement or *inferred* from the defendant's conduct.

b. **Example:** *Gill v McDowell* [1903] 2 IR 463. The defendant placed a hermaphrodite bovine with both male and female animals. It was held that the defendant's actions amounted to a representation that the animal was either male or female.

2. **Opinion or intention**

a. **General rule:** The statement of an opinion or intention does not usually constitute a representation. **[973]**

b. **Exception:** If it can be proved that the defendant did not have that opinion or intent s/he stated. *Ennis v Butterly* [1997] 1 ILRM 28.

3. **Failure to disclose**

a. **General rule:** A failure to disclose facts does not normally amount to a representation — even if one party is working under a mistaken belief on the matter. **[974]**

b. **Exception:** It is a distortion of representation if the non-disclosure distorts the significance of a representation causing deception.

c. **Exception:** Or the law requires disclosure.
Example: Fiduciary relationship — the law requires disclosure.

d. **Statute of Frauds Amendment Act 1828, s. 6 requirements**
[975]

(1) **Reduced to writing and signed:** Misrepresentations fraudulently made to enable another person to obtain credit is not actionable unless the misrepresentation had been reduced to writing and signed by the person making the statement.

(2) **Applies to deceit *only***
Does not apply to other misrepresentations like negligence. *Banbury Bank v Bank of Montreal* [1918] AC 626.

C. Scienter

1. **Definition:** Scienter is having knowledge or being aware. **[976]**

2. **Fraud definition:** A false representation made:

a. Knowingly, or

b. Without belief in its truth, or

c. Recklessly, or

d. Carelessly, with indifference to its truth or falsity.
Derry v Peek [1886–90] All ER 1 — per Lord Herschell.

3. **No requirement of gain**. The defendant is not required to personally gain or benefit from the fraud to commit deceit. **[977]** A third party may benefit or gain instead. *Pasley v Freeman* [1775–1802] All ER 31.

4. **Motive**   **[978]**
The plaintiff is not required to prove the motive of the defendant for his fraud, but a failure to prove could cast a doubt on the credibility of the fraud itself. *Northern Bank Finance Corp. v Charlton* [1979] IR 149.

D. *Intent — to induce plaintiff's reliance*

1. a. The defendant's representation must intend the plaintiff to rely on it in the manner in which the plaintiff did rely upon it. *Bradford Third Equitable Benefit Building Society v Borders* [1941] 2 All ER 205.   **[979]**
   b. **Intent** extends to all intentions objectively inferred from the circumstances.

2. **Class covered**: The plaintiff must be within class of persons covered by the intent by deceit to be actionable. *Peek v Gurney* (1873) LR 6 HL 377.   **[980]**
   (1) To be actionable deceit, the defendant's intent to induce reliance must exactly match the plaintiff's actual reliance. *See Bradford* above.
   (2) **Example:** Mr X tells Sean that his business is going to increase in value due to an important new contract. Mr X's intent is to get Sean to invest in his venture. Relying on the false representations of Mr X, Sean buys stock in the company Mr X stated was going to enter into a contract with his business. Sean's induced reliance does not match Mr X's intent — therefore there is no actionable deceit against Mr X.

E. *Causation — actual reliance*

1. **The false representation** is *not* required to be the *sole* inducement of the plaintiff's detrimental reliance.   **[981]**

2. **General rule**: The representation must have materially influenced the plaintiff's detrimental reliance. *Leyden v Malone* (1968) unrep. (SC).   **[982]**
   a. **No causation**
   The plaintiff cannot prove causation if: **[983]**
   (1) S/he was not *deceived* by the representation.

(2) S/he did not receive the representation until after entering into the transaction, i.e. she could not have relied upon it.

b. **Uncertainty**: This exists in cases where the plaintiff should not have been deceived.

(1) The defect was patent, i.e. obvious.

Example: *Horsfall v Thomas* (1862) 1 H & C 90. A purchaser of goods could not claim reliance on the representation where a patent defect was in contradiction of the representation.

(2) No duty on the plaintiff to inspect.

Phelps v White (1881) 7 LR IR 160. Facts, that the plaintiff had reasonable means of discovering the falsity of the representation, would not defeat his claim.

F. Damages

The plaintiff must suffer damages to maintain an action. **[984]**

a. Damage: There is usually some material harm to the plaintiff but it is not required to be economic in nature.

b. **Personal injuries** are recoverable under deceit.

Langridge v Levy (1838) 4 M & W 337. The defendant misrepresented the safety of a gun that exploded and injured the plaintiff.

c. **Property damages** are recoverable under deceit.

IV. Interference with contractual relations

A. Historical background **[985]**

1. Roman law: Going back to the time of the Romans in Britain the law recognised a citizen's right to seek damages for injuries inflicted on one of his slaves.

2. Expansion: this concept was expanded and extended to employees.

a. Statutory enactment: In 1349 the Black Death had left England with a great labour shortage. The Ordinance of Labourers was enacted in 1349 (1350 25 Edw. III, st. 1) to meet the agricultural crisis.

b. Ordinance Of Labourers 1350 provided a system of compulsory labour. Penalties were provided to:

(1) Keep labourers from running away,

(2) Keep employers from enticing or harbouring another employer's servants.

3. Both actions were enforced in trespass:
   a. The one for injuring an employer's employee, and
   b. The one for enticing away.
4. Eventually both co-mingled and were absorbed into trespass on the case. *Hart v Aldridge* (1774) 98 ER 964.

B. Modern form — in general

1. **Definition:** The modern form of interference with contractual relations is persuading or inducing a contracting party to breach the contract.
2. **Present requirements**   [986]
   a. The defendant's interference with an existing contract,
   b. Intent,
   c. Causation,
   d. Damages,
3. a. The tort of **Interference with Contractual Relations** first appeared in *Lumley v Gye* (1853) 118 ER 749.
   b. **Contracts for personal service**   [987]
   Lumley v Gye. Miss Johanna Wagner, a famous opera singer, was under contract to the plaintiff to sing exclusively in his theatre for a definite term. The defendant enticed Miss Wagner to refuse to perform for the plaintiff. Although she was an opera singer rather than a labourer, the plaintiff was able to maintain an action under the statute for the defendant's acts.
3. Further expansions to include:
   a. **Contracts** *other* than those for personal services. *Temperton v Russell* [1893] 1 QB 715.
   b. **Contracts** broken with no ill will on the part of the defendant. *South Wales Miner's Federation v Glamorgan* [1905] AC 239.

C. Defendant's interference

1. **Direct interference**   [988]
   The defendant may directly prevent the plaintiff from performing her contract, thus causing the breach.
   a. **Example:** Physically restraining the party to the contract, or
   b. Removing an essential piece of equipment.
   GWK Co. Ltd v Dunlop Rubber Co. Ltd (1926) 42 TLR 593. The plaintiff contracted to have its tyres placed on the cars of a manufacturer at a show, but the defendant removed the tyres and replaced them with its own. The defendant was found to

have interfered with the contract between the plaintiff and the manufacturer.

2. **Indirect interference:** Inducing the breach of a contract without having direct dealing with one of the contracting parties. **[989]**

   (1) **Example:** Getting a third party to directly persuade or induce the party to the contract to breach it.

   Note: An employee or agent who is merely performing his job by directly persuading or inducing the party to the contract is not liable to the plaintiff for the tort of interference with contractual relations. His employer or principal is liable. *Montgomery v Shepperton Investment Co. Ltd* (1995) unrep. (HC).

   (2) Inducing the breach of a contract by offering another a more lucrative contract to induce a breach of the original contract with the plaintiff. *De Francesco v Barnum* (1890) 63 LT 514.

3. **No requirement of a legal breach** **[990]**

   a. **Unsettled area:** Disruption of contract is enough for tort to lie, even if the contracting party does not legally breach the contract.

   Example: Inducing a party to legally terminate a contract by invoking an exclusion clause in the contract.

   b. **Note:** A valid contract is essential to this tort.

D. *Intent*

1. The defendant *must intend* to interfere with the plaintiff's contract. **[991]**

2. **Onus** is on the plaintiff to prove that the defendant:

   a. Knew, or

   b. Had constructive knowledge of the contract between the defendant and the plaintiff. *James McMahon Ltd v Dunne* (1964) 99 ILTR 45

E. *Causation*

The interference is a normal and probable result of the defendant's conduct. *James McMahon Ltd v Dunne* (1964) 99 ILTR 45. **[992]**

F. *Damages*

The plaintiff must prove that he suffered damages because of the defendant's conduct in inducing or persuading a third party to breach his/her contract with the plaintiff. **[993]**

a. **Material damage required** for recovery.
b. **Injunctive relief** is available for continued interference with the plaintiff's contracts.

G. Special defence

Justification [994]
a. **Malice** was originally required under this tort.
b. **Justification** was a defence if the defendant could show that he had some legitimate purpose as a motivation for his conduct. *Lumley v Gye* (1853) 118 ER 749.
c. Legal commentators generally agree that:
Justification is *still* available, although is malice no longer required, if the defendant can show his conduct was to further some important personal or public interest.

V. Revision questions

(1) Seedy Cola Company decided to do an advertising campaign to try to gain more of the market. Seedy then hired an infamous convicted paedophile to make false statements that he always enjoyed a glass of Cool Cola with his victims — the sales of Cool Cola plummet. What economic tort, if any, has Seedy Cola committed?

(2) Seedy Cola decided to do a consumer study. Seedy visited four university campuses and asked blindfolded students to compare Seedy Cola to Cool Cola. Eighty per cent of the students surveyed preferred Seedy Cola to Cool Cola. If Seedy Cola uses this statistic in its advertisement and Cool Cola's sales plummet, what economic tort, if any, has Seedy Cola committed?

(3) Polly Politician, during a local speech, labelled herself a compassionate democrat. The local democrat party objects to this label, as Polly is clearly a conservative. Can the local democrat party bring an action for passing off?

(4) Cajun Country is a popular restaurant in Dublin. Recently a restaurant named Cajun County opened across town. Many people are confused as to which restaurant received a rave review in *The Times*. Name the economic tort.

(5) Terry is upset that his worthless brother-in-law Sean is still living with Terry and his wife. Sean assures Terry that he will be able to get a job and leave as soon as he can buy a car. Sean talks Terry into falsely telling the local bank that Sean is employed by Terry.

Based upon Terry's false statement the bank lends Sean money and Sean disappears. Can the bank bring an action against Terry for deceit?

(6) Sebastian is a dancer. He recently signed to tour with a small company across Ireland called the Celtic Cub. While in Dublin, Sebastian is seen by John LaChapelle a world-famous Canadian dance-troupe manager. John LaChapelle wants Sebastian to join his troupe.

   (a) Will John LaChapelle avoid possible liability for interference with contractual relations if he speaks to Sebastian's partner rather than Sebastian about joining his troupe?

   (b) Assume that Sebastian took his contract with the Celtic Cub to a solicitor who told him that the contract was not binding. If Sebastian signs with John LaChapelle can Celtic Cub maintain a cause of action for interference with a contractual relation?

   (c) Assume that all dance companies require their dancers to sign contracts — is this fact important?

(7) Hollywood film director Max Malone, while on holiday in Kilkenny, told a group at the local pub that he would like to shoot his next film in the village of Glenmore using the old schoolhouse.

   (a) Based upon Max's statement Jamsey bought the old schoolhouse, but was disappointed when Max's next film was shot in Wales. Can Jamsey maintain an action in deceit against Max?

   (b) Assume that Nancy overheard Max's plans to film in the old schoolhouse when he was speaking on the phone in the guesthouse where she works. Hoping that a film crew would spend a great deal of money in the village, Nancy bought the local chipper. Can Nancy maintain an action in deceit against Max if his next film is shot in Wales?

   (c) Assume that Darren was thinking of buying the café in Glenmore. Mick told his friend Darren that Max was going to film in Glenmore. When questioned, Mick lied to Darren and said that he had seen the signed contract between Max and the owners of the old schoolhouse. Darren is persuaded to buy the local café. The film is not made in the village of Glenmore but the café makes a substantial profit anyway. Can Darren maintain a cause of action in deceit against Mick?

(8) Tennis racquet designer Bebe Bucks was tired of the standard black, brown or white handgrips on tennis racquets and started using florescent coloured handgrips on his racquets. Within a short time everyone recognised his racquets because of the unique coloured grips. If other manufacturers begin making different coloured grips will they be committing passing off?

(9) Winona is a wedding planner in Waterford. Just as her business has done really well Suzanne moves into Waterford and sets up a rival business.

    (a) Winona is irritated and tells her friend Pat the wedding photographer that, 'Suzanne has a trail of creditors after her a mile long.' The statement is false, but Pat and his friends refuse to take bookings from Suzanne. Suzanne cannot stay in business without photographers. Name the economic tort.

    (b) Winona learns the names of several young women that have recently become engaged from her friend who has one of the local jewellery shops. Winona contacts all the women and finds that two have entered into contracts with Suzanne. Winona quickly makes a deal with the women that she will cut Suzanne's fees by fifty per cent if the women call Suzanne and tell her that their weddings are off. Name the economic tort.

    (c) Winona falsely tells Suzanne that she is pregnant and planning to only handle two weddings a month. Relying on the false statement Suzanne doubles her inventory of centrepieces, candles, ribbons etc. Winona hires two assistants in an attempt to handle every wedding in town. As a result Suzanne experiences a severe cash-flow problem and has to take out a loan. Name the economic tort.

    (d) Winona takes Suzanne's business telephone number and posts it on the Internet as belonging to a stripper for bachelor parties. Has Winona committed the tort of passing off?

SECTION 5:
THE EXAMINATION

9

APPROACHING THE EXAM

Chapter synopsis

I.   Where to concentrate your revision
    A.   Be prepared
    B.   Conquering cases
    C.   Answering the exam questions
        Problem questions
        Planning your answer (problem questions)
        Writing the answer (problem questions)
        Negligence (problem questions)
        Essay questions
II.   Avoiding common mistakes

I. Where to concentrate your revision.

A. Be prepared — early

Step 1: Make certain that you have all the:
(1) Class notes,
(2) Assigned readings,
(3) Past exam papers.
    Note: Past exam papers are useful for answer practice. Do *not* attempt to guess what areas will come up in the exam by reviewing past exam papers.
Step 2: Assess the materials.
(1) What areas did the lecturer *stress*?
    (a) What areas took up the most amount of time?
    (b) What areas appear year after year on exams?
    (c) What areas did the lecturer state were interesting, unusual, in need of change?
(2) Identify the grey areas, e.g. legal questions that are not resolved or are in need of an update.
    Examiners often ask questions regarding the grey areas.
(3) Identify recent changes in the law, such as:
    (a) Cases, and

(b) Statutes.
(4) Identify recent recommendations for change, such as:
   (a) Reports of the Law Reform Commission,
   (b) Law review articles,
   (c) Newspaper articles.
(5) Do *not* neglect the settled areas of the law.
   Without a good knowledge of these areas a student will be unable to make a proper analysis or necessary comparisons.

B. Conquering cases

1. The points that you make in your answers must be backed up with relevant authority.
2. Everyone wrestles with the names of cases.
   If you cannot remember the name of a particular case, *briefly* outline enough facts to enable the examiner to know to which case you are referring.
3. The best way to conquer cases for many students is to test yourself with case flash cards.
   a. Put the name of the case on the front of an index card.
   b. On the back put a brief summary of the facts, holding and the importance of the case.
   c. Look at the name and try to recite the information on the back. If you are correct put the card in a different stack. Keep going through the cards until you have them correct. Now turn the cards over and try reciting the name from the facts.
   d. Case cards are easier to carry and use than a full set of notes or books.

C. Answering the exam questions

1. **Problem questions** test your ability to apply the law to the facts given.
   a. Many students find this type of question the most difficult.
   b. The best way of tackling this type of question is to treat it like a maths problem — *work* your way through it.
      However, unlike a maths problem, there is no one precise correct answer in most law questions.
2. **Planning your answer (problem questions)**
   a. *Read* the question.
   b. *Read* the question again.
   c. **Identify the tort(s).**

Sometimes this is easy: if you find a question difficult ask yourself the questions in d. e. and f. below.

d. **From the facts which tort(s) may be a possible basis of liability?**

Remember: the same facts may give rise to numerous torts.

e. **What interest of the plaintiff has been injured?**

   (1) His person?

   (2) His property?

   (3) His reputation? Etc.

f. **How has the defendant conducted him/herself?**

   (1) Performed an intentional act?

   (2) Performed a negligent act?

   (3) Performed no act? (Failed to act.)

g. **Identify the issues.**

   Sometimes this too is easy. If not, try asking yourself the following questions:

   (a) *What are the essential elements that the plaintiff must establish as a basis of liability for the tort?*

   (b) *Is each and every essential element present in the facts given?*

   (c) *Consider defences and limitations.*

   Does the statute of limitations bar the action?

   (d) *Parties: check the relationship, if any, between the parties.*

      i   Vicarious liability,

      ii   Standard of care issues,

      iii   Publication issues in defamation (spouses).

h. After identifying the issue(s) — *select one issue.*

   It is better to take the issues one at a time than to skip back and forth in your answer.

i. **Briefly outline your answer for each issue.**

   (1) Again, check to make certain that you are answering the question asked.

   Beware: In exams it is easy to go off on a tangent.

   (2) All you want are a few basic *phrases*, *words* and *cases* to jog your memory to keep you from going off track or forgetting something.

   Do not spend more than a few minutes outlining your answers.

   (3) If you do not like the flow of your proposed answer just renumber the points quickly.

3. **Writing the answer (problem questions)**

   Taking one issue at a time:

a. **The beginning** — the introduction
   (1) Many students are at a loss where to begin.
   (2) Unless you are instructed otherwise, a good way to begin may be to *define the tort*.
   Remember: The examiner is always right and if the examiner gives you specific instructions concerning the exam — follow them!
   (3) **Example:** A trespass to land is defined as the intentional or negligent entering or remaining or directly causing anything to come into contact with, land in the possession of another, without lawful justification.
b. *Briefly* **discuss the relevant law concerning trespass to land.**
   (1) What is relevant?
   Example: It would *not* be relevant to discuss chattels remaining on the land if you are dealing with a trespass by entering the land.
   (2) Remember to cite authority for your points, e.g.:
       (a) Cases,
       (b) Statutes.
c. *Apply* **the** *relevant law* **to the** *facts given* **to you in the problem.**
   Do *not* list every fact — just discuss the facts that are important to your analysis.
d. **Apply any relevant defences and limitations.**
   Some students prefer to list all possible defences and eliminate the non-relevant defences quickly.
e. **Reach a conclusion.**
   (1) Even a wrong conclusion is usually better than no conclusion.
   (2) Some students like to start an answer with 'The answer' (conclusion).
       (a) You would not guess the answer to a maths problem and then work the problem; similarly, you should not guess the answer to a law problem question then work the problem.
       (b) If you must start the problem with the conclusion, leave space and fill it in after you work the problem.
f. **Repeat** the above steps until you have covered all the issues presented.
g. **Reach a final conclusion.**
   Tye up all the issues you have covered.

4. Negligence (problem questions)

    a. Generally, negligence is the most important area of tort law, therefore it is a favourite area for law examiners. It also presents some unique application difficulties.

        Carefully read through the facts — make certain that you understand the sequence of events.

    b. Be methodical — analyse each element in order.

        (1) You *must* find an appropriate act or omission before looking for a duty.

        (2) Do *not* conclude that there is a breach of duty before considering causation.

        (3) **Remember**: Look at the relationship between the parties. *Never assume that the defendant owes a duty.*

5. Essay questions

    a. Most students have less difficulty answering essay questions, but they often make the same types of mistakes.

    b. **Read the question.**

    c. **Read the question again.**

    d. **Usually the issue is identified for you.**

        (1) Make certain that you answer the question asked.

        (2) If you have prepared essay answers in the hope that the question will come up in the exam, make certain that you *tailor* your prepared essay to answer the question asked.

    e. **Take a side.**

        Because most essay questions ask you to analysis some legal dilemma or problem you will be required at times to determine which side you want to take, so quickly determine which side you think you can put forward best.

        (a) In doubt? What did your lecturer say about it?

        (b) What do the law commentators write about it?

    f. **Ask yourself questions.**

        (1) Why is this true?

        (2) Why is this important?

        (3) How can this be improved?

        (4) How is this issue handled in other jurisdictions?

    g. **Outline your answer.**

        (1) Again, if you don't think that it flows well just renumber the points until you have it the way you like it.

        Do *not* write out a new outline.

        (2) Remember an instruction in an exam to *discuss, criticise* or *evaluate* does not signify that you should spend three

pages on stating the posture of the law as it now stands and two paragraphs on analysis.

    (3) State the law, but *spend the majority of your time and effort* on the critical analysis.

h. **Start writing your answer**.

    (1) Check to make certain you are answering the question asked.

    (2) Cite authorities to back up your points.

    (3) Cite any relevant works including your textbooks.

i. **Reach a conclusion.**

    (1) The best conclusions tie up many of the points raised in the answer.

    (2) Merely answering the question asked isn't the best approach, but it is probably better than just ending abruptly.

II. Avoiding common mistakes

A. Answer the question asked.

1. Many students spend hours revising by writing out answers to what they hope are the exam questions.

    a. One of the problems with this approach is that students often end up writing out their practice answer in the exam and do not answer what has been asked.

    b. If you find it helpful to write out practice answers make certain that you alter the practice answer to answer the question asked in the exam.

2. Avoid those heart-stopping moments.

Ever leave an exam hall and learn that you advised the wrong person? Make certain you answer the question asked.

3. **Avoid killing your answer** (and grade).

    a. **Shotgun approach**

You will seldom be asked to write everything you know about a particular area of law. Yet, many students spend most of their effort and time on writing every single detail they know about the subject, in the hope that one or more of the points will hit the target. Blasting away with memorised material, writing pages on the subject and two paragraphs on analysis, is not going to earn you many marks if the question asks you to analyse or criticise.

    b. **Shooting yourself in the foot**

(1) Very few examiners will ask you to write an analysis or critique of something in law that is perfectly satisfactory as it stands. *Do not* merely write everything you know about the current status of that area of law and summarise that it does not need to be changed.

(2) Write a relevant summary of the status of the law, then:
  (a) Discuss what is right with it.
  (b) Discuss what is wrong with it.
  (c) What has been proposed to make it better?
  (d) Will the proposed changes make it better?
  (e) What would you propose?

4. **Don't jump the gun**
   (1) Many students lead themselves away from higher marks by jumping to a conclusion under the stress of the exam.
   (2) This often happens when students only revise limited subjects or areas of the law, if they try to pigeonhole the torts, rely on buzz words or key words. **Examples:**
     (a) If a window in your garage is broken, the window is not a chattel but part of the land.
     (b) Just because an animal appears in a question do not assume that animal liability is the correct issue. If you leave your cat, Fluffy, with the vet for an operation and Fluffy escapes out of the open window, remember Fluffy is a chattel. Leaving her with the vet created a bailment, so detinue would be a better place to jump or even professional negligence.
     (c) Every time you see the word 'escape' don't limit your thoughts and answer to *Rylands v Fletcher*.

5. **Time = marks — do not waste it**.
   a. Common time wasters include:
      Copying most of the facts given in the exam into the answer. The examiner knows the facts, so just briefly discuss the important or relevant facts in your exam answer.
   b. The use of two or three different colours of ink.
      The examiner is looking for your knowledge of law, not your knowledge or use of colours. Stick with blue or black ink and save the time you would waste switching pens.
   c. Overuse of correction fluid.
      1. There is nothing worse than picking up an exam script and finding the pages stuck together with correction fluid.
      2. Instead of relying on correction fluid, quickly outline your

answer before you begin to write your answer.
3. If you do make a minor mistake, simply and *neatly* cross through the mistake and continue.
4. For those one-page big mistakes, do not waste time trying to paint over it. Cross through the offending page and continue.
d. Underlining words or phrases.
1. Unless you have been instructed otherwise it is a great waste of time to underline words or phrases.
2. Believe it or not, examiners read the answers and do not skim the papers looking for key words, buzz words, cases or phrases upon which to award marks. Generally, underlining words or phrases is simply a waste of time.

B. Do not make reading your exam answers a trial.

1. Get the basics right.
a. **Spelling**: Every year students make fundamental mistakes with spelling legal and sometimes non-legal words.
If the examiner has any doubts about your ability it will be removed if you:
(a) Confuse 'libel' with 'liable',
(b) Make the 'plaintiff' into a 'paintiff', or
(c) Spell 'defendant' with three Es.
b. **Sentence structure**: Write in complete sentences, but apply the KISS principle — *Keep It Short and Simple.*
(1) Many students try to emulate the styles of some of the great legal writers of the ages. This is quite understandable after spending a year reading their great works. However, the exam answers are *your* work and you must impress the examiner with your knowledge of the law — to do so you must be able to get your points across.
(2) Long, difficult or contorted sentences are not the best way to get your knowledge across to the examiner. If an examiner has to reread a sentence several times to understand what you are trying to say, you are not helping your marks. **Warning**: This study aid is in an outline form and many sentences are not complete. Make certain the sentences in your exam answers are complete.
c. **Paragraphs**
(1) A paragraph gives the examiner a mental pause before continuing to read your exam answers. Unfortunately,

many students fail to see the importance of paragraphs and often write in bullet form or sometimes in a solid block.

Have you ever tried to read a computer printout with words covering the entire page — no margins, no paragraphs, just words and more words? It is not a very pleasurable read.

(2) Writing in paragraph form helps you to organise your answer, allowing you to quickly glance over your answer to assess coverage of a topic.

   d. **Punctuation**

      (1) Is not optional, *use it.*

      (2) Your exam answer is not the time to experiment with new methods of punctuation. Stick to the conventional methods.

2. **Writing in the third person**

   a. Generally, legal writers write in the third person.

     Yes, judges do often write in the first person and, as one of my law professors told our class, when you become a judge you too can write in the first person.

   b. Some lecturers are fanatical about this and others are not.

     Be safe — get in the habit of letting your answer speak for itself.

APPENDIX

ANSWERS TO REVISION QUESTIONS

I. Chapter 1 answers

(1) No tort. Mere words are not an assault. *See Tuberville v Savage* [41].

(2) Assault. Apprehension is not fear. *See* [45].

(3) No tort, as long as Veronica is free to go where she wants there is no false imprisonment. *See* [59].

(4) (a) False imprisonment. If Bertha is sitting on Anthony without his consent she is falsely imprisoning Anthony because he is restrained. *See* [57].

    (b) Battery. If Bertha is sitting on Anthony without his consent she is committing a battery. *See* [21].

    (c) Possible assault. The facts state that Bertha cornered Anthony. If he was placed in reasonable apprehension of an immediate battery from Bertha there may have been an assault. *See* [37].

(5) Yes. Anne consented to the contact. Her consent is not invalidated by Peter's fraud. Peter's fraud did not relate to the nature of the act. *See* [80].

(6) (a) No battery. Battery is the direct application of physical force upon the person of another without consent. There has been no physical force or contact.

    (b) Probably. An assault is an act by the defendant that places the plaintiff in reasonable apprehension of an immediate battery. While words alone can never amount to an assault, words in a particular context (i.e. being in a rowboat in the middle of a river) may be an assault if the words induce a reasonable apprehension of an immediate battery. *See* [40] *et seq.*

    (c) Yes. Grainne is not required to risk injury, humiliation or property damage to avail of the tort of False Imprisonment. *See* [58].

(7) (a) No. The teacher was *in loco parentis* and is allowed to use reasonable chastisement on a pupil. *See* [97].

    (b) No. In order for an assault to occur the victim must be in reasonable apprehension of an imminent battery. Because

Ralphie's back was turned he could not have known that the book was raised.

(8) (a) No. Sinead's consent to Oliver's spankings is invalidated by his fraud. Oliver's fraud concerned the nature of the acts (spankings). He told Sinead that they were treatment for her whiplash when in fact they were not. *See* [80].

(b) Although Ireland has no reported cases of intentional infliction of emotional distress, these facts would probably fall within this tort. *See* [69] *et seq.*

(9) No. The elderly gentleman was not acting with voluntary control. He was asleep. *See* [23].

(10) No. Although it was *obiter* in *Walsh v Family Planning Services* the Supreme Court made it clear that battery will not apply where a doctor exceeds the consent of the patient. Negligence is the proper tort. *See* [82].

(11) No tort, unless Liam placed or induced Santa to use the chimney. *See* [56].

(12) (a) (*i*) Battery. Mike grabbing the handbag. Physical contact extends to any part of the body touched or to anything attached to the body and practically identified with it. *See* [27].

(*ii*) Assault. Ken chasing Mike. *See* [37].

(*iii*) Battery. Ken caught Mike. *See* [26].

(*iv*) Battery. Mike falling on Bob.

(b) (*i*) No defences.

(*ii*) and (*iii*) Ken has a valid defence. He can use reasonable force to defend (retrieve) the lady's chattel (handbag). *See* [111].

(*iv*) No battery because Mike's contact was not voluntary. *See* [23].

II. Chapter 2 answers

(1) Trespass to land. *See* [130].

(2) (a) No, Michael did not act voluntarily. *See* [122].

(b) Yes, Tim, by his negligent act (driving), caused Michael to cross the boundary of Farmer Fred's land. *See* [130].

(3) (a) Trespass to chattels. *See* [181].

(b) No defences. **Note:** Necessity will not be a valid defence because there is a reasonable alternative. Pauline could ask Naomi to move the bag.

(4) (a) Cyril entered under a licence with an interest (i.e. he paid consideration to enter). *See* [146] *et seq.*

    (b) Yes, Cyril's licence expired when the film he paid to see ended.

(5) (a) Yes, Mai Day committed a trespass when she invaded the air space with a stone, *see* [134], also when the stone hit the ground. *See* [130]. **Note:** It is not a trespass to land for the stone to hit the windows for sale.

    (b) No, when Mai Day broke the windows (that were on sale) the windows were chattels. She broke the panes, but generally broken glass does not destroy the character of the window. Mere damage is not enough for conversion, but it may be enough for trespass to chattels. *See* [206] *et seq.*

(6) Assuming that Toulouse was for breeding purposes, the vet committed a conversion by wrongfully neutering her. The character of my pedigree breeding cat has changed, *see* [206]. If Toulouse was not for breeding purposes but was simply a pet or rat warden, the vet has committed a trespass to my chattel by damaging my chattel. *See* [182].

(7) (a) Yes, even though the gentleman does not harm the land his presence is a trespass. *See* [125].

    (b) (*i*) When the gentleman picked the rose he severed realty. Assuming that the rose was planted in the garden (and not in a container) it was realty, *see* [133]. The act of picking it was a severance and hence a conversion. *See* [219].

        (*ii*) The picked rose belonged to Miss M. When the gentleman took the rose that was another act of conversion, *see* [197]. Remember a person may act in such a way as to commit several conversions with the same chattel. *See* [211].

(8) It is a trespass to chattels. *See* [172] *et seq.* and Street's comments in [183].

(9) (a) Drinking John's tea is a conversion. Consuming something destroys the character of the chattel. John wouldn't want the tea back now would he? *See* [206].

    (b) Moving the thermos is a trespass to the chattel. *See* [181].

(10) (a) Acts that are trespass to land include: (*i*) throwing the fire cracker into the sitting room and (*ii*) reaching into the window.

    (b) No. It does not apply to (*i*), nor does it apply to (*ii*) where Sean caused the greater evil or peril (i.e. the fire). *See* [159].

    (c) Curtains are generally considered chattels, rather than land, because they are not permanently attached to the land.

Therefore it was a conversion when the curtains caught fire because of Sean's conduct.

(11) Assuming that Susan and Michael co-owned their wedding photographs Susan has committed a conversion by burning them. *See* [220].

(12) Assuming the stone is an antiquity of importance the State has the best title to it. *Webb v Ireland. See* [228].

(13) (a) (*i*)　Bob snapped off a couple of limbs = trespass to chattels.

　　　　(*ii*)　Bob entered onto the Scrooge farm = trespass to land.

　　　　(*iv*)　Bob chopped down a tree = conversion by severing realty.

　　　　(*v*)　Taking the tree = conversion by taking Scrooge's chattel.

14. (a) Yes. See [154] *et seq.*

　　(b) No. Although Ziggy interfered with Mary's furniture (chattels) by moving the furniture, he has two defences: (i) consent, *see* [235] and (ii) lawful authority, *see* [257}.

15. (a) Yes. *See* [235] *et seq.*

　　(b) No. Sean is not required to make a written demand. All that is required is that Sean must make a demand for the possession of his chattel unless it would be futile to do so. See [243]. When Sean telephoned and learned that his desk was destroyed a demand would have been futile. If the desk was destroyed thorough no fault of ABC, and ABC can prove the absence of fault, ABC may escape liability. See [246] *et seq.*

III. Chapter 3 answers

(1) (a) Pure economic loss. *See* [397] *et seq.*

　　(b) Probably. Using the *Ward v McMaster* requirements of (*i*) Proximity between the parties, (*ii*) Reasonable foreseeable damages and (*iii*) No adverse public policy considerations, it would appear that Margaret should recover. *See* [400] *et seq.*

　　(c) Probably not. Applying the *Kelly v Hennessy* principles — Andy suffered harm from exposure to the aftermath, but he cannot recover unless he had a close personal relationship with Nichola. *See* [416].

　　(d) S. 48(1) of the Civil Liability Act 1961. *See* [425].

　　(e) Wrongful death.

　　(f) S. 6(1) of the Statute of Limitations (Amendment) Act 1991, provides that the action must be brought within three years from the date of the death. *See* [428].

　　(g) No, only one cause of action is allowed under s. 48(2) of the Civil Liability Act 1961. *See* [426].

(2) (a) Yes, under the eggshell skull rule. *See* [516] *et seq.*

(b) No, negligence is not actionable *per se*. Paul suffered no physical injury to himself or to his property. There is nothing in the problem to suggest that he suffered nervous shock.

(c) No. In common law jurisdictions a person is under no general duty to go to the aid of another in peril. There are two general exceptions to this rule: (*i*) if the defendant has a special relationship with the plaintiff — such as between a parent and child, or (*ii*) if the defendant caused or placed the plaintiff in the peril. David was merely a witness to the accident. He does not have a special relationship to Mary, nor did he place her in the peril. Therefore, David did not owe Mary an affirmative duty to help her. *See* [322] *et seq.*

(d) No. New forces must join with Tony's negligence to injure Shelly. There was no new force. The suitcase was set in motion by Tony's negligence. *See* [511].

(e) No. Mary has not performed a negligent act that caused Shelly's injuries. *See* [460].

(3) (a) (*i*) Elmer owed Richard a duty of care.

(*ii*) Elmer breached the duty of care that he owed to Richard.

(*iii*) Because Elmer breached the duty of care that he owed to Richard, Richard suffered an injury, loss or damage.

(*iv*) Richard suffered a loss, damage or injury. *See* [276].

(b) No. Contributory negligence is concerned with the plaintiff's contribution to his own injuries, it is not concerned with his contribution to the incident that caused his injury. *See* [544].

(c) (*i*) But for Elmer leaving his window open Richard would not have been injured. This statement is not true — there is no actual causation.

(*ii*) But for Elmer leaving the keys to the gun safe in his home Richard would not have been injured. This statement is not true — there is no actual causation. Would your answer have been different if the instrumentality causing the death had been a car that Tom stole from Elmer when he found the keys to the car?

(*iii*) But for Tom shooting Richard, Richard would not have been injured. This statement is true — there is actual causation.

(d) No. The cause of Tom's injury is the poor job he performed in cutting off the gun barrel. Did you want to write that Tom was contributorily negligent? This is not the case. To be contributorily negligent means that the defendant (Elmer) had to be negligent. Elmer was not negligent.

(4) (a) A dentist must exercise the skills of a reasonable dentist. *See* [302] *et seq.*

(b) Under *Dunne v National Maternity Hospital* if there are two or more accepted medical treatments it is well settled that the medical practitioner is protected from liability if he follows one of the accepted procedures, *see* [308]. In this instance, it would appear that there are two accepted procedures: (*i*) to send the patient to an oral surgeon, or (*ii*) to remove the impacted wisdom tooth himself. Therefore, the local dentist's decision to remove the tooth himself is not itself a breach of the duty of care owed.

(c) Yes.

(*i*) The defendant had sole control of the incident. (*ii*) The defendant dentist had knowledge denied to the plaintiff. (*iii*) The plaintiff's injuries do not normally happen during a tooth extraction without some element of negligence by the defendant. *See* [446] *et seq.*

(5) (a) Yes. An assault is an act by the defendant that places the plaintiff in reasonable apprehension of an immediate battery. *See* [37] *et seq.*

(b) No. Under the doctrine of *respondeat superior* the general rule is that an employer may be liable for the tortious acts committed by his/her employees within the scope of the employment. Vicarious liability will not apply if the tort is committed outside the scope of the employment. Travel to and from the primary place of employment is outside the scope of employment. *See* [365] *et seq.*

(c) No. An assault is an intentional tort. The general rule is that an employer may be vicariously liable for the intentional torts committed by his/her employees within the scope of the employee's employment if the employee's duties involve the use of physical force on others — examples would be a bodyguard, or bouncer — or where the force is used to further the employer's interests. While Daniel may have been acting within the scope of his employment his duties did not involve the threatened use of physical force on others, nor did the assault he committed further his employer's interest. *See* [367] *et seq.*

IV. Chapter 4 answers

(1) No. Georgia is a visitor, *see* [595]. She is a social guest engaging in recreation but she is still a visitor.

(2) Yes. Premises include a means of transport, *see* [588].

(3) (a) Visitors

   (b) A common law duty in negligence. In other words, the Act requires an occupier to take reasonable care in the circumstances to ensure that a visitor does not suffer any injury or damages because of any danger or unsafe condition on the premises. *See* [596].

   (c) No. Notices to restrict or exclude liability must be reasonably brought to the attention of the visitor. *See* [600].

(4) (a) Recreational user. *See* [605].

   (b) Yes.

   (c) No. While structures provided for recreational users must be maintained in a safe condition there is an exception for entry structures such as gates and stiles. Occupiers are not required to keep entry structures in a safe condition. *See* [611].

(5) (a) (*i*) The court must determine what type of harm the statute was designed to protect.

   (*ii*) Whether the plaintiff is within the class of persons the statute was designed to protect.

   (*iii*) Whether other remedies are available and adequate.

   (b) Yes. The statute wants to keep guns from falling into the hands of criminals to be used in violent crimes.

   (c) Perhaps. If Elmer's gun safe was an approved model he did not breach the statute. If his gun safe was not an approved model he breached the statute.

   (d) Perhaps. It depends on whether Elmer was in breach of the statute and this breach was the cause of the injury to Richard. For example, if Elmer's gun safe was not approved because it is a new superior model, it is doubtful that Richard will prevail. However, if Elmer's gun safe was not approved because it had a key entry instead of a combination, Richard could argue that the law-makers wanted combination locks rather than key entry to avoid the very thing that happened — a person gaining access to the gun by finding the key.

V. Chapter 5 answers

(1) No. There was no escape. *See* [692].

(2) (a) Strict liability will only apply to domestic animals where the defendant had knowledge of the dangerous nature of an animal. *See* [654].

(b) Yes, act of a stranger. *See* [697].

(3) The Accidental Fires Act 1943 provides that no legal action can be initiated by any person who suffers damage because of a fire accidentally occurring in the building of another person. Accidental: means without negligence. Irene was negligent in causing the fire and was also negligent is failing to control the fire. *See* [642] *et seq.*

(4) Not unless the master instructed Cyril to attack the heifer. *See* [642].

(5) Yes. *See* [365] *et seq.*

(6) (a) Yes. *See* [668].

(b) No, there is no causation between Larry and Aine's injury. It may have been different if Aine was running from Larry and fell, but she was clearly not in danger from the lion.

(7) No. Consent would be a complete defence if Michael consented to the risk associated with the dangerous accumulation. Michael did not consent to the risk — he wanted Johnny to remain responsible for building and maintaining the pond. Johnny may have a partial defence. *See* [701].

(8) (a) No. The Act does not apply to repairers. *See* [713].

(b) No. The Act does not apply to repairers. *See* [713].

(c) Yes. *See* [744] *et seq.*

(d) Yes. *See* [746] *et seq.*

(9) (a) Yes, under s. 2(3). *See* [722].

(b) If Schultze's Department Store was the importer of the defective hairdryer, under s. 2 Jane could maintain a cause of action even though she knows the name of the North Korean manufacturer.

(c) Jane was not contributorily negligent. She did not act unreasonable under the circumstances. *See* [736].

(d) No. Damage to the product itself is not covered by the Act. *See* [720].

(e) No. Jane can recover for the cost of replacing the carpeting minus £350. *See* [729].

(f) Yes. Only property damage is reduced by £350. *See* [729].

(10) (a) No. Pursuant to s. 7, a right of action is barred ten years from the date on which the producer put into circulation the actual product that caused the damage — regardless whether or not the right of action accrued during the ten years.

(b) No. Pursuant to s. 5, a defective product is one that fails to provide the safety that a reasonable person is entitled to expect, taking all circumstances into account. Circumstances may include the use to which the product could reasonably be expected to be put. The more unusual or extreme the use the less likely it could be said to be reasonably expected. It is not usual to use rodent traps as paperweights. *See* [716].

VI. Chapter 6 answers

(1) (a) No. If the rights interfered with belong to a person as a member of the public, the act or omission is a public nuisance. *See* [763]. Only the Attorney General can bring a civil action for a public nuisance. *See* [765].

(b) Yes. A private individual (like Felix) may maintain an action if a special, particular or peculiar damage is suffered. Further, the damage must be more serious than the damage suffered by the general public. A special, particular or peculiar damage may consist of an injury to a person's pecuniary interest where his person or property is damaged — or it may include the deprivation of the opportunity to earn a living. Clearly, Felix has suffered a special, particular or peculiar damage that is more serious than the damage (i.e. environmental pollution) suffered by the general public. *See* [766].

(c) Yes. Same as (b).

(2) (a) Yes. A single act can amount to a nuisance. *See* [826].

(b) Yes. *See* [825]

(c) No. Generally, parents are not responsible for the torts of their children, *see* [370]. Also, there are no facts that indicate that Kevin's parents authorised the creation of the nuisance. *See* [794].

(d) No. Generally, the interference to Clean Jean's use and enjoyment of her apartment must be something that a reasonable person would take offence at, rather than a mere annoyance. Any reasonable person would take offence at the stench of rotten eggs in their home, particularly since the bomb left a dirty brown haze on everything. Clean Jean is not being unduly sensitive by trying to force her neighbours into accommodating some unusual need that she has. *See* [814] *et seq.*

(3) (a) No. Prescription requires twenty years. *See* [836].

(b) No. Coming to the nuisance is not a defence. *See* [834].

(c) No. The defence is not available where it is alleged that the plaintiff came to the nuisance. *See* [832].

(d) Perhaps. English authority suggests that planning permission can only be taken as authorising a nuisance if the effect of the permission alters the character of the locale. From the brief facts given in the instant case it is not known if the planning permission did alter the character of the locale.

VII. Chapter 7 answers

(1) (a) Yes. A university is a legal person and legal persons can sue for defamation. *See* [861].

(b) No. *See* [870].

(c) Mary will not be liable for libel if her communication falls under the defence of qualified privilege. Mary, as a lecturer, may have a duty to report her statement and the Academic Council may have a corresponding interest in receiving the statement. So long as the communication was not wider than necessary or motivated by malice Mary's communication should not amount to libel. *See* [928].

(d) No. The maker of an alleged defamatory statement will only be liable if she could have reasonably foreseen the particular publication. It is not reasonably foreseeable that sending a report to an internal university council will be sent on to a foreign newspaper. *See* [874]

(e) No. The newspaper is in the US and the US is not a member of the EU. The convention applies to member states of the EU. *See* [900].

(f) Yes. The statement is in writing and is thus a libel. Libel is actionable *per se*. *See* [898] *et seq*.

(2) (a) Hamish's statements may come under the defence of fair comment. *See* [919].

(b) Probably not. The public has an interest and concern in the cleanliness of eating establishments. *See* [919].

(c) Probably not. The statement must ruin the person's reputation or good name. A statement merely causing anger or upset is not enough. *See* [894].

(d) Yes. Malice destroys the defence of fair comment. *See* [896].

(3) (a) No. Defamation requires a publication to a third person. *See* [873]. Ricky will only be liable if he could have reasonably

foreseen the particular publication, *see* [874]. It is not reasonably foreseeable that when two people retire to a private office the content of their conversation will be learned by a lip reader peering through a window in the door.

(b) Yes, but the plaintiff made the publication rather than the defendant. Therefore, the defendant is not responsible.

(4) (a) Generally, being falsely accused of winning the lottery would not be a defamatory statement. However, Andrew is the founder and president of the Anti-Gambling League. Such a statement would probably cause a reasonable person to form a negative or adverse view of Andrew's reputation or good name. *See* [868].

(b) Perhaps. Susan clearly published the statement to a third person, i.e. Winnie. However, slander is not actionable *per se* and there is no proof of damages in the problem presented. Because the allegation deals with winning the lottery and not to Andrew's abilities in his place of employment it is doubtful that the statement is slander *per se*.

(c) Mere abuse such as name-calling is not slander. *See* [869].

(d) No. Communication between spouses is not defamatory because there is no publication. *See* [884].

(5) (a) No. The privilege generally applies to statements made in the course of the judicial proceedings. This statement was not made in the course of the proceedings, but was made during a recess. *See* [925].

(b) Slander *per se*. *See* [902] *et seq.*

(c) No. Only a living person is able to bring and maintain an action for defamation. *See* [861].

(d) No. Communications between spouses is not defamatory because there is no publication, *see* [884]. There must be a publication to a third party.

VIII. Chapter 8 answers

(1) Injurious falsehood. *See* [947] *et seq.*

(2) None. It is not an injurious falsehood if the statement is not false. *See* [948].

(3) No. Passing off requires that the misrepresentation must take place in a commercial context, *see* [965]. While a charity may bring an action political parties are not allowed.

(4) Passing off. The defendant (Cajun County) opened a restaurant

with almost the identical name to the plaintiff's business (Cajun Country). Even unregistered names may develop a specific association that may easily allow for the confusion of the public. This is clearly the case in the facts presented. *See* [959].

(5) Only if the false statement was made in writing. S. 6 of the Statute of Frauds Amendment Act 1828 requires that a misrepresentation fraudulently made to enable another person to obtain credit is not actionable unless the misrepresentation has been reduced to writing and signed by the person making the statement. *See* [975].

(6) (a) No. Speaking to a third person is an indirect interference. *See* [989].

   (b) No. A valid contract is essential to the tort. *See* [990].

   (c) Yes. The plaintiff has the onus of proving that the defendant intended to interfere with the plaintiff's contract. To do so the plaintiff must show that the defendant knew or had constructive knowledge of the contract. The fact that all dance companies require contracts would show that John LaChapelle, a manager of a dance troupe, would have had constructive knowledge of the contract between Celtic Club and Sebastian. *See* [991].

(7) (a) No. Generally, a statement of opinion or intention is not a representation. *See* [973].

   (b) No. Max did not intend to induce Nancy to rely upon his statement. *See* [979].

   (c) No. Darren has not suffered a resulting damage from relying on Mick's false statement. *See* [984].

(8) It depends on a number of factors including what colours the other manufacturers are using for their handgrips. Do the new coloured handles confuse the public into thinking that the defendant's goods are Bebe's goods? It would also depend whether the grips are seen more as a fashion trend rather than a misrepresentation. *See Adidas v O'Neill* [962].

(9) (a) Injurious falsehood. *See* [948] *et seq.*

   (b) Interference with contractual relations. *See* [986] *et seq.*

   (c) Deceit. *See* [971] *et seq.*

   (d) No. Some aspect of Suzanne's business must be used to confuse the public into thinking that Winona's services are Suzanne's. In the facts presented, Winona is not trying to confuse the public into thinking that her services are Suzanne's. *See* [958].